Thinking About Crime

THINKING
ABOUT
CRIME

REVISED EDITION

JAMES Q. WILSON

VINTAGE BOOKS

A DIVISION OF RANDOM HOUSE

NEW YORK

Library of Congress Cataloging in Publication Data
Wilson, James Q.
Thinking about crime.

Reprint. Originally published: New York : Basic Books, c1983.
Includes bibliographical references and index.
1. Crime and criminals—United States—Addresses, essays,
lectures.   2. Criminal justice, Administration of—United
States—Addresses, essays, lectures.
I. Title.
[HV6789.W53   1985]   364'.973   84-40520
ISBN 0-394-72917-X

9

Contents

PART IV
CRIME AND THE AMERICAN REGIME

Acknowledgments

F OUR of the chapters of this book were written, in their original form, with the aid of co-authors. I wish to thank them for their assistance and for their permission to reprint, slightly amended, these materials. They are Dr. Robert L. DuPont, M.D., with whom I wrote the original version of chapter 1, and Professor Mark H. Moore and Mr. I. David Wheat, Jr., with whom I wrote what now appears as chapter 11. Professor Moore was also the co-author of what is now "A Note on Gun Control." Dr. George L. Kelling, Jr., joined me in writing what is now chapter 5.

I am also indebted to colleagues who read and commented on early versions of some of the chapters added to this edition. They include: Barbara Boland of INSLAW and Jacqueline Cohen of Carnegie-Mellon University, who commented on chapter 8; Michael Block of the University of Arizona, who commented on chapter 7; and Morton Keller of Brandeis University, Roger Lane of Haverford College, Eric Monkkonen of UCLA, and Michael Sandel of Harvard who commented on chapter 12.

Various publishers have kindly allowed me to reprint, with alterations, material that first appeared under their auspices:

Chapter 1: "The Sick Sixties," *Atlantic Monthly*, October 1973, pp. 91–98. Copyright © 1973, by the Atlantic Monthly Company, Boston, Mass. Reprinted by permission.

Chapter 2: "The Urban Unease: Community vs. City," *The Public Interest*, no. 12 (Summer 1968): 25–39. Copyright © 1968 by National Affairs, Inc.; copyright © 1974 by James Q. Wilson.

Chapter 3: "Crime and the Criminologists," *Commentary*, July 1974, pp. 47–53. Copyright © 1974 by James Q. Wilson.

Chapter 4: "Do the Police Prevent Crime?" *New York Times Sunday Magazine*, 6 October, 1974, pp. 18 ff. Copyright © 1974 by The New York Times Company. Reprinted by permission.

Chapter 5: "Broken Windows: The Police and Neighborhood Safety,"

Atlantic Monthly, March 1982, pp. 29–38. Copyright © 1982 by the Atlantic Monthly Company, Boston, Mass. Reprinted by permission.

Chapter 6: "The Police in the Ghetto," in Robert F. Steadman, *The Police in the Community* (Baltimore: Johns Hopkins University Press, 1972) pp. 51–90, copyright © 1972 by the Committee for Economic Development; and "Police Use of Deadly Force," reprinted in part, from the *FBI Law Enforcement Bulletin,* August 1980, pp. 16–21.

Chapter 8: "Incapacitation," *The Public Interest,* no. 72 (Summer 1983). Copyright © 1983 by National Affairs, Inc.

Chapter 9: " 'What Works?' Revisited: New Findings on Criminal Rehabilitation," *The Public Interest,* no. 61 (Fall 1980) pp. 3–17. Copyright © 1980 by National Affairs, Inc.

Chapter 11: "The Problem of Heroin," *The Public Interest,* no. 29 (Fall 1972) pp. 3–28. Copyright © 1972 by National Affairs, Inc.; copyright © 1974 by James Q. Wilson.

Chapter 12: "Crime and American Culture," *The Public Interest,* no. 70 (Winter 1983): 22–48. Copyright © 1983 by National Affairs, Inc.

Chapter 13: "Crime and Public Policy," in James Q. Wilson, ed. *Crime and Public Policy* (San Francisco: Institute for Contemporary Studies, 1983). Copyright © 1983 by the Institute for Contemporary Studies.

Appendix: "Enforcing the Laws We Have," reprinted from *The Washington Post*, April 1, 1981, p. A21.

Thinking About Crime

Introduction

THE common theme of the essays that make up this book is that the proper design of public policies requires a clear and sober understanding of the nature of man and, in particular, of the extent to which that nature can be changed by plan. Crime is not the only issue that evokes this theme, but it is one that does so dramatically, and it happens to be one that I have found myself studying, off and on, for the better part of twenty years.

I might never have brought together the essays that constituted, in 1975, the first edition of this book had it not been for my belief that the public debate then underway about crime and its prevention was dividing the country (or at least its political elites) into diametrically opposed and intellectually untenable positions. To oversimplify a bit, the liberal position on crime in the late 1960s and early 1970s was, first, to deny that crime was rising and to imply that public concern about "crime in the streets" was simply a rhetorical cover for racist sentiments; second, to state that if, by any chance, crime was actually increasing, it was the result of a failure to invest enough tax money in federal programs aimed at unemployment and poverty; and third, to the extent crime might occur even after such investments, the proper strategy was to rehabilitate offenders in therapeutic facilities located in the community rather than in prisons.

The conservative position was that crime was destroying American society but that this could be prevented by "supporting your local police" (bumper stickers with such sentiments were thoughtfully provided as a low-cost way of implementing that support), impeaching Chief Justice Earl Warren and reversing the Supreme Court rules that were "handcuffing" the police, appointing a "get-tough" attorney general, and reviving the death penalty.

Though present-day liberals and conservatives may deny that these views were ever offered by them, I would refer them to the campaign speeches heard in the 1964, 1968, and 1972 presidential elections. The Republicans in those years spoke frequently of crime but claimed that, contrary to what one might suppose would be the position of a party concerned about states' rights and the virtues of federalism, the solution to crime could be found in Washington with a redirected Supreme Court and a new attorney general. The Democrats' position was to reject such solutions, not simply because they were implausible (though they were), but because the problem they were meant to address did not exist. The 1968 Democratic national platform mentioned crime in passing (it is reassuring to learn that the Democrats deplored it), but scarcely anything was said about crime at the convention that produced this platform, and the two major interest groups presumably speaking for the problems of urban America, the AFL–CIO and the Urban Coalition, made no proposals about crime. The incumbent attorney general, Ramsey Clark, was quoted as saying that he did not think we were having a crime wave at all, and two years later, in a book entitled *Crime in America*, he further reassured us that since the typical middle-class city dweller will be victimized by a violent crime only "once every 2,000 years," we can safely afford to turn our attention to the "far more corrosive" effect of white-collar crime.

I believed at the time that the crime issue was in danger of being left to the demagogues who would either deny what were among the plainest facts of everyday experience or claim that crime could best be prevented by reconstituting the Supreme Court. I also believed that some social scientists had some important things to say and that if their findings were attended to, a bit less nonsense might be uttered. Among the social scientists who had the most to say were a (then) small group of economists, operations research analysts, and political scientists who were beginning to use social science methods to test the efficacy of alternative crime control strategies. Finally, I believed then and I believe now that our society does not need to choose between helping the disadvantaged and fighting crime; to the contrary, helping the disadvantaged is desirable in its own right, and reducing crime is in itself a major source of assistance to those disadvantaged persons who are the principal victims of crime.

Today, seven years later, the political debate is vastly different and, on the whole, much improved. The presidential candidates in 1976 and 1980 adopted, by and large, a constructive attitude toward the crime problem —they scarcely mentioned it. In part this was because crime was no longer a partisan issue, the Democrats having caught up with the public's concern about the problem and the Republicans having learned while in power for eight years that the president cannot be a police chief or a prison warden. But in part also, I think, the modest and nonideological attention given to crime in national campaign rhetoric reflected a growing consensus about the major lines along which the problem ought to be approached.

That consensus had much in common with what the first edition of this book said and what the revised edition repeats: rehabilitation has not yet been shown to be a promising method for dealing with serious offenders, broad-gauge investments in social progress have little near-term effect on crime rates, punishment is not an unworthy objective for the criminal justice system of a free and liberal society to pursue, the evidence supports (though cannot conclusively prove) the view that deterrence and incapacitation work, and new crime-control techniques ought to be tried in a frankly experimental manner with a heavy emphasis on objective evaluation.

Though there is today a greater political consensus and more intellectual common sense evident in public discussions of crime, the consensus is still incomplete and the common sense is far from universal. In speaking before various audiences and in responding to criticisms of the previous edition of this book, I have learned that five issues continue to preoccupy many persons and, since they do not preoccupy me, I am judged by these persons to be either insensitive or fainthearted. The first of these issues follows from my giving principal attention to predatory street crime rather than to "white-collar" crime. No matter how fearful the public may be about the prospect of being mugged, raped, burgled, or vandalized, someone is bound to insist that the "real" problem is political corruption, commercial price-fixing, environmental degradation, or defective automobile designs. I am often told that such activities—which are always called "crimes," whether or not there is in fact a statute imposing criminal penalties on those who engage in them—are more serious because they are more costly to society. They may well be more costly than burglary and robbery if we count only monetary losses, but the American people are not concerned about crime simply, or even chiefly, because it is expensive. Crime is not like inflation or high taxes; though it has economic components, it is not an economic issue. Crime arouses fear and often causes injuries. But so does, one might object, a nuclear accident or an unsafe car. True, and these are serious matters because of that. But predatory crime, in particular crime committed by strangers on innocent victims, causes the kind of fear that drives people apart from one another and thus impedes or even prevents the formation of meaningful human communities. Predatory crime violates the social contract. Moreover, we regard these burglaries, robberies, and rapes not merely as bad or costly or dangerous behavior, but as immoral behavior. That is why, in virtually every known society, past or present, theft, rape, murder, and unprovoked assault are universally condemned. By contrast, while some nations punish

5

businessmen who form industrial trusts, others elevate such men to the peerage. Some nations think the quality of the environment or the safety of cars or the corruption of political life are largely private matters; others think they are public ones. But all nations punish, in the name of the state, theft and unjustified violence. To me, and I suspect to most citizens, all this seems obvious, and thus one should not have to apologize for writing a book about predatory crime and leaving to others the important task of writing about "white-collar" crime. But some leftist intellectuals are so preoccupied with turning all discussion of social problems into an attack on the prevailing economic and political order that their customary response to the public's concern with street crime is to change the subject. Since these intellectuals claim to speak for the best interest of the workers, this response is all the more curious.

A second criticism is that one can do little about crime without addressing its "root causes." In the first edition of this book, I said some rather testy things about that line of argument, not because crime has no root causes, but because a free society can do so little about attacking these causes that a concern for their elimination becomes little more than an excuse for doing nothing. I devoted then, and I repeat here, an entire chapter (chapter 3) to the subject of why one can think seriously about anticrime policies without first discovering a cure for the causes of crime. And in a new chapter (chapter 12) I give an account of what some of these causes may be. But it has become increasingly clear to me that what some people who worry about "root causes" really mean is not that such causes should be found by careful investigation and then remedied by imaginative policies, but rather that these causes are already known and that they can be easily addressed by government programs, provided we have the "will" to do so. The root cause of crime, in this view, is poverty and deprivation, which can be ended by social programs. There is certainly more crime in most poor neighborhoods than in most well-off ones and most criminals are less prosperous than most law-abiding citizens. But as I hope to show (in chapter 7), it is far from clear that giving more opportunities or higher incomes to offenders will lead them to commit fewer crimes, and it is even less clear that programs designed to make society as a whole better off will lower the crime rate. I make this point, not to denigrate social progress, but to clarify our thinking. If human behavior is shaped by the tangible utility of alternative courses of action, then there is little reason to assume that it will be shaped only by those utilities called "jobs" and not also by those called "penalties." It cannot be simply the case that "men steal because they are poor." If objective conditions affect crime rates, then the full statement must be: "Men steal because the net benefits of stealing exceed the net benefits of working."

In other words, persons who explain the rise in crime by the absence of jobs should, by the force of their own logic, be prepared to explain it also by the absence of penalties. But they rarely do. Indeed, those who use economic want as an explanation of crime are largely drawn from the ranks of those who vehemently deny that crime can be deterred by sanctions.

But other readers who took exception to my insistence that one can intelligently make policies designed to reduce crime without first understanding the causes of crime surmised that this bespoke a preference on my part for "getting tough" by more vigorous law enforcement. Not at all. If kindness, better housing, improved diets, or lessened child abuse will reduce crime, I favor them. I only ask that the capacity of such measures to reduce crime be demonstrated and that their employment for crime-reduction purposes not be at the expense of society's desire to see justice done to those who have violated its moral imperatives. In chapter 7, I review the evidence on one kind of helping program—supplying jobs and financial aid to ex-offenders and delinquents. The results are not very encouraging, but I take no satisfaction from that. And as far as other helping programs are concerned, I still await evidence that these will change, by plan and in large numbers, the behavior of serious offenders. Since I strongly suspect that cold, erratic, abusive parents create more than their share of delinquent children, I would especially welcome evidence that society knows how to make such parents warm, consistent, and nurturant, but precious little has come to my attention. There is one public enterprise I do not discuss that may have an effect on crime: the schools. The reason for the omission is ignorance—partly mine, partly that of scholars who only recently have tried to discover why some schools produce less misconduct than others, given similar pupils. In future writings, I hope to remedy that omission as best I can.

A third criticism of the first edition is that, even if sanctions might reduce crime, the use of prison as a sanction is wrong except for that tiny proportion of offenders who are truly dangerous. Prisons are bad because they make their inmates more criminal (they are "schools for crime"), because they are inevitably inhumane and brutalizing, and because they cost too much. Unlike the first two criticisms, this one suffers less from a flaw in logic or a political bias than from a failure of empirical analysis. We want to know, factually, whether prisons make inmates worse off or better off (it is not clear they do either), whether they are inevitably brutalizing (no one has ever, to the best of my knowledge, explained why some prisons are humane and others unspeakable), and whether their costs are unreasonable given the many functions (retribution, deterrence, the protection of society) that they may perform. These questions can be answered, within limits, but only by careful inquiry, not by repeating slogans ("Alternatives to prison!" "Prison costs more than Harvard!").

A fourth argument with which I am frequently confronted is that it is important to reinstate the death penalty. This is not so much a criticism of what I have said as of what I have failed to say. Nobody needs to be told what passions can be aroused by a discussion of capital punishment. While I certainly understand the sources of those passions, both among proponents and opponents, I am not certain why public discussion of crime, and especially political campaigns of candidates who wish to appear tough on crime, should involve so much attention to a policy that can have so little effect on crime rates. Serious and thoughtful arguments can be made for and against capital punishment but whichever argument prevails, the level of public safety on our streets will be little affected. I try to explain the grounds for my skepticism in chapter 10; let me anticipate that argument by putting the matter into a larger context. To the extent people favor the death penalty as a crime fighting measure (and not simply on grounds of just deserts), they are embracing the view that increasing the severity of penalties will have as much or more effect on crime than increasing the certainty or swiftness with which penalties of whatever sort are imposed. No doubt, very severe penalties, including death, will deter many people from committing crimes *if* people believe there is a good chance that these more severe penalties will in fact be imposed. But beyond a certain point, increases in the severity of penalties are counterbalanced by greater delays and uncertainties in their imposition. If the passions that have been harnessed in service of getting states to adopt the death penalty had instead been devoted to getting prosecutors and judges in those states to impose more quickly and more certainly the penalties already at their disposal, I suspect (and with some substantial factual support) that crime would have been measurably reduced. But getting the criminal justice system to function properly is slow, hard, politically unrewarding work; changing a statute to read "thirty years in prison" instead of "ten years in prison," or "death" instead of "life imprisonment" is relatively easy and satisfyingly dramatic.

Finally, I am frequently asked what I think about gun control. I have learned to speak carefully in answering that question and as a result have pleased almost no one. When the first edition of this book appeared, I had not given any serious thought to the matter and hence said nothing. Things have improved only slightly since then. I have learned a great deal from the thoughtful, nonideological research of such scholars as Mark Moore and Philip Cook, but I cannot pretend to add anything to what they have discovered. I have appended to this volume a brief note on guns, originally co-authored with Moore, in which we try to show both that there are high social costs attached to leaving matters as they now stand and that few social benefits are likely to accrue to a policy of trying to shrink the total inventory of guns, reduce the rate of their manufacture, or greatly inhibit the opportunities people have for their lawful acquisition. We instead draw the reader's attention to the problem of preventing people at risk—that is, persons likely to use guns—from carrying them about. To the extent this can be done, there may be significant and immediate gains in public safety without having to settle the politically and perhaps constitutionally explosive issue of whether ordinary citizens should have their access to firearms restricted.

I have addressed these criticisms, not to defend myself, but to re-emphasize what I took to be the central message of the first edition, namely, that we can make more progress thinking analytically and experimentally about crime and its control than we can by exchanging slogans, rehearsing our ideology, or exaggerating the extent to which human nature or government institutions can be changed according to plan. Toward that end, I sought in 1975 to show that there was a growing body of scholarly literature, not generally known to the public, which, if taken seriously, could redirect public policy away from a (thus far) futile effort to alter human nature, by either general progress or individual rehabilitation, and toward a more promising effort to protect society by altering the choices facing would-be offenders. Since then, an immense amount of new research, much of it of very high quality, has been completed. We know more in 1983 than we knew in 1975 and, as is inevitably the case when our knowledge becomes richer, what first appeared to be relatively simple now appears somewhat more complex. As a result, this book, which tries to take into account the new findings of the last eight years, tells a more complicated story than did the first edition—there are more qualifications, exceptions, and uncertainties noted here than could have been noted, given the state of our knowledge, in 1975. I have not hesitated to put all these complexities before the reader because I want him or her to learn, if nothing else, how to think about crime and its control, and in particular how one can and cannot use scientific evidence. It was the economist, Harry Johnson, who noted the unhappy fact that "science demands the submergence of social conscience in a welter of statistical squabbles."[1]

Important as these squabbles are, they are not the whole of the matter. They can test but they cannot replace the good sense of the citizen. I am struck now, as I was in 1975, by how keen and sure are the people's awareness of their own problems and interests, so much so that popular concern for crime and neighborhood safety preceded by several years political and intellectual concern for such problems. I am impressed, now as then, with how insightful is the public understanding of the causes of crime. The average person locates the principal cause in the values of young persons which in turn are shaped by familial and social forces. (To many scholars, imbued with a materialist view of the world, this public understanding is still controversial, if not entirely wrong-headed.) Yet I continue to be aware of how uncertain and dubious are many of the popular remedies for crime, such as more police or better rehabilitative programs. It is the duty of the statesman to link the confident instincts, immediate knowledge, and deeply held values of the citizen with the policy analyses of the specialist so as to produce, by informed persuasion, reasonable programs. Only occasionally do American statesmen and scholars do this job very well, though on the whole they do it better today than they did a decade ago.

The first part of this book describes our recent (since the early 1960s) experience with crime and its impact on the community, and then offers, in the form of a critique of some criminological writings, a general perspective on how best to think about crime control policies. Part II describes the police and their struggle with crime, neighborhood disorder, and community relations. Part III discusses five major issues in the debate over crime control policies: penalties and opportunities (sometimes called "deterrence"), incapacitation, rehabilitation, capital punishment, and drug control. Part IV begins with an ambitious (but neither complete nor conclusive) effort to place crime in the context of American history and culture, so as to reveal some of the fundamental forces affecting its incidence. "Root causes" appear here. Part IV ends with a summary discussion of what a decent crime-control policy might look like and why it is so difficult to implement it.

Five of the chapters that appear here did not appear in the first edition and three chapters that did appear earlier have been completely rewritten. The new material includes essays on neighborhood safety (chapter 5), incapacitation (chapter 8), rehabilitation (chapter 9), crime in American culture (chapter 12), and gun control (appendix), each of which has previously been published in a magazine, newspaper, or journal. The material on penalties and opportunities (chapter 7) appears for the first time, while the essays on police-community relations, the death penalty, and crime and public policy (chapters 6, 10, and 13) have been thoroughly revised.

PART
I
CRIME

Chapter 1

Crime Amidst Plenty: The Paradox of the Sixties

I F in 1960 one had been asked what steps society might take to prevent a sharp increase in the crime rate, one might well have answered that crime could best be curtailed by reducing poverty, increasing educational attainment, eliminating dilapidated housing, encouraging community organization, and providing troubled or delinquent youth with counseling services.* Such suggestions would have had not only a surface plausibility, but some evidence to support them. After all, crime was more common in slum neighborhoods than in middle-class suburbs, and the latter could be distinguished from the former by the income, schooling, housing, and communal bonds of their residents. To improve the material conditions of inner-city life would, of course, require a high level of national prosperity combined with programs aimed specifically at inner-city conditions. There was a confident conviction at the highest levels of the administrations of Presidents Kennedy and Johnson that this prosperity would be achieved and these programs devised.

*Original version of this chapter written with Robert L. DuPont.

They were right. Early in the decade of the 1960s, this country began the longest sustained period of prosperity since World War II, much of it fueled, as we later realized, by a semiwar economy. A great array of programs aimed at the young, the poor, and the deprived were mounted. Though these efforts were not made primarily out of a desire to reduce crime, they were wholly consistent with—indeed, in their aggregate money levels, wildly exceeded—the policy prescription that a thoughtful citizen worried about crime would have offered at the beginning of the decade.

Crime soared. It did not just increase a little; it rose at a faster rate and to higher levels than at any time since the 1930s and, in some categories, to higher levels than any experienced in this century. The mood of contentment and confidence in which the decade began was shattered, not only by crime, but by riots and war. American democracy, which seemingly had endured in part because, as David Potter phrased it, we were a "people of plenty" relieved of the necessity of bitter economic conflict, had in the 1960s brought greater plenty to more people than ever before in its history, and the result was anger, frustration, unrest, and confusion.

Various explanations were offered for the apparent failure of the American promise. Liberals first denied that crime *was* rising. Then, when the facts became undeniable, they blamed it on social programs that, through lack of funds and will, had not yet produced *enough* gains and on police departments that, out of prejudice or ignorance, were brutal and unresponsive. It was not made clear, of course, just why more affluence would reduce crime when some affluence had seemingly increased it, or why criminals would be more fearful of gentle cops than of tough ones. Conservatives, exaggerating the crime increase, blamed it on a "soft" Supreme Court and a "permissive" attorney general on the apparent assumption —never defended, and in fact indefensible—that the Supreme Court and the attorney general could effectively manage the day-to-day behavior of the local police, and that the level of police effectiveness was directly related to the level of crime.

Rising crime rates were not the only sign of social malaise during the 1960s. The prosperity of the decade was also accompanied by alarming rises in welfare rates, drug abuse, and youthful unemployment. During the 1960s we were becoming two societies—one affluent and worried, the other pathological and predatory. This development was first noticed by Andrew Brimmer and Daniel P. Moynihan, who separately but with equal dismay noted that, by the second half of the decade, blacks generally were improving their income positions but blacks in the inner slums were becoming worse off, that the educational attainments of the young generally had risen sharply but that many inner-city schools had virtually ceased to function, and that the work force was at an all-time high at the same time as were the welfare rolls.

It all began in about 1963. That was the year, to overdramatize a bit, that a decade began to fall apart.

Crime

IN 1946 there were in this country 6.9 murders per one hundred thousand population, the highest murder rate since 1937.[1] In the seventeen years that followed the end of World War II, the murder rate declined more or less steadily, so that by 1962 it was only 4.5 per one hundred thousand population—less than two-thirds of what it had been in 1946. In 1964 it showed a slight increase to 4.8, in 1965 another slight increase to 5.1, and in 1966 a larger increase to 5.6; by 1972 it stood at 9.4, higher than at any time since 1936.

Robbery is perhaps the most feared crime, inasmuch as it so often occurs among strangers, without warning, and involves the use or threat of force. It is not as accurately counted as murder, but, being serious and not involving friends, most of the serious cases are called to the attention of the police. In 1946 the robbery rate was 59.4 per one hundred thousand population, higher than it had been since 1935. Then robbery, like murder, began to show a long, slow decline in its incidence until, by 1959, the rate was only 51.2—a drop of 14 percent. The following year it went up suddenly to 59.9, the largest one-year increase during any of the preceding seventeen years. For the next two years it held steady at about this same level, and then in 1963 it went up again; in 1964, again; and in 1965, again. By 1968 it had more than *doubled*, to 131.0.

Auto theft is also a more or less accurately counted crime. Cars are insured, and victims must report the loss to collect their payments. This crime followed, until the 1960s, a pattern just the opposite of that of murder and robbery: the mid-1940s were a *low* point for auto theft, probably because the production of automobiles for civilian use had ended during World War II, so that by 1946 there were simply not many cars around that were worth stealing. In 1949, only 107.7 cars per one hundred thousand population were stolen. Then, as the country returned to a peacetime economy and new cars began rolling off the production lines, the auto theft rate began to drift upward. By 1960 it had risen to 181.6, an increase of almost 60 percent. For a year or two the rate paused at this new high—new, at least, for any period since 1935. Then, from 1963 to 1964, it went up by the largest amount of any year since records were kept: over thirty points. In the language of the stock market chart-makers, auto theft had "broken out," and from that year on it showed sharp annual increases. Put another way, from 1949 to 1961 auto theft increased each year on the average by fewer than seven cars stolen per one hundred thousand population. From 1962 to 1963 it increased at a rate two and one-half times faster than in any preceding year, and from 1963 to 1964 at a rate over four times faster.

If the figures are to be believed, the increase in crime assumed epidemic proportions in the first few years of the 1960s. Interestingly, murder was somewhat slower to show this increase than robbery or auto theft. One reason for this difference may be the continued improvement in the delivery of emergency health care to people who have been assaulted: speedy ambulance drivers and skilled doctors and nurses may have kept the homicide rate down by saving the lives of growing proportions of persons who have been shot or stabbed. In 1933 six times as many crimes were listed as aggravated assaults as were listed as homicides. By 1960 the ratio had increased to seventeen to one, a crude measure, perhaps, of the improvements resulting from radio-dispatched ambulances and new medical and surgical techniques.

Drugs

DURING most of the 1950s, the number of narcotic-related deaths reported by the medical examiner in New York City hovered around one hundred a year.[2] In 1960 it touched two hundred for the first time since at least 1918, and perhaps ever. In 1961 there was a sudden, sharp increase to over three hundred, but the following year it dropped back again. In 1963 the number increased sharply again, and by 1967 had passed seven hundred a year and was still climbing. By the end of the decade, over twelve hundred New Yorkers who died each year either had taken a lethal overdose of a narcotic or had died of some other cause while being habitual narcotic users. Furthermore, the proportion of all narcotic-related deaths due to an overdose had increased: less than half of such deaths before 1961, but more than 80 percent after 1971.

Before 1963, Atlanta probably had no more than about five hundred heroin users. By the end of the decade, the number of users had increased tenfold, to five thousand.

In Boston, the estimated number of heroin users never exceeded six hundred in the period between 1960 and 1963. Between 1963 and 1964, there was a sudden estimated increase of more than four hundred users. During the following year the increase was eight hundred. By the end of the decade, the number of Boston users, like the number of those in Atlanta, had increased tenfold.

Welfare

IN MARCH 1965, Daniel P. Moynihan, then an assistant secretary of labor, published a document entitled *The Negro Family*.[3] The study described the weakness of the family structure among a large minority of blacks and argued for a national policy to correct the causes of that weakness and to support processes that would strengthen such families. The conditions he described were not new: since at least 1950 (the earliest figures included in the report), about one-fifth of black married women, as compared to about one twenty-fifth of white married women, were separated from their husbands. A large and growing number of these women with children but without husbands were on welfare (that is, receiving Aid to Families of Dependent Children [AFDC]).

One fact appeared in the Moynihan report, however, that was utterly without precedent. Since 1948, the annual number of new AFDC cases paralleled almost precisely the unemployment rate for nonwhite males. Whenever the nonwhite unemployment rate went up, as it did in 1949, 1954, and 1957, the number of new welfare cases went up. All this was to be expected—indeed, it was exactly what most supporters of the AFDC plan desired. But in 1962–1963, a remarkable thing happened: the number of new persons admitted to AFDC started going up even though the unemployment rate was going *down*.

From 1961 to 1964, the unemployment rate for nonwhite males fell from 12.9 percent to 9.1 percent, but between 1962 and 1964 the number of new AFDC cases opened each year increased by almost sixty thousand. In short, entry onto the welfare rolls was for the first time being influenced by forces independent of general economic conditions and of unemployment in particular. For decades the line plotting unemployment and the line plotting new AFDC cases were parallel; beginning in about 1960, they moved in opposite directions. From its graphic appearance, the phenomenon might be referred to as the "welfare scissors."

If a second edition of the study had been published in 1969, it would have shown that the scissors continued to open. By then, the nonwhite unemployment rate had fallen to 6.5 percent, but the annual number of new AFDC cases had grown by 222 percent.

The reasons for the increase in welfare applicants at a time when economic conditions were improving remains a matter of conjecture. Some saw the increase as the result of the rise in illegitimacy, especially among black children, but it is far from clear that this occurred (there have probably been important changes in the willingness to *report* a birth as illegitimate, but whether the actual *number* of such births has gone up is uncertain). If it occurred, the change took place in the first five years of the 1960s. From 1955 to 1960, the proportion of nonwhite births reported as illegitimate went from 20.2 percent to 21.6 percent, a trifling change; from 1960 to 1965, however, it rose from 21.6 to 26.3 percent, an increase of better than one-fifth.

Nor is it clear that the rise in welfare consumption in the early 1960s was the result of increasing proportions of women being deserted by their husbands. In 1960, 11 percent of married nonwhite women were separated from their husbands; by 1966 it was still 11 percent. (The proportion of divorced remained constant at 5 percent.) The percentage of nonwhite female-headed households increased only slightly between 1960 and 1966.

What *is* clear is that a growing percentage of women eligible for AFDC began to apply for it, and to receive it. Welfare became either socially more attractive or administratively more accessible, or both. While only a minority of illegitimate children receive welfare, and while many women deserted by their husbands never apply for welfare, it now seems clear that in the early 1960s more and more of those eligible for such aid sought it and, in many cities, more and more of those seeking it got it.

Unemployment

THERE WERE only three years between 1947 and 1957 during which there were as many as one million young persons (ages sixteen to twenty-four) who were unemployed. During the 1960s there was no year in which there were *fewer* than one million unemployed young adults; by 1961 they numbered 1.5 million, almost twice as many as there had been in 1955. The rate of unemployment for young workers was on the order of 8 to 10 percent between 1947 and 1957; from 1958 through 1964, it was never below 11 percent. By the mid-1970s, the teenage unemployment rate was 18 percent for whites and 37 percent for blacks.

The United States made enormous strides in providing jobs during the 1960s, but adults benefited more than young people. During a decade when the unemployment rate generally declined, the unemployment rate for persons sixteen to nineteen years of age actually increased, so that whereas the young made up only one-sixth of the unemployed in 1961, they accounted for more than one-quarter of it by 1971. In one year, 1963, the number of unemployed persons aged sixteen to nineteen increased by *one-fourth* to 17 percent. As the Bureau of Labor Statistics was later to write, "In 1963, the relative position of teenagers began to deteriorate markedly."[4] Whereas before 1963 their unemployment was never more than two or three times greater than that of adults, after then it was at least four times greater, and by 1968 was more than five times greater.

The increase in teenage and young adult unemployment was particularly sharp among nonwhites. Not only were a higher proportion of young nonwhites than young whites unemployed, but the increase in youth unemployment was greater for the former than for the latter: between 1960 and 1963, which was the peak year for the decade, the unemployment rate among persons age sixteen to nineteen went up by 23 percent for whites but by 28 percent for nonwhites. In 1963 there were 176,000 unemployed young nonwhites, more than twice as many as had existed eight years earlier; they accounted for almost one-third of all the young nonwhites in the labor force.

The Search for Causes

The early years of the 1960s witnessed a sudden and marked deterioration in certain key social indicators that, taken together, was unprecedented during any of the previous twenty or thirty years. Some of these indicators, such as teenage unemployment, were noticed and believed; others, such as those about crime and families, were noticed but not believed; and still others, such as those pertaining to heroin addiction, were scarcely even noticed. Or, more precisely, "informed opinion" did not notice or believe many of these indicators.

The price that we paid for this oversight—in confusion, frustration, and social divisions—was substantial. At the very time when the United States was embarking on its greatest period of sustained prosperity, a period that was to produce major improvements in the incomes, educational levels, and housing and health conditions of almost every major segment of our population, the quality of life, especially of life in public places, was rapidly worsening. We were achieving the Great Society without producing the good life, enhancing our prosperity without improving our tranquillity.

The crucial years seem to have been 1962 and 1963. Well before the war in Vietnam had engaged us or the ghetto riots had absorbed us, the social bonds—the ties of family, of neighborhood, of mutual forbearance and civility—seem to have come asunder. Why?

That question should be, and no doubt in time will be, seriously debated. No single explanation, perhaps no set of explanations, will ever gain favor. One fact, however, is an obvious beginning to an explanation: by 1962 and 1963 there had come of age the persons born during the baby boom of the immediate postwar period. A child born in 1946 would have been sixteen in 1962, seventeen in 1963.

The numbers involved were very large. In 1950 there were about twenty-four million persons aged fourteen to twenty-four; by 1960 that had increased only slightly to just under twenty-seven million. But during the next ten years it increased by over thirteen million persons. Every year for ten years, the number of young people increased by 1.3 million. That ten-year increase was greater than the growth in the young segment of the population for the rest of the *century* put together. During the first *two* years of the decade of the 1960s, we added more young persons (about 2.6 million) to our population than we had added in any preceding *ten* years since 1930.

The result of this was provocatively stated by Professor Norman B. Ryder, the Princeton University demographer: "There is a perennial invasion of barbarians who must somehow be civilized and turned into contributors to fulfillment of the various functions requisite to societal survival." That "invasion" is the coming of age of a new generation of young people. Every society copes with this enormous socialization process more or less successfully, but occasionally that process is almost literally swamped by a quantitative discontinuity in the numbers of persons involved: "The increase in the magnitude of the socialization tasks in the United States during the past decade was completely outside the bounds of previous experience."[5]

If we continue Professor Ryder's metaphor, we note that in 1950 and still in 1960 the "invading army" (those aged fourteen to twenty-four) were outnumbered three to one by the size of the "defending army" (those aged twenty-five to sixty-four). By 1970 the ranks of the former had grown so fast that they were only outnumbered two to one by the latter, a state of affairs that had not existed since 1910.

The significance of these numbers can scarcely be exaggerated. They are best understood by looking at one city, such as Washington, D.C. It has a large black population, a high crime rate, and is the source of countless stories about popular fears of criminal attack and countless political speeches about the need to get tough. One would think that it is a city whose population deteriorated substantially during the 1960s. In fact, by most measures, quite the opposite was the case.

Consider the black population, which is about three-fourths of the total. Its median educational level increased from 8.8 years of schooling in 1950 to 11.4 years in 1970.[6] In 1950 there were only ten thousand black adults in the city with a college education; in 1970 there were twenty-two thousand. Black median family income, adjusted for inflation, tripled during the two decades. In 1970, when there was substantial unemployment in the country as a whole, the unemployment for black men aged twenty to fifty-nine in Washington was only 4.5 percent, and for black women the same age it was even less—3.6 percent. Washington has manifold problems of poor housing, poverty, and inadequate schooling, but it is not by any conceivable measure a vast lower-class slum or a city that has lost ground economically or educationally. To a substantial degree, it is a black middle-class or lower-middle-class community.

Yet Washington during the 1960s and 1970s was in the grip of a massive crime, heroin, and welfare problem. A large part of the reason was the change in that city's age structure. In 1960 there were about sixty-five thousand persons aged sixteen to twenty-one in the city. Ten years later, as the postwar baby boom left its mark, that number had risen to over eighty-six thousand—an increase of more than 30 percent. During the 1930s there had been only about eight thousand live births each year in the city; by the end of World War II that number had risen to about twenty thousand per year.

The vast majority of these additional children entered the life of the city and its institutions just the way they had always done—they went to school, took jobs, got married, and had children of their own (though far fewer than the number of children their parents had). A small proportion of them did the rebellious things that some young people always do. But this time, it was a small proportion of a very large number.

The schools were among the first institutions to notice the change. The number of dropouts from Washington junior high schools began to increase beginning in 1962 and peaked in 1964.

Then, as the children got older, the number of dropouts from the senior high schools began to rise, peaking in 1968. When those in school or out of school started looking for jobs, they discovered that the number of new young applicants had increased far faster than the number of jobs. In Washington, the unemployment rate for blacks of ages sixteen to twenty-one had been around 8 percent during the 1950s, but during the 1960s it rose steadily until it reached 16 percent for males and 20 percent for females by 1970.

The proportion of young males in Washington who became addicted to heroin before the 1960s had been, as best one can estimate it, less than 3 percent. One might have expected that rate to remain the same for the new, larger population of young people coming of age in the 1960s. If it had, the number of addicts would have gone up by at least a third—a serious problem, to be sure, but nothing like the epidemic that actually struck. In fact, the addiction rate for males born in the decade following 1945 who grew up in Washington was over *ten times* the "normal" level. As the epidemic mounted, certain age groups were devastated. Of the six thousand young Washington men born in 1953, over 13 percent became heroin addicts, and in some areas of the city about one-fourth of the males born in that year became heroin users. In the single year 1969, about 5 percent of all the sixteen-year-old males became addicted to heroin.

Some women were becoming addicts as well, but in absolute and relative terms their numbers were far smaller than those of the male addicts. For young women, or a fraction of them, welfare rather than heroin led to their identification as a significant group. For several decades AFDC had been utilized principally by older women who had lost their husbands. In the 1960s, as large numbers of young women entered child-bearing age, there was both an increase in AFDC utilization and a change in the kind of recipient. The women on AFDC in Washington tripled between 1961 and 1971, from five thousand to over sixteen thousand, and the largest growth occurred among young women. The number on AFDC who were over thirty increased by 140 percent, but the number who were under thirty increased by 300 percent, and the number who were under twenty increased by 800 percent. In ten years, the age of the typical woman on AFDC fell from thirty to twenty-three.

Crime increased rapidly in this same period. Here, of course, even crude estimates of the number of young persons involved is very difficult. We obviously do not know the age of those who commit crimes, only the age of those arrested for crimes. And we do not know how many crimes are committed by the same person. But we can make some guesses. Professor Marvin Wolfgang and his coworkers at the University of Pennsylvania examined the delinquency records of all the males born in 1945 who lived in Philadelphia between their tenth and eighteenth birthdays.[7] They were able to find over ten thousand of them, and learned that more than one-third had at least one recorded contact with the police by the time they were eighteen, and half of these had more than one such contact. Of the delinquent acts recorded, perhaps a quarter could be regarded as relatively serious crimes. Most of the crimes were committed when the boys were fifteen, sixteen, or seventeen.

Suppose those proportions were true for Washington (they are not likely to be exactly the same, because the racial and economic composition of the cities differ). Since the number of persons aged sixteen to twenty-one increased by twenty-one thousand during the 1960s, and if one-third of these committed one or more delinquent acts, then by 1970 there were at least seven thousand more delinquents in the city than there had been when the decade started. Since each delinquent will have committed at least three offenses known to the police before he turns eighteen, twenty-one thousand more offenses resulting in an arrest were committed. There were no doubt many thousands more that did not produce a police contact.

Age Is Not the Whole Story

CHANGES in the age structure of the population cannot alone account for the social dislocations of the 1960s. While the number of persons between the ages of sixteen and twenty-one in the District of Columbia increased by 32 percent between 1960 and 1970, the social problems increased much more: the rate of serious crime went up by over 400 percent, welfare rates by over 200 percent, unemployment rates by at least 100 percent, and heroin addiction by (a best guess) over 1,000 percent. Detroit, to cite another example, had about one hundred murders in 1960 but over five hundred in 1971, yet the number of young persons did not quintuple.

According to a close study of murder rates in various cities, carried out by Arnold Barnett and his associates at the Massachusetts Institute of Technology, the increase in the murder rate during the 1960s was more than ten times greater than what one would have expected from the changing age structure of the population alone. Apparently much more complex forces are at work in almost all large cities. Though Detroit became known, erroneously, as the "murder capital of the world" (actually, Atlanta enjoyed that dubious distinction), the increase in the murder rate was roughly the same in the fifty largest cities—it about doubled between 1963 and 1971. Clearly, some broad national forces were involved, but exactly what they were, no one knows. The results, however, were chilling: if the murder rate held constant at that level, then a child born in 1974 in Detroit and living there all his life had a one in thirty-five chance of being murdered. And if the murder rate continued to increase at its 1970s pace, his chances of meeting a felonious end increased to one *in fourteen.* At 1970 levels, Barnett pointed out, a typical baby born and remaining in a large American city was more likely to die of murder than an American soldier in World War II was to die in combat.[8]

Other analyses confirmed that the rise in crime rates in the 1960s was not wholly the simple result of an increase in the number of young persons in the population. Theodore Ferdinand calculated from published arrest figures that only 13.4 percent of the increase in arrests for robbery between 1950 and 1965 could be accounted for by the increase in the number of persons between the ages of ten and twenty-four.[9]

One possibility is that the sudden increase in the number of persons at risk has an exponential effect on the rate of certain social problems. There is, perhaps, a "critical mass" of young persons such that, when that number is reached, or when an increase in that mass is sudden and large, a self-sustaining chain reaction is set off that creates an explosive increase in the amount of crime, addiction, and welfare dependency.[10] What had once been relatively isolated and furtive acts (copping a fix, stealing a TV) became widespread and group-supported activities.

Heroin addiction is an example. We have had addicts since at least 1900, and we have always had young people who were potential addicts. We also know, as will be explained in chapter 11, that addiction spreads like a contagion, with one friend turning on another. Yet ordinarily this contagion is rather contained and results in no epidemic of the sort that broke out in the 1960s. The sudden, dramatic increase in the number of potential addicts seems to have created a self-sustaining contagion that rapidly produced a more-than-proportional number of actual addicts.

At the same time, our society did a number of things that nurtured this reaction. The media spread the message that a "youth culture" was being born and celebrated the cult of personal liberation that seemed to be central to that culture, a matter on which I will have more to say in chapter 12. Enhanced personal mobility made it easier to carry a contagion from one group to another. Social programs designed to combat poverty brought together groups that once would have been isolated from each other, and thus spread the contagion as surely as bringing men together in the Army during World War I spread influenza. The contacts of upper-middle-class suburban youths with ghetto blacks as a result of civil rights programs increased access to the drug culture, or perhaps created in the eyes of the whites the mistaken view that such a "culture" existed, and was desirable, when in fact only deviant and episodic drug taking existed.

The institutional mechanisms which could handle problems in ordinary numbers were suddenly swamped, and may, in some cases, have broken down so fully as barely to function at all. The deterrent force of the police and the courts may not be great in normal times, but it may have declined absolutely, and not just relatively, in those exceptional times. The increase in crime produced a less-than-proportionate increase in arrests and, of those arrested, a less-than-proportionate increase in penalties. If the supply and value of legitimate opportunities (jobs) was declining at the very time that the cost of illegitimate activities (fines and jail terms) was also declining, a rational teenager might well have concluded that it made more sense to steal cars than to wash them.

One is tempted to ask, "What might have been?" If the age structure of the decade had been normal, if crime and addiction and welfare dependency had not increased so dramatically, could we have come to grips with our problems any more successfully than we did? Indeed, what would we have considered our problems to be? The war and its divisiveness would have occurred in any event. The demand by blacks for equality of opportunity would still have arisen, though the number of young blacks available for militant protest would have been smaller. The ghetto riots might still have occurred—just as it was hard beforehand to predict that they would occur, it is hard after the fact to predict the circumstances under which they would not have erupted.

But perhaps some problems would have been easier to address had not the social structure appeared to collapse. We might have had a more sensible discussion of riots and what to do about them if it had not been so easy for some to link (incorrectly, I think) the existence of rioting with the rise of ordinary criminality. Programs designed to solve teenage unemployment would clearly have been more successful if so large a fraction of the teenagers to be employed were not deeply involved in heroin addiction and remunerative crime. In retrospect, we might not have described certain "Great Society" programs as failures if the problems they sought to remedy—unemployment, school dropouts, low educational achievement—had not been suddenly enlarged in scope and altered in character. Rebuilding or rehabilitating our inner-city neighborhoods might well have been much easier under public auspices—indeed, might have occurred under private auspices—were not so many of these areas destroyed as communities by crime and addiction.

But we are not yet sure we can even explain what did happen; we shall never be able to explain what might have happened.

Chapter 2

Crime and Community

P REDATORY crime does not merely victimize individuals, it impedes and, in the extreme case, prevents the formation and maintenance of community. By disrupting the delicate nexus of ties, formal and informal, by which we are linked with our neighbors, crime atomizes society and makes of its members mere individual calculators estimating their own advantage, especially their chances for survival amidst their fellows. Common undertakings become difficult or impossible, except for those motivated by a shared desire for protection. Coming together for protection may, of course, lead to a greater sense of mutual aid and dependence and provide the basis for larger and more positive commitments. It was out of a desire for self-defense, after all, that many of the earliest human settlements arose. But then it was a banding together against a common *external* enemy. Mutual protection against an enemy within is more difficult to achieve, less sustaining of a general sense of community, and more productive of conflict as disputes arise over who is the victim and who the aggressor.

It was the failure to appreciate the importance of community and the gravity of the threats to it that led to some mistaken views during the 1960s of the true nature of the "urban crisis." Until at least the latter half of that decade, we were told by leaders that the "key problem" facing our cities was, variously, inadequate transportation, declining retail sales, poor housing, or rising taxes. Though the average citizen no doubt shared these and other concerns in some measure, he was increasingly restive that his view of the problem of his city was not taken seriously.

This view was to be found in a number of opinion surveys but, until nearly the end of the decade, it was not taken seriously by many of those in charge of public policy for cities. There was a curious failure of representation in our political system. I first became aware of the gap between what people were saying and leaders were doing in 1966 when a colleague and I conducted a poll of over one thousand Boston homeowners. We asked what each respondent thought was the biggest problem facing the city. The "conventional" urban problems—housing, transportation, pollution, urban renewal, and so on—were a major concern of only 18 percent of those questioned, and these were disproportionately the wealthier, better-educated respondents. Only 9 percent mentioned jobs and employment, even though many of those interviewed had incomes at or below what is often regarded as the poverty level. The issue which concerned more respondents than any other was variously stated: crime, violence, rebellious youth, racial tension, public immorality, delinquency. However stated, the common theme seemed to be a concern for improper behavior in public places.

From some white respondents this was no doubt a covert way of indicating antiblack feelings. But it was not primarily that, for these same forms of impropriety were mentioned more often than other problems by black respondents as well. And those among the whites who indicated, in answer to another question, that they felt the government ought to do more to help blacks were just as likely to mention impropriety as those who felt the government had already done too much.

Nor was this pattern peculiar to Boston. A survey done in 1967 for *Fortune* magazine in which over three hundred black males were questioned in thirteen major cities showed similar results.[1] In this study, people were not asked what was the biggest problem of their city, but rather what was the biggest problem they faced as individuals. When stated this generally, it was not surprising that jobs and education were given the highest priority. What is striking is that close behind came the same "urban" problems found in Boston—a concern for crime, violence, the need for more police protection, and so on. Indeed, these issues ranked ahead of the expressed desire for a higher income. Surveys reported in 1968 by the President's Commission on Law Enforcement and Administration of Justice showed crime and violence ranking high as major problems among both black and white respondents.[2] Today, of course, the importance of crime as a public concern is well known. In the early 1960s, this concern was often denied or ignored. And even today, a concern for crime remains, to some, an indication of a "conservative" inclination despite the fact that the victims of crimes are disproportionately to be found in communities (or increasingly, noncommunities) that support liberal candidates.

The Failure of Community

IN READING the responses to the Boston survey, I was struck by how various and general were the ways of expressing public concern in this area. "Crime in the streets" was not the stock answer, though that came up often enough. Indeed, many of the forms of impropriety mentioned involved little that was criminal in any serious sense—rowdy teenagers, for example, or various indecencies, such as lurid advertisements in front of neighborhood movies and racy paperbacks in the local drug-store.

What these concerns have in common, and thus what constitutes the "urban problem" for a large percentage (perhaps a majority) of urban citizens, is a sense of the failure of community. By "community" I do not mean, as some do, a metaphysical entity or abstract collectivity with which people "need" to affiliate. There may be an "instinct" for "togetherness" arising out of ancient or tribal longings for identification, but different people gratify it in different ways, and for most the gratification has little to do with neighborhood or urban conditions. When I speak of the concern for "community," I refer to a desire for the observance of standards of right and seemly conduct in the public places in which one lives and moves, those standards to be consistent with, and supportive of, the values and life styles of the particular individual.[3] Around one's home, the places where one shops, and the corridors through which one walks there is for each of us a public space wherein our sense of security, self-esteem, and propriety is either reassured or jeopardized by the people and events we encounter. Viewed this way, the concern for community is less the "need" for "belonging" (or, in equally vague language, the "need" to overcome feelings of "alienation" or "anomie") than the normal but not compulsive interest of any rationally self-interested person in his and his family's environment.

A rationally self-interested person will take most seriously those things which affect him most directly and importantly and over which he feels he can exercise the greatest influence. Next to one's immediate and particular needs for such things as shelter, income, and education, one's social and physical surroundings have perhaps the greatest consequence for oneself and one's family. Furthermore, unlike those city-wide or national forces which influence a person, what happens to him at the neighborhood level is most easily affected by his own actions. The way he behaves will, ideally, alter the behavior of others; the remarks he makes and the way he presents himself and his home will shape, at least marginally, the common expectations by which the appropriate standards of public conduct in that area are determined. How he dresses, how loudly or politely he speaks, how well he trims his lawn or paints his house, the liberties he permits his children to enjoy—all those not only express what the individual thinks is appropriate conduct, but in some degree influence what his neighbors take to be appropriate conduct.

Controlling the Immediate Environment

IT IS primarily at the neighborhood level that meaningful opportunities exist for the exercise of urban citizenship. And it is the breakdown of neighborhood controls (neighborhood self-government, if you will) that accounts for the principal concerns of many urban citizens. When they can neither take for granted nor influence by their actions and those of their neighbors the standards of conduct within their own neighborhood community, they experience what to them are "urban problems"—problems that arise directly out of the unmanageable consequences of living in close proximity.

I suspect that this concern for the maintenance of the neighborhood community explains in part the overwhelming preference Americans have for small cities and towns. According to a Gallup Poll taken in 1963, only 22 percent of those interviewed wanted to live in cities, 49 percent preferred small towns, and 28 percent preferred suburbs. (Only among blacks, interestingly enough, did a majority prefer large cities—perhaps because the costs of rural or small town life, in terms of poverty and discrimination, are greater for the black than the costs, in terms of disorder and insecurity, of big city life.) Small towns and suburbs, because they are socially more homogeneous than large cities and because local self-government can be used to reinforce informal neighborhood sanctions, apparently make the creation and maintenance of a proper sense of community easier. At any rate, Americans are acting on this preference for small places, whatever its basis. As Daniel Elazar has pointed out, the smaller cities are claiming a growing share of the population; the largest cities are not increasing in size at all, and some, indeed, are getting smaller.[4]

A rational concern for community implies a tendency to behave in certain ways which some popular writers have mistakenly thought to be the result of conformity, prejudice, or an excessive concern for appearances. No doubt all of these factors play some role in the behavior of many people and a dominant role in the behavior of a few, but one need not make any such assumptions to explain the nature of most neighborhood conduct. In dealing with one's immediate environment under circumstances that make individual actions efficacious in constraining the actions of others, one will develop a range of sanctions to employ against others, and will, in turn, respond to the sanctions that others use. Such sanctions are typically informal, even casual, and may consist of little more than a gesture, word, or expression. Occasionally direct action is taken—a complaint, or even making a scene—but resort to these measures is rare because they invite counterattacks ("If that's the way he feels about it, I'll just show him!") and because, if used frequently, they lose their effectiveness. The purpose of the sanctions is to regulate the external consequences of private behavior and to handle, in the language of economists, "third-party effects," "externalities," and "the production of collective goods." I may wish to let my lawn go to pot, but one ugly lawn affects the appearance of the whole neighborhood, just as one sooty incinerator smudges clothes that others have hung out to dry. Rowdy children raise the noise level and tramp down the flowers for everyone, not just for their parents.

Because the sanctions employed are subtle, informal, and delicate, not everyone is equally vulnerable to everyone else's discipline. Furthermore, if there is not a generally shared agreement as to appropriate standards of conduct, these sanctions will be inadequate to correct such deviations as occur. A slight departure from a norm is set right by a casual remark; a commitment to a different norm is very hard to alter, unless, of course, the deviant party is "eager to fit in," in which case he is not committed to the different norm at all but simply looking for signs as to what the preferred norms may be. Because of these considerations, the members of a community have a general preference for social homogeneity and a suspicion of heterogeneity; a person different in one respect (for example, income, race, or speech) may be different in other respects as well (for example, how much noise or trash he is likely to produce).

Prejudice and Diversity

THIS REASONING sometimes leads to error. People observed to be outwardly different may not in fact behave differently, or such differences in behavior as exist may be irrelevant to the interests of the community. Viewed one way, these errors are exceptions to rule-of-thumb guides or empirical generalizations; viewed another way, they are manifestations of prejudice. And in fact one of the unhappiest complexities of the logic of neighborhood is that it can so often lead one wrongly to impute to another person some behavioral problem on the basis of the latter's membership in a racial or economic group. Even worse, under cover of acting in the interests of the neighborhood, some people may give vent to the most unjustified and neurotic prejudices.

However much we may regret such expressions of prejudice, it does little good to imagine that the occasion for their expression can be wished away. We may even pass laws (as I think we should) making it illegal to use certain outward characteristics (like race) as grounds for excluding people from a neighborhood. But the core problem will remain. Owing to the importance of community to most people and given the process whereby new arrivals are inducted into and constrained by the sanctions of the neighborhood, the suspicion of heterogeneity will only be overcome when a person proves by his actions that his distinctive characteristic is not a sign of any disposition to violate the community's norms.

Such a view seems to be at odds with the notion that the big city is the center of cosmopolitanism, by which is meant, among other things, diversity. And so it is. A small fraction of the population (in my judgment, a very small fraction) may want diversity so much that it will seek out the most cosmopolitan sections of the cities as places to live. Some of these people are intellectuals, others are young, unmarried persons with a taste for excitement before assuming the responsibilities of a family, and still others are "misfits" who have dropped out of society for a variety of reasons. Since one element of this group—the intellectuals—writes the books which define the "urban problem," we are likely to be confused by their preferences and assume that the problem is in part to maintain the heterogeneity and cosmopolitanism of the central city—to attract and hold a neat balance among middle-class families, young culture-lovers, lower-income blacks, "colorful" Italians, and big businessmen. To assume this is to mistake the preferences of the few for the needs of the many. And even the few probably exaggerate just how much diversity they wish. Manhattan intellectuals are often as worried about crime in the streets as their cousins in Queens. The desired diversity is "safe" diversity—a harmless variety of specialty stores, esoteric bookshops, "ethnic" restaurants, and highbrow cultural enterprises. I suspect that the tolerance for social diversity, especially "safe" diversity, increases with education and decreases with age. This tolerance, however, does not extend to "unsafe" diversity; street crime, for example.

On "Middle-Class Values"

AT THIS POINT I had better take up explicitly the dark thoughts forming in the minds of some readers that this analysis is little more than an elaborate justification for prejudice, philistinism, conformity, and (worst of all) "middle-class values." The number of satirical books on suburbs seems to suggest that the creation of a sense of community is at best little more than enforcing the lowest common denominator of social behavior by means of kaffee klatsches and the exchange of garden tools; at worst, it is the end of privacy and individuality and the beginning of discrimination in its uglier forms.

I have already tried to deal with the prejudice argument. Prejudice exists, as does the desire for community; both often overlap. There is no "solution" to the problem, though stigmatizing certain kinds of prejudgments (such as those based on race) is helpful. Since (in my opinion) social class is the primary basis (with age and religion not far behind) on which community-maintaining judgments are made, and since social class (again, in my opinion) is a much better predictor of behavior than race, I foresee the time when racial distinctions will be much less salient (though never absent) in handling community problems. Indeed, much of what passes for "race prejudice" today may be little more than class prejudice, with race used as a rough indicator of approximate social class.

With respect to the charge of defending "middle-class values," let me stress that the analysis of "neighborhood" offered here makes no assumptions about the substantive values enforced by the communal process. On the contrary, the emphasis is on the process itself; in principle, it could be used to enforce any set of values. To be sure, we most often observe it enforcing the injunctions against noisy children and unmown lawns, but I suppose it could also be used to enforce injunctions against turning children into "sissies" and being enslaved by lawn-maintenance chores. In fact, if we turn our attention to the city and end our preoccupation with suburbia, we will find many kinds of neighborhoods with a great variety of substantive values being enforced. Jane Jacobs described how and to what ends informal community controls operate in working-class Italian sections of New York and elsewhere. Middle-class black neighborhoods tend also to develop a distinctive code. And Bohemian or "hippie" sections (despite their loud disclaimers of any interest in either restraint or constraint) establish and sustain a characteristic ethos. But I will go further: to the extent middle-class values include a desire for property and propriety, they are neither exclusively the concern of the middle class nor worthy of the scorn heaped upon them. They are the common interest of almost everyone.

People without Communities

VIEWED historically, the process whereby neighborhoods, in the sense intended in this chapter, have been formed in the large cities might be thought of as one in which order arose out of chaos to return in time to a new form of disorder.

Immigrants, thrust together in squalid central-city ghettos, gradually worked their way out to establish, first with the aid of streetcar lines and then with the aid of automobiles, more or less homogeneous and ethnically distinct neighborhoods of single-family and two-family houses. In the Boston survey, the average respondent had lived in his present neighborhood for about twenty years. When asked what his neighborhood had been like when he was growing up, the vast majority of those questioned said that it was "composed of people pretty much like myself"—similar, that is, in income, ethnicity, religion, and so on. In time, of course, families, especially those of childrearing age, began spilling out over the city limits into the suburbs and were replaced in the central city by persons lower in income than themselves.

Increasingly, the central city is coming to be made up of persons who have no interest, or who face special disabilities, in creating and maintaining a sense of community. There are several such groups, each with a particular problem and each with varying degrees of ability to cope with that problem. One is composed of affluent whites without children (young couples, single persons, elderly couples whose children have left home) who either (as with the "young swingers") lack an interest in community or (as with the elderly couples) lack the ability to participate meaningfully in the maintenance of community. But for such persons there are alternatives to community, principally, inhabiting a special physical environment that insulates the occupant from those threats it is the function of community to control. They move into high-rise buildings in which their apartment is connected by an elevator either to a basement garage or to a lobby guarded by a doorman and perhaps even a private police force. Thick walls and high fences protect such open spaces as exist from the intrusion of outsiders. The apartments may be air-conditioned, so that the windows need never be opened to admit street noises. Interestingly, a common complaint of such apartment-dwellers is that, in the newer buildings at least, the walls are too thin to ensure privacy; in short, the one failure of the physical substitute for community occasions the major community-oriented complaint.

A second group of noncommunal city residents are the poor whites, often elderly, who financially or for other reasons are unable to leave the old central-city neighborhood when it changes character. For many, that change is the result of the entry of blacks or Puerto Ricans into the block, and this gives rise to the number of antiblack or anti-Puerto Rican remarks which an interviewer encounters. But sometimes the neighborhood is taken over by young college students, or by artists, or by derelicts; then the remarks are antiyouth, antistudent, antiartist, or antidrunk. The fact that the change has instituted a new and (to the older resident) less seemly standard of conduct is more important than the attributes of the persons responsible for the change. Elderly persons, because they lack physical vigor and easy access to neighbors, are especially vulnerable to neighborhood changes and find it especially difficult to develop substitutes for community, except, of course, to withdraw behind locked doors and drawn curtains. They cannot afford the high-rise buildings and private security guards that are the functional equivalent of communal sanctions for the wealthier city dweller.

In the Boston survey, the fear of impropriety and violence was highest for those respondents who were the oldest and the poorest. Preoccupation with such issues as the major urban problem was greater among women than among men, among those over sixty-five years of age than among those under, among Catholics than among Jews, and among those earning less than $5,000 a year than among those earning higher incomes. (Incidentally, these were not the same persons most explicitly concerned about and hostile to blacks—antiblack sentiment was more common among middle-aged married couples who had children and modestly good incomes.)

Though the elderly may be more preoccupied with crime and violence than are those who are younger, they are not more likely to be victimized by it. In 1973 the Law Enforcement Assistance Administration (LEAA) of the Department of Justice sponsored a survey by the Census Bureau of about fifty thousand households in the five largest cities. In four of the five cities, persons over the age of fifty were much less likely to be the victim of a robbery than those under fifty, and in all five cities they were much less likely to be the victim of a burglary.[5] But these figures are misleading in at least two ways: they ignore the greater fear that even a minor crime engenders in persons unable to defend themselves, and they do not take into account the extent to which the victimization of the elderly has been reduced by the anticipatory actions of the elderly themselves who have decided to live behind locked doors.

The third group specially afflicted by the perceived breakdown of community are the blacks. For them, residential segregation as well as other factors have led to a condition in which there is relatively little spatial differentiation among blacks of various class levels. Lower-class, working-class, and middle-class blacks are squeezed into close proximity in such a way as to inhibit or prevent the territorial separation necessary for the creation and maintenance of different communal life styles. Segregation in the housing market is probably much more intense with respect to lower-cost housing than with middle-cost housing, suggesting that middle-class blacks may find it easier to move into previously all-white neighborhoods. But the constricted supply of low-cost housing means that a successful invasion of a new area by middle-class blacks often leads to their being followed rather quickly by those of the working and lower classes. As a result, unless middle-class blacks can leapfrog out to distant white (or new) communities, they will find themselves struggling to assert hegemony over a territory threatened on several sides by blacks with quite different life styles.

The black population has become residentially more, not less, segregated in the past twenty years. A Census Bureau survey of twenty large cities found that the proportion of blacks living in census tracts that were three-fourths or more black increased from 36 percent in 1960 to 50 percent in 1970.[6] Though there has been some black migration to the suburbs, the proportion of blacks in metropolitan areas who live in the central cities had actually risen from 77 percent in 1960 to 79 percent in 1970. During this period of increasing residential concentration, the material conditions of black life have generally improved; there have been dramatic gains in real income, housing quality, and educational attainment. Some of the members of the growing black middle class have been able to escape the inner city, but most have not.

This has meant that efforts by blacks to assert and defend a sense of community have been frustrated by their inability to maintain some degree of territorial homogeneity. The territories they occupy have instead been quite heterogeneous—criminals and noncriminals, addicts and nonaddicts, the middle class and the lower class live in close proximity, even side by side. The creation of a middle-class community requires that middle-class values dominate, and this applies with equal force, perhaps with special force, to blacks. If a family sends its children to schools in which many students reject school work, if they live in an area where illegitimacy is as common as marriage, if they regularly encounter on the streets persons for whom self-expression is more attractive than self-control, the family will either find itself conforming to a standard it does not value or isolating itself from its neighbors in ways that reduce even further such influence as that family might have on the behavior of others.

The residential isolation of blacks of various class levels in the central cities is a deeply destructive social phenomenon. As both Sar Levitan and Thomas Sowell have observed, the dominant ethic of many inner-city areas is established by a lower class from which the working class and the middle class cannot escape, and which they cannot publicly repudiate without giving aid and comfort to whites who wish to believe the worst about blacks.[7] Furthermore, it has become fashionable in some quarters to argue that to be "truly black" is incompatible with being middle class; thus the canons of racial pride can lead many families to act other than as their own interests suggest and as the maintenance of community requires. In the long term, of course, racial pride ("black power") may provide that shared sense of self-respect out of which a new and strong sense of community can be forged. No one knows. In the short run, however, many middle-class black families are left with the unhappy choice between despair and rage.

The LEAA survey cited earlier confirms the greater likelihood of black victimization. In all five of the largest cities, blacks are much more likely than whites to be the victims of robbery and burglary, in some cases by a ratio of nearly two to one. In four of the five cities, they are more likely to be the victims of aggravated assault. It is also generally the case that the very poorest persons, regardless of race, are more likely than the better off to be victims of a robbery. The reverse tends to be true of burglary, auto theft, and larceny. Robbery, a crime that depends on threats rather than stealth, is more likely to be committed by persons close to their own neighborhoods where escape is easy, whereas burglars, who operate unobserved, are more inclined to range over a wider territory in search of promising victims. Auto thieves, of course, steal autos from those who own them, and therefore the victims are in general affluent.

It is often said that the greatest price of segregation is the perpetuation of a divided society, one black and the other white. While there is some merit in this view, it overlooks the fact that most ethnic groups, when reasonably free to choose a place to live, have chosen to live among people similar to themselves. (I am thinking especially of the predominantly Jewish suburbs.) The real price of segregation, in my opinion, is not that it forces blacks and whites apart but that it forces blacks of different class positions together. A black writer, Orde Coombs, has vividly portrayed the despair and terror that has come to be the daily lot of the residents of Harlem and, no doubt, of many other ghettos. The streets are no longer controlled by either the respectable residents or by the police, but by the members of an "underclass" who "viciously prey upon the weak, the old, and the unsuspecting," for whom fear is "something palpable that walks among us every day and will not leave us alone."[8]

What City Government Cannot Do

COMMUNAL social controls tend to break down either when persons with an interest in and the competence for maintaining a community no longer live in the area, or when they remain but their neighborhood is not sufficiently distinct, territorially, from areas with different or threatening life styles. In the latter case especially, the collapse of informal social controls leads to demands for the imposition of formal or institutional controls—demands for "more police protection," more or better public services, and so on. The difficulty, however, is that there is relatively little government can do directly to maintain a neighborhood community. It can, of course, assign more police officers to it, but a city has only so many officers, and those assigned to one neighborhood must often be taken away from another. Perhaps more important is *what* the police in a given neighborhood do; as will be suggested in chapter 5, foot patrol that is linked to community self-help efforts may be worthwhile. But even in these cases, the police can rarely manage all relevant aspects of conduct in public places. Juvenile rowdiness, quarrels among neighbors, landlord-tenant disputes, the unpleasant side effects of a well-patronized tavern—all these are matters which may be annoying enough to warrant police intervention but not to warrant arrests. Managing these kinds of public disorder is a common task for the police, but one that they can rarely manage to everyone's satisfaction, precisely because the disorder arises out of a dispute among residents over what ought to be the standard of proper conduct.

City governments, during the 1950s and early 1960s, became increasingly remote from neighborhood concerns. In part this was the consequence of the growing centralization of local government—mayors were getting stronger at the expense of city councils, city-wide organizations (such as newspapers and civic associations) were getting stronger at the expense of neighborhood-based political parties, and new "superagencies" were being created in city hall to handle such matters as urban renewal, public welfare, and antipoverty programs. Mayors and citizens in many cities have begun to react against this trend and to search for ways of reinvolving government in neighborhood concerns; officials are setting up "little city halls," going on walking tours of their cities, and meeting with neighborhood and block clubs. But there is a limit to how effective such responses can be, because whatever the institutional structure, the issues that most concern a neighborhood are typically those about which politicians can do relatively little.

These issues involve disputes among the residents of a neighborhood or between the residents of two adjoining neighborhoods, and the mayor takes sides in these matters (such as busing) only at his peril. Many of the issues involve no tangible stake; they concern more the quality of life and competing standards of propriety and less the dollars-and-cents value of particular services or programs. Officials with experience in organizing little city halls or police-community relations programs often report that a substantial portion (perhaps a majority) of the complaints they receive concern people who "don't keep up their houses," or who "let their children run wild," or who "have noisy parties." Sometimes the city can do something (sending building inspectors to look over a house that appears to be a firetrap, for example, or having the health department require that someone clean up a lot he has littered), but just as often the city can do little except offer its sympathy.

Poverty, Race, and Community

INDIRECTLY, and especially over the long run, government can do much more. First and foremost, it can help persons enter into those social classes wherein the creation and maintenance of community is easiest. Lower-class persons (by definition, I would argue) attach little importance to the opinions of others; they are preoccupied with the daily struggle for survival and the immediate gratifications that may be attendant on survival and are inclined to uninhibited, expressive conduct. A lower-*income* person, of course, is not necessarily lower-*class;* the former condition reflects how much money he has, while the latter indicates the attitudes he possesses. Programs designed to increase prosperity and end poverty (defined as having too little money) will enable lower-income persons who care about the opinions of others to leave areas populated by lower-income persons who don't care (that is, areas populated by lower-class persons).

Governments and private organizations should continue to insure that, by law and in fact, citizens are not barred from moving from one neighborhood to another or from one community to another on grounds of race. To limit the housing opportunities available to blacks and other minorities to inner-city areas is to deny these people, on grounds other than their personal behavior, a chance to participate in or create for themselves a viable communal order.

In fact, there has been a dramatic increase in the number of persons who are middle-class, and a substantial (though not dramatic) increase in the number of blacks who have been able to move out of inner-city or slum areas. Those who have benefited from these social changes have for the most part enhanced their personal safety and community tranquillity. But we must recognize that, in the short run at least, the areas left behind by this migration have often been made worse off, not because those who remained behind in the slums and deteriorating neighborhoods found themselves suddenly earning less money or living in worse housing, but because the human infrastructure of their communities had departed.

Many persons who once headed the block clubs, ran the PTAs, complained of poor garbage collection, manned the neighborhood political apparatus, and kept the streets under some degree of surveillance have moved out. They left a void, sometimes literally a physical one. The growing number of abandoned buildings in the central parts of New York and other cities is grim evidence of the reduction in population densities and the increased purchasing power of former slum-dwellers.

With the more affluent having departed and the community-maintenance functions they once served now undermanned, the rates of predatory crime in inner-city areas rose. At the same time, because some of those persons who moved out, white and black, were not yet (by the standards of their new communities) fully middle-class, the reported rates of crime in these areas also went up. Hence the development of the (mislabeled) phenomenon, "suburban crime." It is not so much that "the suburbs" (by which we usually mean middle-class white suburbs) are becoming more criminal, but that the population of the various kinds of suburbs is changing.

If this line of argument is correct—and I stress that the social process

I have just described is based on informed conjecture but not on established fact—then the population migrations from city to suburb, made possible by rising incomes and lessening racial barriers, have created conditions that contribute to the apparent paradox of rising crime rates in a period of prosperity.

Chapter 3

Thinking About Crime

THE "social science view" of crime is thought by many, especially its critics, to assert that crime is the result of poverty, racial discrimination, and other privations, and that the only morally defensible and substantively efficacious strategy for reducing crime is to attack its "root causes" with programs that end poverty, reduce discrimination, and meliorate privation. Certainly this was in part the view of President Johnson's Commission on Crime and Administration of Justice[1] and emphatically that of former Attorney General Ramsey Clark.[2] Both the former's report and the latter's book seemed to draw heavily on social science theories and findings.

Such a theory, if it is generally held by social scientists professionally concerned with crime, ought to be subjected to the closest scrutiny, because what it implies about the nature of man and society are of fundamental significance. Scholars would bear a grave responsibility if, by their theoretical and empirical work, they had supplied public policy with the assumption that men are driven primarily by the objective conditions in which they find themselves. Such a view might be correct, but it would first have to be reconciled with certain obvious objections—for example, that the crime rate increased greatly during the very period (1963 to 1970) when there were great advances made in the income, schooling, and housing of almost all segments of society.

In fact, social scientists had not, at the time when their views on crime were sought by policy makers (roughly, the mid-1960s), set forth in writing a systematic theory of this sort. I asked three distinguished criminologists to nominate the two or three scholarly books on crime which were in print by mid-1960 and were then regarded as the most significant works on the subject. There was remarkable agreement as to the titles: *Principles of Criminology*, by Edwin H. Sutherland and Donald R. Cressey, and *Delinquency and Opportunity*, by Richard A. Cloward and Lloyd E. Ohlin, were most frequently cited.[3] Other works, including articles and symposia, were mentioned, and no claim was made that there was complete agreement on the validity of the views expressed in these books. Quite the contrary; criminologists then and now debate hotly and at length such issues as "the cause of crime." But these two books are alike in the way questions are posed, answers sought, and policies derived—alike, in short, not in their specific theories of delinquency, but in the general perspective from which those theories flow. And this perspective, contrary to popular impression, has rather little to do with poverty, race, education, housing, or the other objective conditions that supposedly "cause" crime.

It is the argument of this chapter that in the mid-1960s, and perhaps today as well, social scientists concerned with crime shared a common perspective, but not one that emphasized the material condition of society; that this shared perspective led to a policy stalemate and an ethical dilemma; that when social scientists were asked for advice by national policy-making bodies, they could not respond with suggestions derived from and supported by their scholarly work; and that as a consequence such advice as was supplied tended to derive from their general political views as modified by their political and organizational interaction with those policy groups and their staffs.

This is a large argument, each step of which would require for its support substantial research and a lengthy paper. I have not done that research nor do I intend to write all those papers. Here I can only explain the reasoning behind the argument and show that a close reading of the relevant texts is consistent with it. I can also draw on the experiences of some criminologists who have worked with both the crime commission and the violence commission and who have written their reflections on that relationship.

The Criminological Perspective

THE TREATISE by Sutherland and Cressey is widely viewed as the leading text on the subject of crime. Its seventh edition appeared in 1966, just after President Johnson appointed his crime commission. Professor

Lloyd Ohlin, an associate director of the commission's staff, testified to the impact of many of the book's ideas on the work of the commission.[4]

The central theme of *Principles of Criminology* is that "criminal behavior results from the same social processes as other social behavior."[5] The task of the student of crime is twofold: to show how crime varies with social structure and social processes (how it is influenced by class, neighborhood, mobility, or density) and to explain how persons are inducted into crime (by social imitation, "differential association," and attitude formation). Sutherland and Cressey review various perspectives on crime (or "schools of criminology") but fault all but the "sociological" approach. The "classical" theories of Bentham and Beccaria are rejected because their underlying psychological assumption—that individuals calculate the pains and pleasures of crime and pursue it if the latter outweigh the former—"assumes freedom of the will in a manner which gives little or no possibility of further investigation of the causes of crime or of efforts to prevent crime." The hedonistic psychology suffers from being "individualistic, intellectualistic, and voluntaristic."[6] All "modern" schools of crime, Sutherland and Cressey suggest, reject this perspective and accept instead "the hypothesis of natural causation," by which they appear to mean that all other theories assume that crime is to some degree determined beyond the capacity of the individual freely, or at least easily, to resist.

Theories based on body type or mental capacity are rejected because Sutherland and Cressey claim, wrongly, in my view, that the available data are inconsistent with them. But at least a factual argument is attempted. In the few brief pages devoted to alternatives to the sociological approach, it is striking that the argument that individuals choose crime freely because it is profitable is rejected on *theoretical* grounds, not for *empirical* reasons. Nor are the theoretical objections to the "classical" or "individualistic" perspective developed beyond the revealing statement that such a perspective forecloses the search for the causes of crime because it denies that crime is "caused."

There are, of course, many sociological theories of the causes of crime. Sutherland and Cressey prefer one, the "theory of differential association," but they (or rather Cressey, since Sutherland died before publication of this edition) do not insist that it has been established beyond dispute. We need not dwell on the details of "differential association," however, for its essential premises are not radically different from those of rival sociological theories; namely, that criminal behavior is learned by a person in intimate interaction with others whose good opinion he values, and that this learning places him in "normative conflict" with the larger society.

Sutherland and Cressey do not claim that poverty or racial discrimination cause crime, though crime may be higher in poor or segregated areas. Their references to the impact of poverty, defined as having little money, are few and skeptical. Sutherland is quoted from his earlier writings as observing that while crime is strongly correlated with geographic concentrations of poor persons, it is weakly correlated (if at all) with the economic cycle. That is, crime may be observed to increase as one enters a poor neighborhood, but it is not observed to increase as neighborhoods generally experience a depression, or to decrease as they experience prosperity. "Poverty as such," Sutherland concludes, "is not an important cause of crime."[7]

Being a member of a minority group and experiencing the frustrations produced by discrimination cannot explain crime for Sutherland and Cressey; while the experience of blacks, whose crime rate is high, might support such a theory, that of the Japanese, whose crime rate is low, refutes it.[8] Poverty and racial segregation may serve to perpetuate crime, however, to the extent that these factors prevent persons from leaving areas where crime is already high and thus from escaping those personal contacts and peer groups from which criminal habits are learned. Furthermore, Albert K. Cohen (to whom Sutherland and Cressey refer, approvingly) claims that much of the delinquency found among working-class boys is "non-utilitarian," that is, consists of expressive but financially unrewarding acts of vandalism and "hell-raising," and that these acts are more common among this group than among middle-class boys.[9] If economic want were the cause of crime, one would predict that delinquency for gain would be more common among those less well-off, and delinquency for "fun" more common among the better-off, but the opposite seems to be the case.

There were other major theories of crime in 1966 in addition to those of Sutherland and Cressey. Most of these are reviewed in their treatise, and though criticisms are sometimes made, the governing assumptions of each are quite compatible with what the authors describe as the sociological approach. Sheldon and Eleanor Glueck, for example, produced in the 1950s a major effort to predict delinquency. While the idea of predicting delinquency became controversial on grounds of both fairness and feasibility, their empirical data on factors that helped "cause" delinquency were not seriously challenged. They argued and supplied data to show that among the key variables distinguishing delinquents from nondelinquents (holding age, neighborhood, and intelligence constant) are those related to family conditions—chiefly stability, parental affection, and the discipline of children.[10] Walter B. Miller has argued that delinquency is in large part an expression of the focal concerns of lower-class youth. Toughness, masculinity, "smartness," the love of excitement, and a desire for personal autonomy are valued by lower-class persons to a greater degree than by middle-class ones, and acting on the basis of these values, which are maintained by street-corner gangs, inevitably places many lower-class boys (and some girls) in conflict with the laws of the middle class.[11] Albert K. Cohen suggested that delinquency is in part the result of lower-class youth striving, not simply to assert their focal values, but to repudiate those middle-class values which they secretly prize.[12]

These and other sociological theories of crime, widely known and intensely discussed in the 1960s, have certain features in common. All sought to explain the causes of delinquency, or at least its persistence. All made attitude formation a key variable. All stressed that these attitudes are shaped and supported by intimate groups—the family and close friends. All were serious, intelligent efforts at constructing social theories, and while no theory was proved empirically, all were consistent with at least some important observations about crime. *But none could supply a plausible basis for the advocacy of public policy.*

This was true for several reasons. By directing attention toward the subjective states that preceded or accompanied criminal behavior, the sociological (or more accurately, social-psychological) theories directed attention toward conditions that cannot be easily and deliberately altered. Society, of course, shapes attitudes and values by its example, its institutions, and its practices, but slowly and imprecisely, and with great difficulty. If families inculcate habits of virtue, law-abidingness, and decorum, it is rarely because the family is acting as the agent of society or its government, but rather because it is a good family. If schools teach children to value learning and to study well, it is not simply because the schools are well designed or generously supplied, but because attitudes consistent with learning and study already exist in the pupils. One may wonder what government might do if it wished to make good families even better or successful pupils even more successful: more resources might be offered to reduce burdens imposed by want, but the gains, if any, would probably be at the margin.

If it is hard by plan to make the good better, it may be impossible to make the bad tolerable so long as one seeks to influence attitudes and values directly. If a child is delinquent because his family made him so or his friends encourage him to be so, it is hard to conceive what society might do about his attitudes. One can imagine families being changed through the expert intervention of skilled and patient counselors. But no one knows how a government might restore affection, stability, and fair discipline to large numbers of families lacking these characteristics; still less can one imagine how a family once restored could affect a child who has passed the formative years and has developed an aversion to one or both of his parents.

If the lower class has focal concerns that make crime attractive or even inevitable, it is not clear how government would supply "the lower class" with a new set of values consistent with law-abidingness. Indeed, the very effort to inculcate new values would, if the sociological theory is true, lead the members of that class to resist such alien intrusions all the more vigorously and to cling to their own world view all the more strongly. One could supply the lower class with more money, of course, but if a class exists because of its values rather than its income, it is hard to see how, in terms of the prevailing theory, increasing the latter would improve the former.

Peer groups exist, especially for young people, as a way of defending their members from an alien, hostile, or indifferent larger society, and for supplying their members with a mutually satisfactory basis for self-respect. A deviant peer group—one that encourages crime or hell raising—would regard any effort by society to "reform" it as confirmation of the hostile intent of society and the importance of the group. For the members of a group to believe in a "we," they must believe in the existence of a "they"; the more a "they" asserts its difference or superiority, the more important the "we" is likely to become.

The problem lies in confusing causal analysis with policy analysis. Causal analysis attempts to find the source of human activity in those factors which themselves are not caused—which are, in the language of sociologists, "independent variables." Obviously nothing can be a cause if it is in turn caused by something else; it would then only be an "intervening variable." But ultimate causes cannot be the object of policy efforts precisely because, being ultimate, they cannot be changed. For example, criminologists have shown beyond doubt that men commit more crimes than women and younger men more (of certain kinds) than older ones. It is a theoretically important and scientifically correct observation. Yet it means little for policy makers concerned with crime prevention, since men cannot be changed into women or made to skip over the adolescent years.

Not every primary cause is unchangeable nor does the discovery of the primary causes of crime mean that criminality involves no element of choice. For example, if frustration resulting from doing poorly in school contributes to criminality, reducing school failure may reduce crime. Moreover, since not every person who does poorly in school becomes either angry or criminal, we cannot say that school failure *determines* crime, and thus we need not abandon our view—essential for the operation of any system of law—that behavior is in some sense freely chosen.

Indeed, if the search for the causes of crime should implicate schools (as in the opinion of many it does), then causal analysis can help direct the policy analyst's attention to a possible opportunity for change. But the more we understand the causes of crime, the more we are drawn into the complex and subtle world of attitudes, predispositions, and beliefs, a world in which planned intervention is exceptionally difficult. In the case of schooling, the policy maker will no doubt discover that reducing failure involves much more than merely providing better facilities or more expensive teachers. Though social institutions can be changed, the important changes are usually the result of broad—and slow—social processes.

It is the failure to understand this point that leads statesman and citizen alike to commit the causal fallacy—to assume that no problem is adequately addressed unless its causes are eliminated. The preamble to the UNESCO charter illustrates it: "Since wars begin in the minds of men it is in the minds of men that the defenses of peace must be constructed." The one thing we cannot easily do, if we can do it at all, is change, by plan and systematically, the minds of men. If peace can only be assured by doing what we cannot do, then we can never have peace. If we regard any crime-prevention or crime-reduction program as defective because it does not address the "root causes" of crime, then we shall commit ourselves to futile acts that frustrate the citizen while they ignore the criminal.

Sutherland and Cressey commit the fallacy, yet, being honest scholars, provide evidence in their own book that it *is* a fallacy. "At present," they write, "the greatest need in crime prevention is irrefutable facts about crime causation and sound means for transforming that knowledge into a program of action."[13] Suppose it could be shown that their own theory of crime causation is irrefutably correct (it may well be). The theory is that individuals commit crime when they are members of groups (families, peers, neighborhoods) that define criminal behavior as desirable.[14] The policy implication of this, which the authors draw explicitly, is that the local community must use the school, the church, the police, and other agencies to "modify" the personal groups in which crime is made to appear desirable. No indication is given as to how these agencies might do this and, given what the authors and other sociologists have said about the strength and persistence of family and friendship ties, it is hard to see what plan might be developed.

But we need not merely raise the theoretical difficulties. A series of delinquency-prevention programs have been mounted over the decades, many, if not most, of which were explicitly based on the strategy of altering primary group influences on delinquents. On the basis of careful, external evaluation, almost none can be said to have succeeded in reducing delinquency. Sutherland and Cressey describe one of the most ambitious of these, the Cambridge-Somerville Youth Study begun in the late 1930s. The differences in crime between those youth who were given special services (counseling, special educational programs, guidance, health assistance, camping trips) and a matched control group were insignificant: " 'the treatment' had little effect."[15]

Perhaps a better program would have better results, though it is striking, given the analysis presented so far, that for some a "better" youth project is one that goes beyond merely providing concentrated social welfare services because these services do not address the "real" causes of crime. McCord and McCord, for example, draw the lesson from the Cambridge-Somerville study that the true causes of delinquency are found in the "absence of parental affection" coupled with family conflict, inconsistent discipline, and rebellious parents.[16] They are quite possibly correct; indeed, I am quite confident they are correct. But what of it? What agency do we create, what budget do we allocate, that will supply the missing "parental affection" and restore to the child consistent discipline supported by a stable and loving family? When it comes to the details of their own proposals, they speak of "milieu therapy" in which the child is removed from his family and placed in a secure and permissive therapeutic environment of the sort developed by Dr. Bruno Bettelheim for autistic children. Conceding that such a program is frightfully expensive, they urge us to attempt to reach fewer children than under conventional programs, and presumably to keep each child for a relatively long period. That parents, children, taxpayers, or courts might object to all this is not considered.[17]

Attempts to explain the causes of crime not only lead inevitably into the realm of the subjective and the familial, where both the efficacy and propriety of policy are most in doubt, they also lead one to a preference for the rehabilitative (or reformation) theory of corrections over the deterrence or incapacitation theories. Sutherland and Cressey recognize this: "On a formal level it may be observed that attempts to explain criminal behavior have greatly abetted at least the official use of the treatment reaction."[18] One may deter a criminal by increasing the costs or reducing the benefits of crime, but that strategy does not deal with the "causes" of criminality, and hence does not go to the "root" of the problem. Stated another way, if causal theories explain why a criminal acts as he does, they also explain why he *must* act as he does, and therefore they make any reliance on deterrence seem futile or irrelevant. Yet when Sutherland and Cressey come to consider the consequences of treating criminals in order to reform them, as opposed to punishing in order to deter them, they admit forthright that "there is no available proof" that treatment increases or decreases crime,[19] and that "the methods of reformation . . . have not been notably successful in reducing crime rates."[20] Careful reviews of the major efforts to rehabilitate criminals amply support this judgment.[21]

Policy analysis, as opposed to causal analysis, begins with a very different perspective. It asks not what is the "cause" of a problem, but what is the condition one wants to bring into being, what measure do we have that will tell us when that condition exists, and what policy tools does a government (in our case, a democratic and liberal government) possess that might, when applied, produce at reasonable cost a desired alteration in the present condition or progress toward the desired condition. In this case, the desired condition is a reduction in specified forms of crime. The government has at its disposal certain (rather few, in fact) policy instruments: it can redistribute money, create (or stimulate the creation of) jobs, hire persons who offer advice, hire persons who practice surveillance and detection, build detention facilities, illuminate public streets, alter (within a range) the price of drugs and alcohol, require citizens to install alarm systems, and so on. It can, in short, manage to a degree money, prices, and technology, and it can hire people who can provide either simple (for example, custodial) or complex (for example, counseling) services. These tools, if employed, can affect the risks of crime, the benefits of noncriminal occupations, the accessibility of things worth stealing, and (perhaps) the mental state of criminals or would-be criminals. A policy analyst would ask what feasible changes in which of these instruments would, at what cost (monetary and nonmonetary), produce how much of a change in the rate of a given crime. He would suspect, from his experience in education and social services, that changing the mental state of citizens is very difficult, quite costly, hard to manage organizationally, and liable to produce many unanticipated side effects. He would then entertain as a working hypothesis that, given what he has to work with, he may gain more by altering risks, benefits, alternatives, and accessibility. He would not be sure of this, however, and would want to analyze carefully how these factors are related to existing differences in crime by state or city, and then try some experimental alterations in these factors before committing himself to them wholesale.

There is nothing that requires criminologists, as that profession is currently defined, to be policy analysts. Searching for the causes of crime is an intellectually worthy and serious undertaking, though one pursued so far in ways that are often long on theory and short on facts. I only make the point that a commitment to causal analysis, especially one that regards social processes as crucial, will rarely lead to discovering the grounds for policy choices, and such grounds as are discovered (for example, taking children away from their parents) will raise grave ethical and political issues. Furthermore, searching for the social causes of crime will direct attention away from policy-relevant ways of explaining differences in crime rates. It was not until 1966, fifty years after criminology began as a discipline in this country and after seven editions of the leading text on crime had appeared, that there began to be a serious and sustained inquiry into the consequences of differences in the certainty and severity of penalties on crime rates.[22] Now, to an increasing extent, that inquiry is being furthered by economists rather than sociologists. This is in part because economists are by and large not interested in causality in any fundamental sense—they do not care, for example, why people buy automobiles, only that they buy fewer as the cost rises.

That criminologists gave little serious empirical attention until recently to the deterrence and accessibility aspects of crime is unfortunate; that some of them, on virtually no evidence, asserted that deterrence (usually described as "punishment") is of no value is inexcusable. Walter Reckless, for example, in the 1967 edition of his text on crime, states flatly that punishment "does not . . . prevent crime," though he adduces no systematic evidence to warrant such a conclusion.[23] Tittle and Logan provide other examples of this unsupported policy view in their survey of the more recent literature on deterrence, a survey that concludes by observing that "almost all research since 1960 supports the view that negative sanctions are significant variables in the explanation of conformity and deviance. . . . Sanctions apparently have some deterrent effect under some circumstances."[24] More recent research supports this tentative conclusion, though it does not conclusively establish it (see chapter 7). What is clear is that modern criminology, as an intellectual enterprise, did not until rather recently give serious empirical attention to the question.

In sum, the criminologist, concerned with causal explanations and part of a discipline—sociology—that assumes that social processes determine behavior, has operated largely within an intellectual framework that makes it difficult or impossible to develop reasonable policy alternatives, and has cast doubt, by assumption more than by argument or evidence, on the efficacy of those policy tools, necessarily dealing with objective rather than subjective conditions, which society might use to alter crime rates. A serious policy-oriented analysis of crime, by contrast, would place heavy emphasis on manipulation of objective conditions, not necessarily because of a belief that the "causes of crime" are thereby being eradicated, but because behavior is easier to change than attitudes, and because the only instruments society has by which to alter behavior in the short run require it to assume that people act in response to the costs and benefits of alternative courses of action. The criminologist assumes, probably rightly, that the causes of crime are determined by attitudes that in turn are socially derived, if not determined; the policy analyst is led to assume that the criminal acts *as if* crime were the product of a free choice among competing opportunities and constraints. The radical individualism of Bentham and Beccaria may be scientifically questionable but prudentially necessary.

Some readers will be dismayed by my argument that, for policy reasons, it is a mistake to direct our crime-reduction efforts chiefly at the causes of crime. To these readers, trying to change behavior without first changing the causes of that behavior is at best superficial and at worst hardhearted. Let me remind them that they often accept—indeed, endorse enthusiastically—my approach when it comes to certain kinds of crime. The sponsors of civil rights laws did not withdraw their bills punishing racist behavior because they dealt only with "symptoms" rather than with the life circumstances that were the true causes of racism. They rejected the view that "you can't legislate morality" when it comes to denying blacks the right to vote or buy a home, and they were right to do so. Nor did most legislators accept the argument that one must first deal with the "root causes" of political corruption, commercial price-fixing, or marketing dangerous drugs. They instead set about changing corrupt, manipulative, and harmful *behavior,* and they did so—again, rightly—by increasing the risks facing people who engaged in this behavior. By devising effective policies rather than postponing action until causes had been eliminated, the advocates of these measures not only changed the behavior in question, they probably changed the causes also. I suspect that there are today somewhat fewer racists, bribers, price-fixers, and unscrupulous drug merchants than once was the case in part because people have been taught, by the law and its resolute enforcement, that such behavior is not only risky, it is wrong.

A major apparent exception to the general perspective of criminologists is the work of Cloward and Ohlin. Writing in 1960, they developed an influential theory of delinquency in big cities. A delinquent gang (or "subculture"—the terms are used, for reasons not made clear, interchangeably) arises in response to the conflict that exists between socially approved goals (primarily monetary success) and socially approved means to realize those goals. Certain youth, notably lower-class ones, desire conventional ends but discover that there are no legitimate means to attain them; being unable (unwilling?) to revise these expectations downward, they experience frustration, and this may lead them to explore illegitimate ("nonconforming") alternatives.[25] Some lower-class youth may aspire to middle-class values ("money and morality," as the authors put it), while others may aspire only for success in lower-class terms (money alone).[26] The barriers to realizing those aspirations are found in part in cultural constraints derived from the immigrant experience (southern Italians and Sicilians, for example, allegedly do not value schooling highly), but in larger part in structural difficulties, chiefly the fact that education is costly in money outlays and foregone earnings.

In its brief form, the theory of Cloward and Ohlin would seem to be in sharp contrast to the general sociological perspective. Delinquency may be learned from peers, but it is learned because of the gap between aspirations and opportunities, and opportunities in turn are objective conditions determined by government and the social system. Education, they claim, is the chief source of opportunity. One expects Cloward and Ohlin to end their book with a call for cheaper, more readily available educational programs. But they do not. Indeed, less than one page is devoted to policy proposals, amounting essentially to one suggestion: "The major effort of those who wish to eliminate delinquency should be directed to the reorganization of slum communities."[27] No explanation is offered of what "slum reorganization" might be, except for several pages that decry the presence of "slum disorganization." Their analysis leads the reader toward the material desires of life (indeed, that is all the lower classes are supposed to value), but stops short of telling us how those material desires are realized. Their theory states that "each individual occupies a position in both legitimate and illegitimate opportunity structures" (they rightly note that this is a "new way" of viewing the problem), but they do not speak of the costs and benefits of illegitimate as opposed to legitimate opportunities.[28] Instead, the individual who is confronted with a choice among kinds of opportunities does not *choose*, he "learns deviant values" from the "social structure of the slum."[29] When the authors come to speak of policy, they have little to say about what determines the choice of illegitimate opportunities (nobody has chosen anything, he has only "learned" or "assimilated"), and thus they have no theoretical grounds for suggesting that the value of legitimate opportunities should be increased (for example, better-paying jobs for slum youth), or that the benefits of illegitimate ones be decreased (for example, more certain penalties for crime), or that "opportunities" for goal gratification be replaced by direct goal gratification (for example, redistributing income). They can only write of those structures or groupings that affect learning and values, and this requires an (unexplained) "social reorganization."

The Perspective Applied

EXPLAINING human behavior is a worthwhile endeavor; indeed, for intellectuals it is among the most worthwhile. Those who search for such explanations need not justify their activity by its social utility or its policy implications. Unfortunately, neither intellectuals nor policy makers always understand this. If the government becomes alarmed about crime, it assumes that those who have studied it most deeply can contribute most fully to its solution. Criminologists have rarely sought to show statesmen the error of this assumption. To a degree, of course, criminological knowledge may assist criminologists' actions; careful study and conscientious learning can help one avoid obvious errors, attack popular myths, and devise inventive proposals. But it is also likely that the most profound understanding may impede or even distort, rather than facilitate, choice, because much of this knowledge is of what is immutable and necessary, not what is variable or contingent.

In the mid-1960s, when the federal government turned toward social scientists for help in understanding and dealing with crime, there was not in being a body of tested or even well-accepted theories as to how crime might be prevented or criminals reformed, nor was there much agreement on the "causes" of crime except that they were *social,* not psychological, biological, or individualistic. Indeed, there was not much agreement that crime was a major and growing problem—scholars noted the apparent increase in crime rates, but (properly) criticized the statistical and empirical weaknesses in these published rates. While these weaknesses did not always lead critics to conclude that crime was in fact not increasing, some scholars did draw that conclusion tentatively, and their criticisms encouraged others to draw it conclusively.

Nor were scholars very foresighted. Having established beyond doubt that crime rates are strongly related to age differences, few scholars (*none* that I can recall) noted the ominous consequences for crime of the coming-of-age in the 1960s of the postwar "baby boom." Similarly, while some scholars had shown by cross-sectional studies that the proportion of a city's population that was nonwhite was powerfully correlated with assaultive crimes, few, to my knowledge, drew the obvious implication that, unless this correlation was spurious, the continued in-migration of blacks to large cities would inflate crime rates. Once the various national commissions were underway, however, scholars associated with them (notably the group associated with the Task Force on the Assessment of Crime, under the direction of Lloyd Ohlin) began to work vigorously on these issues, and produced a number of reports that showed vividly the impact of demographic changes on crime rates.

The major intellectual difficulty governing the relationship of social scientists to policy makers with respect to crime was not the presence or absence of foresight, however, but rather the problem of how to arrive at policy proposals in the absence of scientific knowledge that would support them. The crime commission did not develop new knowledge as to crime prevention or control; as Professor Ohlin later described it, existing "social science concepts, theories and general perspectives were probably of greater utility to the staff and the Commission in forming the final recommendations than the inputs from new knowledge development efforts."[30] What were these "concepts, theories and general perspectives"? One, cited by Ohlin, consisted of "grave doubts" about the effectiveness of the criminal justice system and of rehabilitation and treatment programs. From this, Ohlin and his colleagues drew the conclusion that "the criminal justice system should be used only as a last resort in the control of undesirable conduct." From that inference, in turn, the commission adopted the view that offenders should be "diverted" from the system, and recommended a broad policy of "de-prisonization."[31]

There are no doubt ample grounds, by reason of humanity, why one would find fault with prisons, but at the time of the commission's work there were scarcely any well-established *scientific* grounds. That "treatment" had failed seemed clear, but it was equally clear that "nontreatment" had failed as well: persons on probation may be no more likely to recidivate than those in prison, but neither are they much less likely. As for deterrence, there was, when the commission deliberated and Professor Ohlin advised, virtually *no* scientific material on whether prison did or did not deter. But the commission scarcely dealt with the deterrence or incapacitation functions of prison.

In short, criminology could not form the basis for much policy advice to the commission, but that did not prevent criminologists from advising. Professor Ohlin is entirely honest about this: "The relevant social science literature was descriptive and analytical. There were relatively few experimental or controlled studies of the effectiveness of particular programs or policies. . . . Sociologists serving as consultants to the Commission proved reluctant to draw out . . . action recommendations. . . . When they did try to do this, the recommendations were often *more influenced by personal ideological convictions than by appropriately organized facts and theories* [italics added]. . . ."[32]

What were these ideologies? After an earlier version of this chapter appeared in print, one criminologist, the late Robert Martinson, wrote in response that his colleagues had become "advocates and spokesmen for the treatment interest and the treatment ideology, and did everything in their power to ridicule the very idea of deterrence."[33] Since he knew his professional associates better than I, there is no reason for me to reject his conclusions. Surely their role on public commissions tends to confirm it. But there is also a good deal of criminological literature that has little policy value, not because it is ideologically pro-treatment (much is in fact quite skeptical of treatment), but because it derives from an intellectual paradigm that draws attention to those features of social life least accessible to policy intervention.

Social scientists did not carry the day on the commission (they could not, for example, get their view on marijuana accepted), but the effect of their advice, based on personal belief rather than scholarly knowledge, was clear. Working with sympathetic commission members in small task forces, the advisers stimulated and participated in a "process that led to far more liberal recommendations by the Commission than one would have thought possible at the outset given the conservative cast of its membership."[34]

There is nothing wrong with social scientists trying to persuade others of their policy beliefs, just as there is nothing wrong with conservative commission members trying to persuade sociologists of their beliefs. There *is* something wrong with a process of persuasion colored by the belief that one party to the process is an "expert" whose views are entitled to special consideration because of their evidentiary quality. There is no way of knowing to what extent commission members believed what the sociologists were saying was true, as opposed to merely plausible or interesting. But based on my own experience in advising national commissions, including the crime commission, I am confident that few social scientists made careful distinctions, when the chips were down, between what they knew as scholars and what they believed as citizens, or even spent much time discussing the complex relationships between knowledge and belief. I certainly did not, and I do not recall others doing so.

Having alluded to my own role as a policy adviser, let me amplify on that experience to reinforce, by self-criticism, the point I am making. I was not in 1966 a criminologist, nor am I now. I came to crime, if I may put it that way, as a consequence of my study of police administration and its political context, and found myself labeled an "expert" on crime because of that interest, and perhaps also because of the desire of governmental consumers of "expertise" to inflate, by wishful thinking, the supply of such persons to equal the demand for their services.

Once I found myself in the crime business, I found that my ideas on the subject—apart from those formed by my empirical research on policing—were inevitably influenced by the currents of academic opinion about me. The effect of these currents is not to persuade one of what is important, but to persuade one of what is interesting. In my case, I did not absorb from criminological writings a set of policy conclusions about whether criminals can be deterred or rehabilitated, but I did absorb a set of "interesting facts" about crime: for example, crimes are age-specific, victims contribute to their victimization in most assaultive crimes, and published crime rates are unreliable. All of these things were (and are) true, but of course they are not directly related to the policy question of what is to be done about crime.

These things were thought important by social scientists with whom I spoke because they were not widely known; they constituted, so to speak, the "unconventional wisdom." Social scientists generally, and practitioners of the "softer" social sciences in particular, are in their day-to-day work preoccupied with things they know that others do not, rather than (as their critics sometimes allege) with their cherished ideologies or favorite policy nostrums. This preoccupation arises in part out of the natural pleasures of discovery and in part out of both the professional rewards that accrue to originality and critical skills and the professional penalties that are imposed on naïveté and conventionality. It was only gradually, as I became involved in various advisory roles, that I realized that what is interesting is not necessarily useful.

In short, I did not, any more than Professor Ohlin, have in 1966–1968 empirically supported policy advice to offer statesmen dealing with crime. What I then realized, as did Professor Ohlin, was that many of those seated about me, urging in the strongest tones various "solutions" to crime, were speaking out of ideology, not scholarship. Only later did I realize that criminologists, and perhaps all sociologists, are part of an intellectual tradition that does not contain built-in checks against the premature conversion of opinion into policy, because the focal concerns of that tradition are with those aspects of society that are, to a great extent, beyond the reach of policy and even beyond the reach of science. Those matters that are within the reach of policy have been, at least for many criminologists, defined as uninteresting because they were superficial, "symptomatic," or not of "causal" significance. Sociology, for all its claims to understand structure, is at heart a profoundly subjectivist discipline. When those who practice it are brought forward and asked for advice, they will say either (if conservative) that nothing is possible, or (if liberal) that everything is possible. That most sociologists are liberals explains why the latter reaction is more common, even though the presuppositions of their own discipline would more naturally lead to the former.

Since the 1960s, there has been a great improvement in how social scientists address policies on crime. There have been serious, competent efforts by national review panels to assess the quality of evidence regarding the possibility of deterring crime (see chapter 7), rehabilitating criminals (see chapter 9), and reducing crime through incapacitation (see chapter 8). The possible effects of the death penalty have received the most careful scrutiny (see chapter 10). But above all, a growing number of social scientists have adopted an experimental attitude toward crime control; they have become, in effect, policy analysts trying to find out what works in the real world. In no area of law enforcement has more ingenuity and effort been marshaled toward this end than in the attempt to discover by what means policing can be improved. To the results of these efforts we now turn.

PART
II
POLICING

Chapter 4

The Police and Crime

THE average citizen thinks of the police as an organization primarily concerned with preventing crime and catching criminals. When crime increases or criminals go uncaught, the conventional public response is to demand more or better policemen. When the crime rate goes down or a particularly heinous crime is solved, the police often get, or at least try to take, the credit.

For some time, persons who run or study police departments have recognized that this public conception is misleading. The majority of calls received by most police are for services that have little to do with crime but a great deal to do with medical emergencies, family quarrels, auto accidents, barking dogs, minor traffic violations, and so on. And those calls that do involve serious crimes, such as burglaries, robberies, and auto thefts, typically occur after the event has taken place and the trail is cold; the officer who responds can often do little more than fill out a report that will contain few if any leads for further investigation.[1] The police themselves wish it were otherwise; most patrolmen would prefer to stop a crime in progress or catch a major felon, but only infrequently do they have the chance.

The growing realization among scholars and administrators of the importance of the service provision, order-maintenance function of patrolmen has led some experts to dismiss or downplay the crime control function. A police department is often thought "advanced" or "progressive" to the extent it emphasizes community service rather than crime prevention. To a degree, this is well and good: for too long, police officers were given little training and no supervision in the performance of their most frequent duties, with the result that many citizens felt poorly treated and many officers felt frustrated and unsure of their mission.

But progress along these lines does not constitute an answer to the citizen's concern with crime. He believes, with reason, that if there were no police at all there would be more crime, and therefore he supposes that if there were more police there would be less crime. When he sees a policeman on a street corner, the citizen often feels more secure and assumes that the burglar or mugger seeing the same officer will feel less secure. If a crime is committed, the citizen believes that the police should diligently look for the criminal, even if it means neglecting their community service functions. The citizen is impatient with theories that argue that crime can only be prevented by reforming prisons or ending poverty. He thinks that crime, or at least crime that affects him, will be prevented if sufficient policemen walk by his home or business often enough.

There have been some attempts to test that belief, but until recently these efforts had serious shortcomings. One of the first was carried out in 1954 by the New York City Police Department (NYPD) under the direction of Commissioner Francis W. H. Adams.[2] Beginning on September 1 of that year, the police strength assigned to the twenty-fifth precinct in Manhattan (comprising much of East Harlem) was more than doubled. Most of the additional men were inexperienced patrolmen taken straight from the Police Academy who were assigned to foot posts, although experienced detectives and traffic, juvenile, and narcotics officers were also added to the precinct. Before the experiment, called "Operation 25," began, as many as two-thirds of the foot posts (or beats) in the area were unmanned. During the experiment, no post was left vacant, the number was increased from fifty-five to eighty-nine, and their average length was shortened.

Operation 25 lasted four months. During that time serious crimes declined and the reduction was greatest for "street crimes"—those that either occurred in public places or involved entry from the street into private places. Muggings fell from sixty-nine during the same period in 1953 to seven in the experimental part of 1954, and auto thefts dropped from seventy-eight to twenty-four. Burglaries declined as well, especially those for which the entry was made from the front of the residence or store. Murder, essentially a "private" crime, did not decline at all; indeed, it increased from six to eight cases. Felonious assault, which, like murder, frequently occurs in private places among "friends," did decline, but not nearly as much as street robberies or auto thefts.

Operation 25 was used to justify to the mayor and city council police demands for increases in manpower. The increases were forthcoming. Between 1954 and 1974, the size of the NYPD increased by 54 percent, while the total population remained about constant. However, crime increased even more rapidly than the police.

The subsequent increase in crime despite the growth in the size of the police force does not necessarily repudiate the findings of Operation 25. After all, the composition of the population had changed substantially during the years since 1954. Furthermore, not all officers added to a police department are added to the effective street force of that department. Thus, for every hundred officers added to the force, only a few may represent net increments to street patrol.

But if later history did not disprove Operation 25, problems in its design raised questions about its significance. There was no direct measure of true crime rates, only counts of reported crimes. More important, the comparison in crime rates was made with crime the preceding year. It is possible that crime might have declined during 1954 for reasons other than the increased police presence. But most important, no effort was made to discover whether crime in surrounding precincts increased as a result of the increased police activity of Operation 25. Perhaps crime was not reduced, only displaced. Finally, police administrators, if not citizens, want to know whether increases in police manpower short of doubling the previous number will have any effect, and whether patrolmen in cars are more or less effective than those on foot.

In the 1960s, there were some fresh efforts to answer these questions. In Great Britain, J. A. Bright of the Home Office reported on the "Beat Patrol Experiments" carried out in 1965 to discover whether the number of crimes in an urban area would be affected by the number of foot patrolmen in that area.[3] In four British cities a number of foot beats were designated as experimental areas, and over successive four-week periods the number of officers walking those beats was varied systematically between zero and four. At the end of one year, Bright and his colleagues concluded that the number of reported crimes on a beat decreased when the officers patrolling it on foot increased from zero to one, but that there were no further decreases resulting from raising the number of patrolmen to two per beat. There was some tentative evidence that a really sharp increase—say, from one to three or even four officers on a single beat—would produce still further reductions in crime, but the evidence supporting this was weak, and in any event it is not generally feasible to triple or quadruple a city's police force. In sum, Bright rejected the view that having more foot patrolmen in a neighborhood will produce a reduction in crime. Unfortunately, the beats in which the experiment was conducted were so small and the periods during which the changes were made so brief that the Home Office results could at best be regarded as tentative.

At about the same time, another project was underway in New York that sought to measure the results of having more cops on the beat. One of the objectives of this study, carried out by S. J. Press for the New York City Rand Institute, was to look closely at the possibility, overlooked in Operation 25, that reported crime rates might change for reasons having nothing to do with the additional officers on patrol.[4] To this end, Press studied two nearby precincts similar to the one (the twentieth precinct) in which, beginning in October 1966, police manpower was increased by 40 percent, while the manpower assigned in the rest of the city remained about what it had always been.

The results, though not quite as dramatic as those claimed for Operation 25, were on the whole quite consistent with it. In the twentieth precinct, street robberies per week fell by 33 percent, auto theft by 49 percent, and grand larcenies "visible from the street" by 49 percent. There were no appreciable decreases in serious crimes that occurred in private places, such as burglary and assault. Most important, these were *net* reductions in crime, over and above such changes as may have occurred in the similar precincts in which no additional policemen were deployed. Furthermore, these reductions seemed to be genuine—that is, little evidence was found that crime had simply been displaced to adjoining precincts.

Though the data from the twentieth precinct were better analyzed than had been those from the twenty-fifth precinct, the results were still inconclusive. Only changes in reported crimes, not in actual crimes, could be observed, and the reporting system itself changed early in the project, perhaps affecting the results in unknown ways. The time period was short —four months in the case of Operation 25, eight months in the twentieth precinct. Perhaps a sudden increase in police manpower will make criminals lie low or go elsewhere for a while, but then, as they become accustomed to the new situation, they resume their activities. This is often exactly what happens when better street lights are installed; crime decreases for a while but then returns to its previous level. Only rudimentary efforts were made to match socioeconomically the areas in which the police were strengthened with those in which they were not. In short, neither project was a true experiment.

Nonetheless, even discounting the findings substantially to allow for these imperfections, the results in the two New York projects were sufficiently striking and consistent to warrant entertaining the belief that very large increases in police patrols may reduce "outside" or "street" crime significantly, at least for a short period of time.

Some of the limitations of the early studies were overcome in a careful analysis of subway robberies in New York City and the effect of increased assignment of police to the subway system. The proportion of crimes committed that are actually reported is probably much higher in the subway than in the city as a whole, because many victims are transit employees who must report crimes if they are to account for missing cash and tokens. And citizen victims are delivered by the subway to stops where police, dispatchers, and change-booth clerks are readily available, thus facilitating the reporting of a loss.

The two most common major crimes in subways are the robbing of passengers, an offense typically committed by young black boys of school age who, though unarmed, often use violence, and the robbing of change-booth clerks, a crime typically committed by somewhat older males, frequently narcotics users, who, though armed with guns, rarely use violence.

In the two years preceding 1965, subway felonies were increasing at an annual rate of about 50 percent. In April of that year, Mayor Robert Wagner ordered a substantial increase in police patrols in the subways, from twelve hundred persons to over thirty-one hundred, with the objective, which was by and large met, of having a police officer on every subway train and at every station between the hours of 8 P.M. and 4 A.M.

The results of this manning schedule over an eight-year period were later analyzed by Jan M. Chaiken, Michael W. Lawless, and Keith A. Stevenson at the New York City Rand Institute.[5] This evaluation covered the longest period of patrol work ever studied in a comparable fashion. Following the introduction of heavy police coverage in 1965, there was a short-term decline in total subway crime. Within a year or so, however, the number of subway robberies began to rise again at a rapid rate, so that by 1970 there were six times as many robberies occurring as had occurred in 1965, when the extra police were first hired.

This discouraging result in total subway robberies concealed, however, a remarkable success story. The extra police were primarily deployed during the evening. The number of subway felonies occurring per hour during the night fell in 1965 *and remained low,* while the number of felonies occurring during the day, after a brief decrease in 1965 when the publicity about more transit police was at its peak, rose more or less steadily from 1966 on.

The Rand authors concluded that, though subway crime had tended to rise year after year, the addition of uniformed officers to the trains and platforms during the evening hours has caused a substantial decline in crime at those times, and that this deterrent effect of the police has persisted for several years. The cost was high, however—about $35,000 per deterred felony. And the circumstances were quite special: the subway is an enclosed place with few exits. A would-be robber, seeing a police officer on a train or platform, will find it difficult to select a victim sufficiently removed from the officer as to eliminate the chance of being caught in the act and to discover an escape route sufficiently convenient as to give him a good chance of getting away once a hue and cry is set up. In short, the subway patrol plan, while apparently of considerable value when it is in effect, offers few guidelines for patrolling the city streets.

In the late 1960s there was being developed a major new research technique of great potential value in studying police effectiveness. This was the "victimization survey," pioneered by the Task Force on the Assessment of Crime of President Johnson's Commission on Law Enforcement and Administration of Justice. A national survey of ten thousand households was carried out in 1966 by Philip H. Ennis and the National Opinion Research Center of the University of Chicago.[6]

These surveys provided for the first time convincing evidence of the extent of unreported crime, a fact now widely accepted. There were, we learned, about twice as many major crimes being committed in the United States every year than appeared in official police statistics. In 1972–1973, the United States Bureau of the Census began to conduct even larger victimization surveys that in general confirmed the earlier finding.

The 1966 surveys, being one-shot enterprises, could not tell us anything about *changes* in true crime rates. But they offered a technique which, though quite expensive, could be applied to experiments in police patrol. By measuring victimization rates of individuals and business firms in experimental areas before and after changes in police deployment, and also in carefully matched control areas where no changes in deployment occurred, more reliable conclusions could be drawn about the extent to which various police strategies could affect crime.

In the early 1970s a few big-city police departments began such experiments with funds, technical assistance, and evaluation studies provided by the Police Foundation, a private, independent foundation in Washington, D.C., created in the summer of 1970 by the Ford Foundation.

The first to be completed was done in Kansas City, Missouri, to test the effect of different levels of "preventive patrol." Preventive patrol, for long the fundamental assumption of police deployment, means having officers walk or drive through their beats whenever they are not answering a specific call for service or assistance. By their continuous, moving presence, so the theory goes, crime will be prevented because would-be criminals will be aware of and deterred by the police presence. Furthermore, this patrolling may enable the officer to witness a crime in progress or to discover and stop fugitives, suspicious persons, and stolen cars.

Officers in Kansas City designed an experiment to test these assumptions. In the southern part of the city, fifteen police beats were sorted into five groups of three matched beats each. Each group was made up of beats that were as similar as possible in population characteristics (income, ethnicity, transiency, and so on), reported crime levels, and calls for police services. Within each group, three different patrol strategies were used for a one-year period. One beat (chosen at random) was patrolled in the customary fashion by a single patrol car that cruised the streets whenever it was not answering calls. These were the "control" beats. A second beat in each group had a greatly increased level of preventive patrol—cars were visible cruising these streets two to three times more frequently than in the control areas. This strategy was called "proactive patrol." In the third beat in each group, preventive patrol was eliminated altogether—a police car would enter the area only in answer to a specific request for service. When that run was completed, the car would either return to the periphery of the beat or cruise streets outside it. This was called "reactive patrol." Before and after the experiment, individuals and businessmen were interviewed to learn whether they had been the victims of crime, what they thought of the quality of police service, and to what extent they were fearful of crime.

The results analyzed by George L. Kelling and others were startling. After a year, no substantial differences among the three areas were observed in criminal activity, amount of reported crime, rate of victimization as revealed in the follow-up survey, level of citizen fear, or degree of citizen satisfaction with the police. For all practical purposes, the changes in the level of preventive patrol made no difference at all.

For reasons that are still hard to understand, citizen respect for the police increased somewhat in the control beats, where nothing was changed, and did not increase at all (indeed, declined slightly) on the proactive beats, where more police became available. And strangest of all, perhaps, the citizen living on the proactive beats felt more apprehensive than those living on others about the likelihood of being robbed or raped.

It is easy to misinterpret these results, and so it is important to state what was *not* found. The experiment did *not* show that the police make no difference and it did *not* show that adding more police is useless in controlling crime. All it showed was that changes in the amount of random preventive patrol in marked cars did not, by itself, seem to affect, over one year's time in Kansas City, how much crime occurred or how safe citizens felt. Very different results might have been obtained if important changes were made in *how* the police were used: for example, by having them patrol in unmarked cars, by having them walk beats out of uniform, by directing them to place under continuing surveillance frequently victimized homes or stores, or by assigning them to do more thorough follow-up investigations of crimes.

Even so, the Kansas City results offer an important opportunity for police administrators and public officials. If true generally and not just in one city, then these findings mean that there is no compelling reason to tie up large numbers of uniformed officers in the monotonous and apparently unproductive task of driving through the streets waiting for something to happen. By cutting back on preventive patrol, a substantial amount of manpower (in Kansas City, perhaps as much as one-third of all patrol man-hours) could be made available for other tasks, such as investigation, surveillance, or community service.

The key question, therefore, is whether other ways of using patrolmen will be more effective in terms of crime control or citizen satisfaction. Two kinds of patrol strategies have been designed to replace preventive patrol. One is the "community service" approach. It is based on the assumption that if officers are encouraged to become familiar with the neighborhoods in which they work and to take larger responsibilities for following through on citizen requests for assistance as well as on complaints of crime, they will win the confidence of and thus the cooperation of the public and will gather better intelligence about criminal activities. The other is the "crime attack" model which, while not logically incompatible with the former, is based on the assumption that the best use of patrolmen is to place them as close as possible, not to the citizens, but to either a known offender or the scene of a potential crime, in ways that will enable them to apprehend the criminal in the act, or at least to cut short his crime almost as soon as it begins.

The community service model is variously called "team policing," the "beat commander project," the "basic car plan," or the "neighborhood police team." Variants of it have been tried in Syracuse, Los Angeles, New York, Cincinnati, Detroit, and elsewhere.[7] The essential idea is to assign a team of patrolmen and supervisors to a small area, say, one precinct or a few beats, and to leave them there with broad latitude to learn about the neighborhood, alter their own working hours to meet the demands of the area, conduct much of their own follow-up investigation on crimes, and serve as active intermediaries between citizens and various social service agencies. Instead of moving patrolmen about through many neighborhoods in response to radio calls for service, each team of patrolmen is expected to handle all the calls in their own neighborhood. Instead of turning all crime complaints, once the initial report is taken, over to detectives or other specialists from "downtown," the team is expected to do much of the initial investigation. The immediate objective is to develop among the officers a strong sense of territoriality—their beats are "their turf"—out of which will arise, it is hoped, a stronger sense of identification with the community and the fostering of reciprocity in information and service.

The crime attack model takes a much wider variety of forms, ranging from "Operation Identification" (designed to mark valuable items so as to simplify their recovery and thus discourage their theft) to stakeout squads stationed in the back rooms of liquor stores waiting for an armed robber to enter. In each case, the strategy is to make an object harder to steal or a thief easier to catch. Little effort goes into developing information from the community, because the police recognize that since the vast majority of citizens commit no serious crimes and know no serious criminals, they have little information to offer. A common crime attack tactic is the use of decoys, that is, officers disguised as derelicts, cab drivers, hippies, and other frequent targets of criminal activity. Some cities, such as New York, have used community service or team policing methods in some areas and decoys and stakeout squads in others.

Although there is no logical conflict, there sometimes appears to be tension between the two approaches. Stakeout squads and decoys may produce dead criminals rather than arrests. Decoys sometimes have difficulty convincing either criminals or innocent bystanders that they are police officers; indeed, there have even been instances in which a decoy has been unable to convince a fellow officer that he was a cop. As a result, police decoys have sometimes been attacked by citizens and shot at by skeptical officers. In racially tense areas, aggressive law enforcement, unless well managed, can give rise to community criticism.

At the same time, team policing may improve the morale of the officers or the image of the department without producing any increase in arrests or any decrease in crime. If crime rates are insensitive to the number of officers driving around on preventive patrol, they may also be unaffected by efforts to get to know the community.

The evaluations done so far of various crime-attack strategies have mixed results. In 1971 the NYPD formed an "anticrime patrol" of about one thousand officers dressed in civilian clothes or in disguises. They worked the streets of high-crime areas on the theory that, since criminals recognize uniformed patrol officers (hence the ineffectiveness of random preventive patrol) and commit many crimes that cannot be solved owing to the absence of clues (hence the low clearance rate of detectives), crime could best be reduced by catching the criminals in the act. Although the disguised officers represented only about 5 percent of the men and women assigned to each precinct, they made in 1973 over 18 percent of the felony arrests, including over half the arrests for robbery and about 40 percent of those for burglary and auto theft. Three-fourths of the arrests resulted in convictions, far higher than the city-wide rate.[8] But because the anti-crime patrol was not designed as an experiment (there were no matched control groups of officers and no effort to assign the special units to randomly selected neighborhoods), it is hard to say whether the effort produced a genuine impact on crime rates.

A more careful attempt was made to test the value of police decoy units in Birmingham, Alabama. For a variety of reasons, including the fact that there may not be enough street robberies in Birmingham to permit one to assess the effect of different police tactics designed to reduce them, the results of the experiment were inconclusive.

Several variants of these crime-attack strategies were tested in Kansas City, in part to discover how to make better use of patrol officers than simply assigning them to random preventive patrol. The Kansas City Police Department improved the distribution to regular patrol personnel of detailed information about the most active robbers and burglars in the area (the criminal information strategy), it assigned a specialized unit to stakeout locations known to be likely targets of criminal activities (location-oriented patrol, or "LOP"), and it assigned another unit to place under close surveillance known criminals (perpetrator-oriented patrol, or "POP"). The evaluation of these efforts by Tony Pate and his colleagues suggests that the criminal information strategy is worthwhile, that LOP seemed to produce an increase in arrests (as well as an increase in citizen complaints), and that POP was the less effective tactic in large part because the suspects quickly recognized and easily evaded the police surveillance efforts.[9]

LOP and POP are expensive; they involve devoting many police hours to watching and waiting. But there is a lower-cost alternative, already employed by many departments. This involves "field interrogations," police jargon for stopping and questioning suspicious persons or known offenders whenever they are encountered on the streets. Some departments require their officers not only to make such street stops, but to fill out and file a field contact report as a way of building up a tactical intelligence file on street activity. In San Diego, the police, in cooperation with a research team, divided the city into similar experimental areas. In some, routine field interrogation activity continued; in others, these interrogations were stopped for a nine-month period. The areas in which street stops were halted experienced a significant increase in those kinds of crimes most readily suppressed by police activity, such as robbery, burglary, auto theft, and disturbing the peace. When the field interrogations were resumed, the number of such offenses dropped to its pre-experiment level. Moreover, there seemed to be no adverse community reaction, as measured by opinion surveys, to the police use of street stops. In his report, John E. Boydstun concluded that field interrogations deterred potential offenders, especially young, opportunistic ones. The reduction in crimes was not the result of an increase in arrests but of an increase in aggressive police activity.[10]

Many citizens may be interested in these findings but still believe that the most important crime-attack strategy the police can employ is to respond promptly when citizens call. Whatever the effect of rapid response on the overall crime rate, surely the chances of solving any particular crime are better if the police get there promptly. Many police believe this as well and use this argument to justify requests for more personnel, cars, and radios. Unfortunately, the evidence does not support this view. In research carried out in five different cities—Kansas City, San Diego, Jacksonville (Florida), Peoria (Illinois), and Rochester (New York)—and based on interviews with victims, witnesses, bystanders, and police officers, there appeared little evidence that, beyond a certain point, quick police response was a factor influencing the number of arrests. If the crime was actually in progress when the police were called, there was a good chance of an arrest. But if the police were called after the crime had been committed, how fast the police got to the scene of the crime made little difference. The reason was simple: most of the delays between the commission of the crime and the arrival of the police are the result of what *citizens* (victims, witnesses) do. The citizen must discover the crime, cope (often with the aid of a friend) with the shock of the loss, make up his mind to call, find a telephone, and dial the number. If up to half the delay in the police arriving is the result of what the citizen does, even for those crimes in which the victim directly confronts the criminal (the citizen delay will, of course, be much longer if the citizen discovers he was burgled while he was away on a two-week vacation), then making the police more alert or swifter will not make much of a difference.[11]

Much more needs to be learned, but the central theme of the studies made so far of crime-attack strategies is that *what* the police do may be more important than how many there are, that patrol focused on particular persons or locations may be better than random patrol, and that speed may be less important than information.

The lessons from studies of the community service model are equally complex. The most ambitious experiment of this kind was undertaken in Cincinnati, where the police implemented in District One (the downtown, inner-city area) a "Community Sector Team Policing Program," or COMSEC. Under COMSEC there was a slight increase (about 16 percent) in police manpower assigned to District One, but a profound change in the way the police were organized and directed.

Formerly, motorized patrol officers in District One handled calls from throughout the area, even from a place outside their normal "sector" (i.e., beat). When particular problems arose, specialized units from headquarters were called in to handle juveniles, burglary reports, narcotics, and so on. The officer who took the initial call for service often performed no function beyond that of making a routine report. At the start of a tour of duty, the officers assigned to the district would muster together and listen to such information as a supervisor may have had; much of it might not have applied to their beat. There was little opportunity to exchange information in any systematic way with officers covering the same sector. Nor was there always a close correspondence between the number of officers on patrol in a sector and the workload at a given time in that sector. Finally, "community relations" was the responsibility of a community relations unit that worked out of headquarters. In all these respects, the Cincinnati police were organized in much the same way as other big-city police.

COMSEC changed much of that. Each sector in District One was now covered by a team that remained in that sector and handled almost all (91 percent) of the calls for service from it. The team rarely called on specialized units for help on any matter except homicide. Not even the central traffic unit operated within District One except for some patrolling of the expressways. Detectives rarely appeared. The Tactical Patrol Unit was disbanded. Community relations became part of the ongoing responsibilities of each patrol officer, to be discharged by involving local citizens in crime prevention and service activities. Officers on the beat appeared at meetings in that neighborhood to answer questions and to gather information by, for example, showing pictures of known burglars operating in the area. Information developed by each officer was shared among his colleagues under the guidance of an information "collator." Working hours were changed frequently to adjust to actual workloads and neighborhood needs.

The eighteen-month experiment began in March 1973; the results were analyzed by Alfred I. Schwartz and his colleagues from the Urban Institute. The number of reported burglaries decreased in Division One while it increased in the rest of the city. But with respect to other serious crimes, Division One did not do much better than did Cincinnati as a whole.

Citizen fears of crime were not greatly allayed by the COMSEC program. The proportion of those living in District One who felt unsafe when out alone at night did not change substantially; the proportion who thought their neighborhood more dangerous than others actually went up;

the proportion (about half) who believed their chances of being robbed had gone up in the past few years did not change. And this lack of any greater sense of security was not the result of the invisibility of the police: there was a significant increase in the percentage of citizens in District One who reported having seen police officers walking the area. Nor was it the result of any lack of public confidence in the police—about 90 percent of the citizens interviewed thought the police handling of various incidents was "good" or "very good." In fact, even among those *arrested* by the police, 80 percent thought the officers were basically honest, and more than half thought they were properly respectful to persons such as themselves.[12]

Another experiment, this one in Rochester, New York, suggested that one aspect of the team policing model may have another advantage, namely, improving police effectiveness in investigating crimes that have been reported. In Rochester, two or three teams were allowed to combine the patrol and investigative (or detective) functions, instead of having separate units do each, as in most departments. The theory was that immediate follow-up on crime reports by officers assigned to a neighborhood permanently would lead to more crimes being solved (or as the police put it, "cleared") than if the follow-up was done by detectives sent in some time later to work independently of the patrolmen.

After two years, outside evaluators, led by Peter Bloch of the Urban Institute, concluded that there had been an impressive increase in the number of crimes cleared by the experimental teams as compared to the number cleared in other parts of the city by conventional detective units. The ability of the experimental teams to make more arrests was the result of better use of information, more intensive follow-up investigation, and concentrating efforts on those cases that seemed promising (and quickly closing out those that offered no leads).[13]

At this stage of our understanding of police work, it is hard to draw any comprehensive conclusions about the ability of the police to prevent crime that are not so guarded and cautious as to be useless. Since 1954, we have gathered more questions than answers. In general, however, these observations seem warranted:

First, a massive increase in police presence on foot in densely settled areas will probably lead to a reduction in those crimes, such as muggings and auto theft, that require the perpetrators to use the city streets. This seems to be supported by Operation 25, the manpower increase in the twentieth precinct, and the New York subway experience. No one can yet say with any confidence, however, how long this reduction will persist (except in the special case of the subway project, where it endured for many years), and how much crime is merely displaced to another location.

The suggestion from the twentieth precinct that there is little displacement remains just that—only a suggestion, inadequately supported by data. And the cost of any massive increase is—well, massive.

Second, substantial increases in random preventive patrol by police in marked cars do not appear to have any effect on the crime rates, nor do they tend to reassure the citizenry about their safety. Police time spent driving the streets waiting for something to happen is not time well spent.

Third, the community service model of neighborhood team policing appears, on the basis of preliminary results from Cincinnati, to be of some value in reducing burglaries even without massive increases in police manpower. Ironically, the effort by the police to get closer to the community has not as yet reassured the community about its safety or made much difference in what the community thinks about the police, or vice versa.

Finally, a crime-attack strategy, employing frequent street stops and the use of decoys, stakeouts, and close surveillance of known offenders, may hold great promise, but so far it has been the least well tested of all police methods. More careful experimentation is needed.

It may be, however, that judging the police solely or even chiefly by their ability to reduce crime is a mistake. Most police work involving crime occurs after the crime is committed and reported (in the jargon of police analysts, it is "reactive") and depends crucially for its success on the subsequent actions of prosecutors and judges. The traditional function of the police—indeed, the purpose for which they were originally created about 150 years ago—was to maintain order in urban neighborhoods. In our concern over crime, we may have mistakenly though understandably turned for help to the most visible and familiar part of the criminal justice system and thereby made the police both the object of our hopes and the target of our frustrations. Perhaps we should stand back and view the police in a broader perspective, one which assigns them an important part, to be sure, in crime control, but an even more important part in the maintenance of orderly neighborhoods.

Chapter 5

Broken Windows: The Police and Neighborhood Safety

I N the mid-1970s, the state of New Jersey announced a "Safe and Clean Neighborhoods Program," designed to improve the quality of community life in twenty-eight cities.* As part of that program, the state provided money to help cities take police officers out of their patrol cars and assign them to walking beats. The governor and other state officials were enthusiastic about using foot patrol as a way of cutting crime, but many police chiefs were skeptical. Foot patrol, in their eyes, had been pretty much discredited. It reduced the mobility of the police, who thus had difficulty responding to citizen calls for service, and it weakened headquarters control over patrol officers.

Many police officers also disliked foot patrol, but for different reasons: it was hard work, it kept them outside on cold, rainy nights, and it reduced their chances for making a "good pinch." In some departments, assigning officers to foot patrol had been used as a form of punishment. And academic experts on policing doubted that foot patrol would have any impact on crime rates; it was, in the opinion of most, little more than a sop to public opinion. But since the state was paying for it, the local authorities were willing to go along.

*Original version of this chapter written with George L. Kelling, Jr.

Five years after the program started, the Police Foundation, in Washington, D.C., published an evaluation of the foot-patrol project. Based on its analysis of a carefully controlled experiment carried out chiefly in Newark, the foundation concluded, to the surprise of hardly anyone, that foot patrol had not reduced crime rates. But residents of the foot-patrolled neighborhoods seemed to feel more secure than persons in other areas, tended to believe that crime had been reduced, and seemed to take fewer steps to protect themselves from crime (staying at home with the doors locked, for example). Moreover, citizens in the foot-patrolled areas had a more favorable opinion of the police than did those living elsewhere. And officers walking beats had higher morale, greater job satisfaction, and a more favorable attitude toward citizens in their neighborhoods than did officers assigned to patrol cars.[1]

These findings may be taken as evidence that the skeptics were right —foot patrol has no effect on crime; it merely fools the citizens into thinking that they are safer. But in my view, and in the view of the authors of the Police Foundation study, the citizens of Newark were not fooled at all. They knew what the foot-patrol officers were doing, they knew it was different from what motorized officers do, and they knew that having officers walk beats did in fact make their neighborhoods safer.

But how can a neighborhood be "safer" when the crime rate has not gone down—in fact, may have gone up? Finding the answer requires first that we understand what most often frightens people in public places. Many citizens, of course, are primarily frightened by crime, especially crime involving a sudden, violent attack by a stranger. This risk is very real in Newark, as in many large cities. But we tend to overlook or forget another source of fear—the fear of being bothered by disorderly people (not violent people, nor, necessarily, criminals, but disreputable or obstreperous or unpredictable people: panhandlers, drunks, addicts, rowdy teenagers, prostitutes, loiterers, the mentally disturbed).

What foot-patrol officers did was to elevate, to the extent they could, the level of public order in these neighborhoods. Though the neighborhoods were predominantly black and the foot patrolmen were mostly white, this "order-maintenance" function of the police was performed to the general satisfaction of both parties.

George Kelling, one of the Police Foundation researchers, spent many hours walking with Newark foot-patrol officers to see how they defined "order" and what they did to maintain it. One beat was typical: a busy but dilapidated area in the heart of Newark, with many abandoned buildings, marginal shops (several of which prominently displayed knives and straight-edged razors in their windows), one large department store, and, most important, a train station and several major bus stops. Though the area was run-down, its streets were filled with people, because it was a major transportation center. The good order of this area was important not only to those who lived and worked there but also to many others, who had to move through it on their way home, to supermarkets, or to factories.

The people on the street were primarily black; the officer who walked the street was white. The people were made up of "regulars" and "strangers." Regulars included both "decent folk" and some drunks and derelicts who were always there but who "knew their place." Strangers were, well, strangers, and viewed suspiciously, sometimes apprehensively. The officer (call him Kelly) knew who the regulars were, and they knew him. As he saw his job, he was to keep an eye on strangers and make certain that the disreputable regulars observed some informal but widely understood rules. Drunks and addicts could sit on the stoops, but could not lie down. People could drink on side streets, but not at the main intersection. Bottles had to be in paper bags. Talking to, bothering, or begging from people waiting at the bus stop was strictly forbidden. If a dispute erupted between a businessman and a customer, the businessman was assumed to be right, especially if the customer was a stranger. If a stranger loitered, Kelly would ask him if he had any means of support and what his business was; if he gave unsatisfactory answers, he was sent on his way. Persons who broke the informal rules, especially those who bothered people waiting at bus stops, were arrested for vagrancy. Noisy teenagers were told to keep quiet.

These rules were defined and enforced in collaboration with the "regulars" on the street. Another neighborhood might have different rules, but these, everybody understood, were the rules for *this* neighborhood. If someone violated them, the regulars not only turned to Kelly for help but also ridiculed the violator. Sometimes what Kelly did could be described as "enforcing the law," but just as often it involved taking informal or extralegal steps to help protect what the neighborhood had decided was the appropriate level of public order. Some of the things he did probably would not withstand a legal challenge.

A determined skeptic might acknowledge that a skilled foot-patrol officer can maintain order but still insist that this sort of "order" has little to do with the real sources of community fear—that is, with violent crime. To a degree, that is true. But two things must be borne in mind. First, outside observers should not assume that they know how much of the anxiety now endemic in many big-city neighborhoods stems from a fear of "real" crime and how much from a sense that the street is disorderly, a source of distasteful, worrisome encounters. The people of Newark, to judge from their behavior and their remarks to interviewers, apparently assign a high value to public order and feel relieved and reassured when the police help them maintain that order.

Second, at the community level, disorder and crime are usually inextricably linked, in a kind of developmental sequence. Social psychologists and police officers tend to agree that if a window in a building is broken *and is left unrepaired,* all the rest of the windows will soon be broken. This is as true in nice neighborhoods as in run-down ones. Window-breaking does not necessarily occur on a large scale because some areas are inhabited by determined window-breakers whereas others are populated by window-lovers; rather, one unrepaired broken window is a signal that no one cares, and so breaking more windows costs nothing. (It has always been fun.)

Philip Zimbardo, a Stanford psychologist, reported in 1969 on some experiments testing the broken-window theory. He arranged to have an automobile without license plates parked with its hood up on a street in the Bronx and a comparable automobile on a street in Palo Alto, California. The car in the Bronx was attacked by "vandals" within ten minutes of its "abandonment." The first to arrive were a family (father, mother, and young son) who removed the radiator and battery. Within twenty-four hours, virtually everything of value had been removed. Then random destruction began—windows were smashed, parts torn off, upholstery ripped. Children began to use the car as a playground. Most of the adult "vandals" were well-dressed, apparently respectable whites. The car in Palo Alto sat untouched for more than a week. Then Zimbardo smashed part of it with a sledgehammer. Soon, passersby were joining in. Within a few hours, the car had been turned upside down and utterly destroyed. Again, the "vandals" appeared to be primarily respectable whites.[2]

Untended property becomes fair game for people out for fun or plunder, and even for people who ordinarily would not dream of doing such things and who probably consider themselves law-abiding. Because of the nature of community life in the Bronx—its anonymity, the frequency with which cars are abandoned and things are stolen or broken, the past experience of "no one caring"—vandalism begins much more quickly than it does in staid Palo Alto, where people have come to believe that private possessions are cared for, and that mischievous behavior is costly. But vandalism can occur anywhere once communal barriers—the sense of mutual regard and the obligations of civility—are lowered by actions that seem to signal that "no one cares."

I suggest that "untended" behavior also leads to the breakdown of community controls. A stable neighborhood of families who care for their homes, mind each other's children, and confidently frown on unwanted intruders can change in a few years, or even a few months, to an inhospitable and frightening jungle. A piece of property is abandoned, weeds grow up, a window is smashed. Adults stop scolding rowdy children; the children, emboldened, become more rowdy. Families move out, unmarried adults move in. Teenagers gather in front of the corner store. The merchant asks them to move; they refuse. Fights occur. Litter accumulates. People start drinking in front of the grocery; in time, an inebriate slumps to the sidewalk and is allowed to sleep it off. Pedestrians are approached by panhandlers.

At this point it is not inevitable that serious crime will flourish or violent attacks on strangers will occur. But many residents will think that crime, especially violent crime, is on the rise, and they will modify their behavior accordingly. They will use the streets less often, and when on the streets will stay apart from their fellows, moving with averted eyes, silent lips, and hurried steps. "Don't get involved." For some residents, this growing atomization will matter little, because the neighborhood is not their "home" but "the place where they live." Their interests are elsewhere; they are cosmopolitans. But it will matter greatly to other people, whose lives derive meaning and satisfaction from local attachments rather than from worldly affairs; for them, the neighborhood will cease to exist except for a few reliable friends whom they arrange to meet.

Such an area is vulnerable to criminal invasion. Though it is not inevitable, it is more likely that here, rather than in places where people are confident they can regulate public behavior by informal controls, drugs will change hands, prostitutes will solicit, and cars will be stripped. Drunks will be robbed by boys who do it as a lark, and the prostitutes' customers will be robbed by men who do it purposefully and perhaps violently. Muggings will occur.

Among those who often find it difficult to move away from this are the elderly. Surveys of citizens suggest that the elderly are much less likely than younger persons to be the victims of crime,[3] and some have inferred from this that the well-known fear of crime voiced by the elderly is an exaggeration: perhaps we ought not to design special programs to protect older persons; perhaps we should even try to talk them out of their mistaken fears. This argument misses the point. The prospect of a confrontation with an obstreperous teenager or a drunken panhandler can be as fear-inducing for defenseless persons as the prospect of meeting an actual robber; indeed, to a defenseless person, the two kinds of confrontation are often indistinguishable. Moreover, the lower rate at which the elderly are victimized is a measure of the steps they have already taken —chiefly, staying behind locked doors— to minimize the risks they face. Young men are more frequently attacked than older women, not because they are easier or more lucrative targets, but because they are on the streets more.

Nor is the connection between disorderliness and fear made only by the elderly. This is made clear in a number of surveys on the sources of public fear. One, done in Portland, Oregon, indicated that three-fourths of the adults interviewed cross to the other side of a street when they see a gang of teenagers; another survey, in Baltimore, discovered that nearly half would cross the street to avoid even a single strange youth.[4] When an interviewer asked people in a housing project where the most dangerous spot was, they mentioned a place where young persons gathered to drink and play music, despite the fact that not a single crime had occurred there. In Boston public housing projects, the greatest fear was expressed by persons living in the buildings where disorderliness and incivility, not crime, were the greatest.[5] Knowing this helps one understand the significance of such otherwise harmless displays as subway graffiti. As Nathan Glazer has written, the proliferation of graffiti, even when not obscene, confronts the subway rider with the "inescapable knowledge that the environment he must endure for an hour or more a day is uncontrolled and uncontrollable, and that anyone can invade it to do whatever damage and mischief the mind suggests."[6]

In response to fear, people avoid one another, weakening controls. Sometimes they call the police. Patrol cars arrive, an occasional arrest occurs, but crime continues and disorder is not abated. Citizens complain to the police chief, but he explains that his department is low on personnel and that the courts do not punish petty or first-time offenders. To the residents, the police who arrive in squad cars are either ineffective or uncaring; to the police, the residents are animals who deserve each other. The citizens may soon stop calling the police, because "they can't do anything."

The process we call urban decay has occurred for centuries in every city. But what is happening today is different in at least two important respects. First, in the period before, say, World War II, city dwellers—because of money costs, transportation difficulties, familial and church connections —could rarely move away from neighborhood problems. When movement did occur, it tended to be along public-transit routes. Now mobility has become exceptionally easy for all but the poorest and those who are blocked by racial prejudice. Earlier crime waves had a kind of built-in self-correcting mechanism: the determination of a neighborhood or community to reassert control over its turf. Areas in Chicago, New York, and Boston would experience crime and gang wars, and then normalcy would return as the families for whom no alternative residences were possible reclaimed their authority over the streets.

Second, the police in this earlier period assisted in that reassertion of authority by acting, sometimes violently, on behalf of the community. Young toughs were roughed up, people were arrested "on suspicion" or for vagrancy, and prostitutes and petty thieves were routed. "Rights" were something enjoyed by decent folk, and perhaps also by the serious professional criminal, who avoided violence and could afford a lawyer.

This pattern of policing was not an aberration or the result of occasional excess. From the earliest days of the nation, the police function was seen primarily as that of a night watchman: to maintain order against the chief threats to order—fire, wild animals, and disreputable behavior. Solving crimes was viewed not as a police responsibility but as a private one. The police role has slowly changed from maintaining order to fighting crimes. The change began with the creation of private detectives (often ex-criminals), who worked on a contingency-fee basis for individuals who had suffered losses. In time, the detectives were absorbed into municipal police agencies and paid a regular salary; simultaneously, the responsibility for prosecuting thieves was shifted from the aggrieved private citizen to the professional prosecutor. This process was not complete in most places until the twentieth century.[7]

In the 1960s, when urban riots were a major problem, social scientists began to explore carefully the order-maintenance function of the police and to suggest ways of improving it—not to make streets safer (its original function) but to reduce the incidence of mass violence. Order-maintenance became, to a degree, coterminous with "community relations." But, as the crime wave that began in the early 1960s continued without abatement throughout the decade and into the 1970s, attention shifted to the role of the police as crime-fighters. Studies of police behavior ceased, by and large, to be accounts of the order-maintenance function and became, instead, efforts to propose and test ways whereby the police could solve more crimes, make more arrests, and gather better evidence. If these things could be done, social scientists assumed, citizens would be less fearful.

A great deal was accomplished during this transition, as both police chiefs and outside experts emphasized the crime-fighting function in their plans, in the allocation of resources, and in deployment of personnel. The police may well have become better crime-fighters as a result. And doubtless they remained aware of their responsibility for order. But the link between order-maintenance and crime-prevention, so obvious to earlier generations, was forgotten.

That link is similar to the process whereby one broken window becomes many. The citizen who fears the ill-smelling drunk, the rowdy teenager, or the importuning beggar is not merely expressing his distaste for un-seemly behavior, he is also giving voice to a bit of folk wisdom that happens to be a correct generalization—namely, that serious street crime flourishes in areas in which disorderly behavior goes unchecked. The unchecked panhandler is, in effect, the first broken window. Muggers and robbers, whether opportunistic or professional, believe they reduce their chances of being caught or even identified if they operate on streets where potential victims are already intimidated by prevailing conditions. If the neighborhood cannot keep a bothersome panhandler from annoying pass-ersby, the thief may reason, it is even less likely to call the police to identify a potential mugger or to interfere if the mugging actually takes place.

Some police administrators concede that this process occurs, but argue that motorized-patrol officers can deal with it as effectively as foot-patrol officers. I am not so sure. In theory, an officer in a squad car can observe as much as an officer on foot; in theory, the former can talk to as many people as the latter. But the reality of police-citizen encounters is power-fully altered by the automobile. An officer on foot cannot separate himself from the street people; if he is approached, only his uniform and his personality can help him manage whatever is about to happen. And he can never be certain what that will be: a request for directions, a plea for help, an angry denunciation, a teasing remark, a confused babble, a threatening gesture.

In a car, an officer is more likely to deal with street people by rolling down the window and looking at them. The door and the window exclude the approaching citizen; they are a barrier. Some officers take advantage of this barrier, perhaps unconsciously, by acting differently in the car than they would on foot. I have seen this countless times. The police car pulls up to a corner where teenagers are gathered. The window is rolled down. The officer stares at the youths. They stare back. The officer says to one, "C'mere." He saunters over, conveying to his friends by his elaborately casual style the idea that he is not intimidated by authority. "What's your name?" "Chuck." "Chuck who?" "Chuck Jones." "What'ya doing, Chuck?" "Nothin'." "Got a P. O. [parole officer]?" "Nah." "Sure?" "Yeah." "Stay out of trouble, Chuckie." Meanwhile, the other boys laugh and exchange comments among themselves, probably at the officer's ex-pense. The officer stares harder. He cannot be certain what is being said, nor can he join in and, by displaying his own skill at street banter, prove that he cannot be "put down." In the process, the officer has learned almost nothing, and the boys have decided the officer is an alien force who can safely be disregarded, even mocked.

Most citizens like to talk to a police officer. Such exchanges give them a sense of importance, provide them with the basis for gossip, and allow them to explain to the authorities what is worrying them (whereby they gain a modest but significant sense of having "done something" about the problem). You approach a person on foot more easily, and talk to him more readily, than you do a person in a car. Moreover, you can more easily retain some anonymity if you draw an officer aside for a private chat. Suppose you want to pass on a tip about who is stealing handbags, or who offered to sell you a stolen TV. In the inner city, the culprit, in all likelihood, lives nearby. To walk up to a marked patrol car and lean in the window is to convey a visible signal that you are a "fink."

The essence of the police role in maintaining order is to reinforce the informal control mechanisms of the community itself. The police cannot, without committing extraordinary resources, provide a substitute for that informal control. On the other hand, to reinforce those natural forces the police must accommodate them. And therein lies the problem.

Should police activity on the street be shaped, in important ways, by the standards of the neighborhood rather than by the rules of the state? Over the past two decades, the shift of police from order-maintenance to law-enforcement has brought them increasingly under the influence of legal restrictions, provoked by media complaints and enforced by court decisions and departmental orders. As a consequence, the order-maintenance functions of the police are now governed by rules developed to control police relations with suspected criminals. This is, I think, an entirely new development. For centuries, the role of the police as watchmen was judged primarily not in terms of its compliance with appropriate procedures but rather in terms of its attaining a desired objective. The objective was order, an inherently ambiguous term but a condition that people in a given community recognized when they saw it. The means were the same as those the community itself would employ, if its members were sufficiently determined, courageous, and authoritative. Detecting and apprehending criminals, by contrast, was a means to an end, not an end in itself; a judicial determination of guilt or innocence was the hoped-for result of the law-enforcement mode. From the first, the police were expected to follow rules defining that process, though states differed in how stringent the rules should be. The criminal-apprehension process was always understood to involve individual rights, the violation of which was unacceptable because it meant that the violating officer would be acting as a judge and jury—and that was not his job. Guilt or innocence was to be determined by universal standards under special procedures.

Ordinarily, no judge or jury ever sees the persons caught up in a dispute over the appropriate level of neighborhood order. That is true not only because most cases are handled informally on the street but also because no universal standards are available to settle arguments over disorder, and thus a judge may not be any wiser or more effective than a police officer. Until quite recently in many states, and even today in some places, the police made arrests on such charges as "suspicious person" or "vagrancy" or "public drunkenness"—charges with scarcely any legal meaning. These charges exist not because society wants judges to punish vagrants or drunks but because it wants an officer to have the legal tools to remove undesirable persons from a neighborhood when informal efforts to preserve order in the streets have failed.

Once we begin to think of all aspects of police work as involving the application of universal rules under special procedures, we inevitably ask what constitutes an "undesirable person" and why we should "criminalize" vagrancy or drunkenness. A strong and commendable desire to see that people are treated fairly makes us worry about allowing the police to rout persons who are undesirable by some vague or parochial standard. A growing and not-so-commendable utilitarianism leads us to doubt that any behavior that does not "hurt" another person should be made illegal. And thus many of us who watch over the police are reluctant to allow them to perform, in the only way they can, a function that every neighborhood desperately wants them to perform.

This wish to "decriminalize" disreputable behavior that "harms no one," and thus remove the ultimate sanction the police can employ to maintain neighborhood order, is, I think, a mistake. Arresting a single drunk or a single vagrant who has harmed no identifiable person seems unjust, and in a sense it is. But failing to do anything about a score of drunks or a hundred vagrants may destroy an entire community. A particular rule that seems to make sense in the individual case makes no sense when it is made a universal rule and applied to all cases. It makes no sense because it fails to take into account the connection between one broken window left untended and a thousand broken windows. Of course, agencies other than the police could attend to the problems posed by drunks or the mentally ill, but in most communities, especially where the "deinstitutionalization" movement has been strong, they do not.

The concern about equity is more serious. We might agree that certain behavior makes one person more undesirable than another, but how do we ensure that age or skin color or national origin or harmless mannerisms will not also become the basis for distinguishing the undesirable from the desirable? How do we ensure, in short, that the police do not become the agents of neighborhood bigotry?

I can offer no wholly satisfactory answer to this important question. I am not confident that there *is* a satisfactory answer, except to hope that by their selection, training, and supervision, the police will be inculcated with a clear sense of the outer limit of their discretionary authority. That limit, roughly, is this: the police exist to help regulate behavior, not to maintain the racial or ethnic purity of a neighborhood.

Consider the case of the Robert Taylor Homes in Chicago, one of the largest public-housing projects in the country. It is home for nearly twenty thousand people, all black, and extends over ninety-two acres along South State Street. It was named after a distinguished black man who had been, during the 1940s, chairman of the Chicago Housing Authority. Not long after it opened in 1962, relations between project residents and the police deteriorated badly. The citizens felt that the police were insensitive or brutal; the police, in turn, complained of unprovoked attacks on them. Some Chicago officers tell of times when they were afraid to enter the Homes. Crime rates soared.

By the 1980s, the atmosphere had changed. Police-citizen relations improved—apparently, both sides learned something from the earlier experience. When a boy stole a purse and ran off, several young persons who saw the theft voluntarily passed along to the police information on the identity and residence of the thief, and they did this publicly, with friends and neighbors looking on. But problems persisted, chief among them the presence of youth gangs that terrorized residents and recruited members in the project. The people expected the police to "do something" about this, and the police were determined to do just that.

But do what? Though the police can obviously make arrests whenever a gang member breaks the law, a gang can form, recruit, and congregate without breaking the law. And only a tiny fraction of gang-related crimes can be solved by an arrest; thus, if an arrest is the only recourse for the police, the residents' fears will go unassuaged. The police will soon feel helpless, and the residents will again believe that the police "do nothing." What the police in fact do is to chase known gang members out of the project. In the words of one officer, "We kick ass." Project residents both know and approve of this. The tacit police-citizen alliance in the project is reinforced by the police view that the cops and the gangs are the two rival sources of power in the area, and that the gangs are not going to win.

None of this is easily reconciled with any conception of due process or fair treatment. Since both residents and gang members are black, race is not a factor. But it could be. Suppose a white project confronted a black gang, or vice versa. We would be apprehensive about the police taking sides. But the substantive problem remains the same: how can the police strengthen the informal social-control mechanisms of natural communities in order to minimize fear in public places? Law enforcement, per se, is no answer. A gang can weaken or destroy a community by standing about in a menacing fashion and speaking rudely to passersby, without breaking the law.

We have difficulty thinking about such matters, not simply because the ethical and legal issues are so complex, but because we have become accustomed to thinking of the law in essentially individualistic terms. The law defines *my* rights, punishes *his* behavior, and is applied by *that* officer because of *this* harm. We assume, in thinking this way, that what is good for the individual will be good for the community, and what doesn't matter when it happens to one person won't matter if it happens to many. Ordinarily, those are plausible assumptions. But in cases where behavior that is tolerable to one person is intolerable to many others, the reactions of the others (fear, withdrawal, flight) may ultimately make matters worse for everyone, including the individual who first professed his indifference.

It may be their greater sensitivity to communal as opposed to individual needs that helps explain why the residents of small communities are more satisfied with their police than are the residents of similar neighborhoods in big cities. Elinor Ostrom and her co-workers at Indiana University compared the perception of police services in two poor, all-black Illinois towns, Phoenix and East Chicago Heights, with those of three comparable all-black neighborhoods in Chicago. The level of criminal victimization and the quality of police-community relations appeared to be about the same in the towns and the Chicago neighborhoods. But the citizens living in their own villages were much more likely than those living in the Chicago neighborhoods to say that they do not stay at home for fear of crime, to agree that the local police have "the right to take any action necessary" to deal with problems, and to agree that the police "look out for the needs of the average citizen."[8] It is possible that the residents and the police of the small towns saw themselves as engaged in a collaborative effort to maintain a certain standard of communal life, whereas those of the big city felt themselves to be simply requesting and supplying particular services on an individual basis.

If this is true, how should a wise police chief deploy his meager forces? The first answer is that nobody knows for certain, and the most prudent course of action would be to try further variations on the Newark experiment to see more precisely what works in what kinds of neighborhoods. The second answer is also a hedge—many aspects of order-maintenance in neighborhoods can probably best be handled in ways that involve the police minimally, if at all. A busy, bustling shopping center and a quiet, well-tended suburb may need almost no visible police presence. In both cases, the ratio of respectable to disreputable people is ordinarily so high as to make informal social control effective.

Even in areas that are in jeopardy from disorderly elements, citizen action without substantial police involvement may be sufficient. Meetings between teenagers who like to hang out on a particular corner and adults who want to use that corner might well lead to an amicable agreement on a set of rules about how many people can be allowed to congregate, where, and when.

Where no understanding is possible, or if possible, not observed, citizen patrols may be a sufficient response. There are two traditions of communal involvement in maintaining order. One, that of the "community watch-men," is as old as the first settlement of the New World. Until well into the nineteenth century, volunteer watchmen, not policemen, patrolled their communities to keep order. They did so, by and large, without taking the law into their own hands—without, that is, punishing persons or using force. Their presence deterred disorder or alerted the community to disorder that could not be deterred. There are hundreds of such efforts today in communities all across the nation. Perhaps the best known is that of the Guardian Angels, a group of unarmed young persons in distinctive berets and T-shirts, who first came to public attention when they began patrolling the New York City subways but who claim now (late 1982) to have chapters in more than thirty American cities. Unfortunately, we have little information about the effect of these groups on crime. It is possible, however, that whatever their effect on crime, citizens find their presence reassuring, and that they thus contribute to maintaining a sense of order and civility.

The second tradition is that of the "vigilante." Rarely a feature of the settled communities of the East, it was primarily to be found in those frontier towns that grew up in advance of the reach of government. More than 350 vigilante groups are known to have existed; their distinctive feature was that their members did take the law into their own hands, by acting as judge, jury, and often executioner, as well as policeman.[9] Today, the vigilante movement is conspicuous by its rarity, despite the great fear expressed by citizens that the older cities are becoming "urban frontiers." But some community-watchmen groups have skirted the line, and others may cross it in the future. An ambiguous case, reported in *The Wall Street Journal*, involved a citizens' patrol in the Silver Lake area of Belleville, New Jersey. A leader told the reporter, "We look for outsiders." If a few teenagers from outside the neighborhood enter it, "we ask them their business," he said. "If they say they're going down the street to see Mrs. Jones, fine, we let them pass. But then we follow them down the block to make sure they're really going to see Mrs. Jones."

Though citizens can do a great deal, the police are plainly the key to order-maintenance. For one thing, many communities, such as the Robert Taylor Homes, cannot do the job by themselves. For another, no citizen in a neighborhood, even an organized one, is likely to feel the sense of responsibility that wearing a badge confers. Psychologists have done many studies on why people fail to go to the aid of persons being attacked or seeking help, and they have learned that the cause is not "apathy" or "selfishness" but the absence of some plausible grounds for feeling that one must personally accept responsibility.[10] Ironically, avoiding responsibility is easier when a lot of people are standing about. On streets and in public places, where order is so important, many people are likely to be "around," a fact that reduces the chance of any one person acting as the agent of the community. The police officer's uniform singles him out as a person who must accept responsibility if asked. In addition, officers, more easily than their fellow citizens, can be expected to distinguish between what is necessary to protect the safety of the street and what merely protects its ethnic purity.

But the police forces of America are losing, not gaining, members. Some cities have suffered substantial cuts in the number of officers available for duty. These cuts are not likely to be reversed in the near future. Therefore, each department must assign its existing officers with great care. Some neighborhoods are so demoralized and crime-ridden as to make foot patrol useless; the best the police can do with limited resources is respond to the enormous number of calls for service. Other neighborhoods are so stable and serene as to make foot patrol unnecessary. The key is to identify neighborhoods at the tipping point—where the public order is deteriorating but not unreclaimable, where the streets are used frequently but by apprehensive people, where a window is likely to be broken at any time and must quickly be fixed if all are not to be shattered.

Most police departments do not have ways of systematically identifying such areas and assigning officers to them. Officers are assigned on the basis of crime rates (meaning that marginally threatened areas are often stripped so that police can investigate crimes in areas where the situation is hopeless) or on the basis of calls for service (despite the fact that most citizens do not call the police when they are merely frightened or annoyed). To allocate patrol wisely, the department must look at the neighborhoods and decide, from first-hand evidence, where an additional officer will make the greatest difference in promoting a sense of safety.

One way to stretch limited police resources is being tried in some public-housing projects. Tenant organizations hire off-duty police officers for patrol work in their buildings. The costs are not high (at least not per resident), the officer likes the additional income, and the residents feel safer. Such arrangements are probably more successful than hiring private watchmen, and the Newark experiment helps us understand why. A private security guard may deter crime or misconduct by his presence, and he may go to the aid of persons needing help, but he may well not intervene against—that is, control or drive away—someone challenging community standards. Being a sworn officer (a "real cop") seems to give one the confidence, the sense of duty, and the aura of authority necessary to perform this difficult task.

Patrol officers might be encouraged to go to and from duty stations on public transportation and, while on the bus or subway car, enforce rules about smoking, drinking, disorderly conduct, and the like. The enforcement need involve nothing more than ejecting the offender (the offense, after all, is not one with which a booking officer or a judge wishes to be bothered). Perhaps the random but relentless maintenance of standards on buses would lead to conditions on buses that approximate the level of civility we now take for granted on airplanes.

But the most important requirement is to think that maintaining order in precarious situations is a vital job. The police know this is one of their functions, and they also believe, correctly, that it cannot be done to the exclusion of criminal investigation and responding to calls. We may have encouraged them to suppose, however, on the basis of our oft-repeated concerns about serious, violent crime, that they will be judged exclusively on their capacity as crime-fighters. To the extent that this is the case, police administrators will continue to concentrate police personnel in the highest-crime areas (though not necessarily in the areas most vulnerable to criminal invasion), emphasize their training in the law and criminal apprehension (and not their training in managing street life), and join too quickly in campaigns to decriminalize "harmless" behavior (though public drunkenness, street prostitution, and pornographic displays can destroy a community more quickly than any team of professional burglars).

Above all, we must return to our long-abandoned view that the police ought to protect communities as well as individuals. Our crime statistics and victimization surveys measure individual losses, but they do not measure communal losses. Just as physicians now recognize the importance of fostering health rather than simply treating illness, so the police—and the rest of us—ought to recognize the importance of maintaining, intact, communities without broken windows.

Chapter 6

The Police and Community Relations

ONE of the chief constraints on the effectiveness of the police in dealing with crime and neighborhood order is thought to arise out of their relations with the community they serve. It is not only that the police must perform for the community many tasks unrelated to law enforcement, but that the very effort to enforce the law will bring the police into conflict with the citizens they are supposed to serve, to the detriment of both. In this view, the citizens are fearful of and hostile toward the police, and the police reciprocate by displaying unjustified suspicion and harsh and even brutal behavior. The harder the police try to catch criminals, the more they are likely to rub raw the sores of community discontent.

During the 1960s, bad police-community relations were described as a chief cause of black riots. The police were variously described as an "army of occupation" and "pigs"; the neighborhood residents as "rioters" and "lawless" or worse. At the height of the concern, it seemed as if the inner cities were in a perpetual state of war, and in some places that was not very far from the truth.

If matters were always and everywhere this bad, then nothing could be done. One cannot ameliorate with government programs a problem that arises out of the rejection of the legitimacy of government itself. If police and cities are, in the slums, implacable enemies utterly beyond reconciliation, then all the talk of improving matters with community relations programs, better trained officers, and more effective "communication" seems pointless and trivial.

In fact, police-community relations were neither so bad as the "war" theory proclaimed nor so good that we can dismiss the matter as a nonproblem. Furthermore, many of the favorite methods for improving police-community relations *are* either pointless or trivial, not because the problem they address is of catastrophic proportions, but for a much simpler and more common reason: they are based on a misunderstanding of the day-to-day relationships and attitudes that exist between the police and a poor neighborhood.

Citizen Views of the Police

THE SINGLE most striking fact about the attitudes of citizens, black and white, toward the police is that in general these attitudes are positive, not negative. A study done in 1964 of blacks living in several large cities showed that a majority of those interviewed in Atlanta, Chicago, and New York City thought the police treated blacks "very well" or "fairly well."[1] A study done in 1967 for the President's Commission on Law Enforcement and Administration of Justice indicated that among several thousand men, the overwhelming majority of both whites and blacks believed that the police were "very good" or "pretty good" at being respectful to "persons like yourself."[2] A survey of residents of Washington, D.C., disclosed that among the persons who had reported having a recent contact with the police, 78 percent thought the officer had acted properly.[3] In this study, 80 percent of the black men said that the police "deserve a lot more respect and thanks than they get."[4] In two largely black precincts in Boston and Chicago, only 10 percent of those citizens interviewed said that they had little or no respect for the way the police did their job.[5] Finally, a survey done in 1968 for the Kerner Commission indicated that about one-third of the blacks interviewed were critical of the police in their city (believing that the police use insulting language, that they search without reason, and that they rough people up unnecessarily), but not only was this group much less than a majority, it was also about the same size as the group that was critical of the mayor, the state government, the federal government, and local merchants.[6]

Of course, interpreting these findings depends a good deal on how big one thinks a third or a quarter is. With respect to the last study, for example, one could report it either as saying "two-thirds of the blacks were not critical of the police" or as saying "fully (or 'a whopping') one-third of the blacks were highly critical of the police." Whatever adjectives one chooses to append to these numbers, however, one thing is clear—they offer little support for the view that the great majority of blacks are seething with resentment against the police on grounds of injustice or abuse.

But if a majority of blacks are not critical of police conduct, a significant minority are, and this minority is composed chiefly of the young. A study of the Watts area of Los Angeles, done shortly after the riot, questioned persons of all ages about the police (among other things). It found that only 31 percent of the blacks over the age of forty-five, but 60 percent of those between the ages of fifteen and twenty-nine, thought there was some or a great deal of police brutality. Of the males under the age of thirty-five, over half claimed that they had been subjected to insulting language, almost half to a "roust, frisk, or search without good reason," and almost a quarter to "unnecessary force while being arrested."[7]

It is not surprising that young men, whether for good reason or not, should dislike the police. Most crimes, so far as we know, are committed by young men; brawls and rowdiness in which the police must intervene typically involve young males; riot participants tend to be youthful; complaints from citizens about neighborhood nuisances are often directed at the behavior of young men. In any community, black or white, rich or poor, the young man and the police are natural adversaries. The crucial question is whether young black males feel, rightly or wrongly, more aggrieved than their white counterparts. From such evidence as we have, the answer is that they do.

In a study for the Kerner Commission nearly six thousand persons, black and white, living in fifteen large cities were interviewed. Their attitudes toward and experiences with the police were tabulated by race and age. The results are sufficiently interesting to warrant reporting in full. Tables 6–1, 6–2, and 6–3 show that at all age levels, blacks are more critical of the police than whites; that is, they are much more likely to believe that the police use insulting language, that they frisk and search for no reason, and that they rough people up.[8] In the youngest age group (sixteen to twenty), blacks are twice as likely as whites to have these beliefs, but in the older age groups they are *three or four* times as likely as whites to think this way. Stated another way, a sixty-five-year-old black has the same beliefs about the police as an eighteen-year-old white.

For both blacks and whites, beliefs critical of the police decline in frequency as one grows older, but the decline is greater for the whites. By the time they are about thirty-five years old, the great majority of blacks

Table 6–1
"Police Use Insulting Language"

AGE GROUP (BOTH SEXES)	BELIEVE IT HAS HAPPENED		HAPPENED TO THEM	
	WHITE	BLACK	WHITE	BLACK
16–19	24%	55%	14%	24%
20–29	24	45	11	19
30–39	14	37	7	14
40–49	13	36	3	15
50–59	9	26	6	7
60–69	8	24	3	5

Table 6–2
"Police Frisk and Search Without Good Reason"

AGE GROUP (BOTH SEXES)	BELIEVE IT HAS HAPPENED		HAPPENED TO THEM	
	WHITE	BLACK	WHITE	BLACK
16–19	25%	51%	12%	22%
20–29	15	43	5	18
30–39	7	33	2	11
40–49	9	32	2	9
50–59	7	28	1	4
60–69	4	24	1	8

Table 6–3
"Police Rough People Up Unnecessarily"

AGE GROUP (BOTH SEXES)	BELIEVE IT HAS HAPPENED		HAPPENED TO THEM	
	WHITE	BLACK	WHITE	BLACK
16–19	25%	49%	3%	8%
20–29	13	43	1	7
30–39	7	33	3	3
40–49	5	30	0	2
50–59	6	26	1	4
60–69	3	20	0	1

and whites do not have strong antipolice views, but while for the whites criticism is confined to a tiny fraction of the population (about one-tenth), for the blacks it remains the active concern of about a quarter or more.

Experience with the police, unlike beliefs about them, follows a somewhat different pattern. In the youngest age group, about twice as many blacks as whites report that they personally experienced insulting police language, an unreasonable search, or a roughing up. Past the age of fifty, however, there is not much difference in white and black experience—only an infinitesimal fraction of both races claim to have been the victims of police malpractice. If this cross-section of current black opinion is any guide to how attitudes develop over time (and it may not be), then age does not produce a reconciliation between beliefs and experiences for blacks to the same extent that it does for whites. By the time whites are in their fifties, there are only trivial differences between the proportions reporting an antipolice belief and those reporting an antipolice experience (less than 10 percent in both cases); at the same age, by contrast, the proportion of blacks with antipolice beliefs (20 to 28 percent) continues to be larger than that with antipolice experiences (8 percent or less).

It is easy to become preoccupied with black criticisms of alleged police abuse; it is easy to forget that there is as much or more black criticism of inadequate police protection and service. In the Kerner Commission survey, for example, a majority of black respondents believed that the police "don't come quickly," and about one-fourth say that this slow response has happened to them. Moreover, these attitudes and experiences, unlike those concerning abuses, do *not* change much with age. About half of all blacks aged twenty to twenty-nine think the police are too slow; about half of those aged sixty to sixty-nine feel the same way. About a quarter of those aged twenty to twenty-nine say they have experienced a slow response; about a quarter of those aged sixty to sixty-nine say the same thing.[9]

The president's crime commission cited a number of studies showing that in many areas blacks view "crime in the streets" as one of the most important problems afflicting their neighborhood.[10] A *Fortune* magazine survey of three hundred urban blacks in 1967 indicated they felt the same way—"better police protection" was the most frequent *neighborhood* need mentioned (personal concerns, such as better jobs and schooling, had the highest priority).[11] In December 1968 the New York branch of the NAACP issued a report demanding a halt to "the reign of criminal terror in Harlem" and called for assigning more police to the area, placing armed guards in housing projects, handing out harsher sentences to those convicted, and disposing more swiftly of criminal cases. The author of the report told a reporter that "it is not police brutality that makes people afraid to walk the streets at night," it is "criminal brutality."[12] In Detroit, the Urban League launched a community attack on crime that has attracted wide initial support among blacks and whites. One black leader spoke of the need for more policemen and sentences "that will disturb the criminal, shaking him from criminal acts."[13] In the National Opinion Research Center study of ten thousand citizens and their attitudes toward the police, black men at every income level were more likely to believe that the police were very good or pretty good at being "respectful to people like yourself" than they were to believe that the police did a very good or pretty good job at "giving protection to the people in the neighborhood." In both cases, the highest-income blacks (those earning over $10,000 a year) were the most critical.[14]

In sum, blacks are more likely than whites to be critical of the police on grounds of both abuse and inadequate protection. While criticism of inadequate protection is voiced by close to a majority of all blacks, criticism of police abuse is expressed by a minority of perhaps one-fourth to one-third, and experience of police abuse is confined to a very small minority. Antipolice attitudes are strongest among young black males. Older blacks are much less likely to report police abuses but just as likely to report inadequate protection, perhaps because an older person is less likely to come into contact with the police as a suspect but just as likely to come into contact with a criminal as his victim. Finally, there are growing indications of outspoken black demands for *more,* not less, police activity.

Police Views of the Citizen

THE VIEWS of many police officers seem to confirm the "war" theory of police-community relations. Data gathered at least as far back as 1960 suggest that most big-city officers see the citizenry as at best uncooperative and at worst hostile. For example, a majority of Chicago police sergeants questioned in 1960 and again in 1965 felt that civilians generally did not cooperate with the police, that the department did not have the respect of most citizens, that their civilian friends would criticize the department to their faces, and that most people obey the law only from fear of being caught.[15] The COMSEC experiment in Cincinnati (see chapter 4) revealed that whereas 90 percent of the citizens thought the police behaved well in incidents they had witnessed, 85 percent of the officers thought the chances of being abused by the citizens were high.

In fact, as the previous section indicated, the majority of all citizens, and the vast majority of white citizens, have a generally good opinion of the police and are in favor of measures designed to help them. The apparent contradiction between actual citizen opinion and police perception of it stems, I believe, from the fact that the average patrolman in a big city is most frequently in contact not with the "average citizen," but with a relatively small number of persons who are heavy users of police services (willingly or unwillingly), and his view of citizen attitudes is strongly influenced by this experience. By the nature of his job, the police officer is disproportionately involved with the poor, the black, and the young, partly because young males, especially poor ones, are more likely to be involved in criminal activities and breaches of the peace, and partly because even the law-abiding poor (who are, after all, the majority of the poor) must rely on the police for a variety of services which middle-class families do not require or, if they require them, obtain from nonpolice sources. The police, for example, are routinely expected in poor areas to deal with family quarrels; in more affluent neighborhoods, such disputes are either less threatening to the participants or are kept out of public view.

In a study done for the Kerner Commission, Peter H. Rossi and his colleagues at Johns Hopkins University interviewed over four hundred police officers working in largely black sections of eleven major cities. When asked in general terms what they felt was their major problem to be faced, more officers mentioned a lack of public support than any other factor.[16] Fifty-four percent were dissatisfied with the respect they received from citizens; 30 percent believed that the average citizen in these neighborhoods held them in contempt. But when the police were asked about the views of *particular groups* in the neighborhood, a different picture emerged. The vast majority (between 72 and 94 percent) felt that older persons, storekeepers, school teachers, and whites were "on their side"; the police were divided as to whether most blacks saw them as friends, enemies, or were indifferent; a majority believed that most adolescents saw the police as enemies.[17]

Interestingly, black police officers (about one hundred were interviewed) had the same opinion as their white colleagues—to them, the chief source of hostile citizen attitudes was to be found, in increasing order of importance, among "most Negroes," "most young adults," and "most adolescents."[18] The black officers were generally more sympathetic to the problems of blacks than were white officers—they were much more likely to believe that blacks were badly treated by the city as a whole and by the police in particular—but their conception of the problems facing the police officer tended to be quite similar to that of their white colleagues.[19]

In sum, when questioned closely, the community and the police tend to agree as to the source of their difficulties, though clearly they disagree over who is to blame. The chief problem is to be found in the relations between young males, especially black young males, and ghetto police officers. But if this is true, why is there not a tacit alliance between older black residents, interested in better police protection and fearful of rising rates of crime (especially juvenile crime), and police officers who are also concerned about crime and who want "more cooperation" in ending it? In part, there is such a convergence of views; one night spent in a ghetto police precinct will provide graphic evidence of the extent to which the older black residents, especially the women, regularly turn to the police for help. But to a considerable degree the alliance is never forged, at least not to the extent one finds in a middle-class white suburb. The reasons are skin color and the conditions of ghetto life.

Blackness conceals, for some police officers, the important differences in social class and respectability among blacks. Because the urban lower class is today disproportionately black (just as it was once disproportionately Irish), a dark skin is to the police a statistically significant cue to social status, and thus to potential criminality. If arrest figures are to be believed, blacks are ten times as likely to commit a murder and eight times as likely to commit an assault as whites. The possibility that social class and family background, not race as such, explain these differences in rate is less apparent than the association between skin color and crime; understandably (though often injustly), a black skin is taken as grounds for police suspicion and therefore for questioning and frisking.

However race may contribute to police suspicions, it is not clear that it produces a discriminatory pattern in the proportion of suspicious persons who are arrested. During 1966, independent observers watched police-juvenile encounters in three large cities and noted that only 15 percent resulted in an arrest. In comparable situations the police were no more likely to arrest the black than the white. One factor that made the situations noncomparable was the presence of a complainant, usually an adult. When a black adult was present when the police dealt with a black juvenile, an arrest was more likely than when the adult was absent, usually because black adults, unlike whites, were more likely to insist upon an arrest.[20]

Even if arrest decisions are made fairly, there is no denying the tensions produced by mutual suspicions. The conditions of ghetto life, especially the fact of residential segregation, intensify the problem by leading blacks of various classes, and thus of various degrees of law-abidingness, to live in close proximity. To the police, this heterogeneity makes it difficult to perceive and act upon relevant differences in social position. Because so many urban blacks live in or near high-crime areas, they may innocently become not only the victims of crime but also the objects of police suspicion.

This problem, serious in any case, becomes acute if the police feel themselves obliged to intensify their crime prevention activities. There are very few strategies by which the police can reduce crime rates—indeed, for some "private" crimes, such as murder, there is almost nothing they can do—but such strategies as they have require them to place a community under closer surveillance and thus to multiply the occasions on which citizens are likely to be stopped, questioned, or observed. Inevitably, the great majority of the persons stopped will be innocent of any wrongdoing; inevitably, many of these innocent persons will believe the police are "harassing" them; inevitably, innocent blacks will believe that they are being "harassed" because of their race.

Thus, if the law-abiding majority in a black community demand "more police protection," they are likely to be calling for police activity that will increase the frequency of real or perceived police abuses. If, on the other hand, they demand an end to "police harassment," they are likely to be ending police practices that have some (no one knows how much) crime prevention value.

Citizen Attitudes and Crime Control

HOW CITIZENS feel about the police may be the result of either their experiences (as crime victims, arrestees, ticketed motorists, or witnesses), their general beliefs about police behavior (as gleaned from television, newspapers, and friends), or both. If their feelings derive mainly from experiences, then there is something the police can do about the problem; if they derive from the media, there is rather little that can be done. Unfortunately, the evidence we have so far does not permit a simple answer to the question.

The data in tables 6–1, 6–2, and 6–3 suggest rather strongly that unfavorable *views* about the police are much more common, especially among young blacks, than unfavorable *experiences* with the police. There is thus a good deal of evidence consistent with the view that general beliefs, acquired from the media or friends, are very important in shaping attitudes toward the police. But there are also data that show the effect on citizen attitudes of first-hand experience with the police.

A follow-up study of citizens served by the Baltimore Police Department showed that when the officer who answered a citizen's call for assistance took the trouble to explain his actions and to describe what was likely to happen, and followed up the initial contact with additional effort (investigation, another call), the citizen (either black or white) later reported a more favorable attitude toward the police than he did when the officer seemed unconcerned about the victim.[21] A similar finding was reported from a survey of residents of Seattle: of those who had called the police to report a crime, the citizens who were satisfied with the way the police responded expressed more favorable general attitudes about the police than those who were dissatisfied.[22]

Getting a traffic ticket, on the other hand, appears to make little difference in citizen attitudes toward the police. The Seattle study found no relationship between such attitudes and whether a person had been ticketed in the preceding year, except for very low-income persons.[23] No doubt those of us who are ticketed often feel momentarily chagrined or irritated, but this seems to have no lasting effect on our attitudes toward the police.

Though citizen experiences with the police (except for most traffic violations) affect citizen attitudes toward the police, they do not fully explain them. In the Baltimore study, for example, blacks were more critical of the police even when they reported that they had been treated the same as whites—that is, when they said the police responded promptly and handled the complaint satisfactorily.[24] In these cases, they may be expressing a view of the police that is more a product of the general burdens under which blacks have labored in our society.

Though one might presume that attitudes critical of the police impede law enforcement and order maintenance, this widespread belief is difficult to confirm with any systematic evidence. One way to test the theory is to ask whether persons with a low opinion of the police are less likely to call on them for help than persons who hold a high opinion. Obviously, if people refuse to call the police because of their attitudes toward them, then these attitudes are a major impediment to law enforcement. In two separate studies, however, the findings failed to support the theory; in each case, there was no difference in willingness to call the police between citizens with favorable and unfavorable attitudes.[25]

Nor do sharp differences in the perceived quality of the local police department seem to make much difference in how citizens evaluate police fairness. In one of the studies done for President Johnson's crime commission, people were interviewed in two cities. One had a "traditional" police force with older patrolmen, a decentralized administrative structure, poor equipment and facilities, low pay, few blacks on the force, almost no community relations program, and weak internal discipline. The other was nationally famous for its "modernized," "professional" style with young patrolmen, good pay, highly centralized administration, an active internal inspection and discipline system, a large community relations program, and a high proportion of blacks serving in the ranks. In each city, residents of a predominantly black area were interviewed. The results showed that the citizens were aware of the kind of department they had—in the professional city only 18 percent thought that the police were not doing a good job, while in the traditional city 35 percent had this view. And when storekeepers in the area were asked how fast the police would respond to a call, only 19 percent of those in the traditional city but 40 percent of those in the professionalized city believed the police would arrive in less than five minutes.

But when asked how they evaluated the fairness, honesty, and abusiveness of the two forces, the citizens of the two communities displayed little difference in attitude. In both places 43 percent said that being black means a difference in how you are treated by the police; in both cities 10 percent said that they had little respect for the police; in both cities 16 percent said they had seen the police use unnecessary force. Slightly more persons in the professionalized city (53 percent) had "great respect" for the police than did residents of the traditional city (43 percent), but the difference was not large.[26] The head of the professionalized department may wonder whether his efforts have been worth the candle—either he had improved the department but the citizens did not realize it or the "improvements" had not affected the behavior of patrolmen.

For their part, the police are convinced that lack of citizen cooperation and support is a major barrier to crime control. Any patrol officer can recount many stories of an investigation being frustrated because bystanders claimed they "saw nothing," witnesses refused to testify, victims dropped charges, and no one would come to an officer's aid when he was being overpowered in a scuffle. To the police, a suspicious and skeptical attitude in dealing with citizens is amply justified by the facts, however that attitude might be interpreted by those who observe it.

The tension and dissatisfaction that characterize some police-citizen encounters arise out of the differing definitions of the situation held by officer and citizen. The most common calls for police help involve domestic disturbances and property losses (for example, burglaries). In a disturbance, the citizen wants a "solution" that vindicates his "rights"; the officer sees only a conflict for which he can supply no solution and in which who has what rights is quite unclear. The citizen views the police as an all-purpose emergency service; the officer is acutely aware of the differences between civil and criminal matters, of the impropriety of his intervening authoritatively in purely private ones, and of his inability to command or even influence the delivery of other public services.[27] In a property crime, the citizen wants his television set back, but the officer knows he is not likely to find it. The former wishes to see a prompt and vigorous investigation; the latter has no leads on which to base such an investigation and no time or resources with which to develop them. In both these cases, the citizen wants "action" but gets instead aloofness and apparent indifference. The officer wants peace and an orderly supply of information but confronts instead conflict, emotion, and confusion.

In short, the sources of police-citizen antagonisms are to some extent inherent in the situation and not the product of—though they may be exacerbated by—the accidental personal qualities and attitudes of either citizen or officer. The police see conflict and unrecoverable losses where the citizen expects vindication and restitution, and all of this under circumstances that make certain citizens (young males, especially black ones) particularly suspect. It is easy to see why each side concludes that the problem arises out of the moral failings of the other: "insensitive" or "bigoted" police, "disorderly" and "belligerent" citizens.

Deadly Force

NO ASPECT of police-community relations raises more passionate concerns or more divided opinions than the use of deadly force. Many community groups and minority organizations believe police killings of civilians are excessive and even "genocidal"; many police agencies are apprehensive and angry about unprovoked fatal assaults on their officers.

The official data on fatalities, gathered by the National Center for Health Statistics, indicate that in a typical year (such as 1974), about 375 civilians are killed by the police and between 100 and 130 police officers are killed by civilians. However, evidence gathered by Lawrence W. Sherman and Robert H. Langworthy suggest that the official count of civilians killed is much lower than the true number. Based on their study of police department records in several cities, they estimate that the actual number of civilians killed by the police may be as much as 50 percent higher than that shown in the NCHS reports. If true, this means that between 3 and 4 percent of all homicides are police-caused.[28]

The angry debates about deadly force do not depend on the accuracy of national data, however. They arise out of the circumstances of particular dramatic incidents. When two white officers shoot and kill a 39-year-old black woman named Eulia Love who was apparently brandishing a kitchen knife, blacks are outraged. When a black police officer named Cecil Sledge is shot from ambush while going about his routine duties, the police are outraged.

Over the last ten years or so, the use of deadly force has become the most important source of police-community conflict. And since the typical victim of deadly force employed in police-civilian contacts has been a young black male,[29] it is natural that black organizations have made this issue a central theme of their criticism of police practice.

The fact that blacks (and other minorities) are disproportionally the victims of police shootings has led some critics to charge that this disproportionality is the result of antiblack sentiments—in short, of racism. Defenders of the police retort that this pattern merely reflects the greater likelihood of blacks committing crimes, especially violent ones, and in the process threatening police officers or innocent bystanders. Whether either explanation is correct cannot, of course, be determined from the circumstances of a single dramatic case, nor even from gross statistics that compare shootings to either the race or the criminal patterns of victims. What is wanted is a closer look at the pattern of shooting.

We have no such look for the nation as a whole, but we do have it for at least some important cities. James J. Fyfe has done, in New York City, the best study we now have. He found that there was a very high correlation ($+.78$) between the total homicide rate of an area and the rate of police shootings. Even more interestingly, however, he found that black police officers were about twice as likely to shoot at civilians as white or hispanic officers. Moreover, this difference persisted when he controlled for the race of the victim—black officers were about twice as likely to kill a black civilian as were white officers.[30]

One should not conclude from this that black officers in New York are trigger-happy. Much of the difference between their behavior and that of their white colleagues could be explained by the area of the city to which they were assigned. Blacks are much more likely to be assigned to the most hazardous precincts, partly because of their relative lack of seniority (many blacks have only recently joined the force) and partly because of a departmental policy of placing black officers in black precincts (which are disproportionally of the hazardous variety). Once one controls for duty assignment, the rate at which black, white, and hispanic officers shoot at civilians is virtually identical. Of course, the situation may be very different in other cities. But in New York at least, the evidence does not suggest that white police are waging "genocide" against black civilians.

But even if police shootings are not the result of racist attitudes, they still may be unjustified. Answering that question depends on first reaching some agreement as to what constitutes an unjustified shooting, and that is quite difficult. Catherine H. Milton and her colleagues at the Police Foundation studied police shootings in seven cities (Birmingham, Detroit, Indianapolis, Kansas City [Missouri], Oakland, Portland [Oregon], and Washington, D. C.) during the period 1973–1974. After reviewing several hundred shooting incidents, Milton and her associates concluded that the "substantial majority appeared to be clearly justified under the applicable state laws and department policies."[31] Of course, this leaves open the question of whether existing laws and policies provide reasonable standards. Milton and her colleagues noted that in some cases an officer was found to have shot in self-defense but used (in their judgment) force out of proportion to the threat he faced; in other cases, a fleeing suspect was shot without the officer having probable cause to believe the suspect had committed a felony, but he could not otherwise be apprehended.

There is no objective standard, and thus there are no systematic data, that can resolve such issues. But we can shed light on the matter by asking a slightly different question—not what proportion of shootings are justified, but whether there are inexplicable differences among cities (or in one city over time) in the rate at which police shoot at civilians. If differences exist and if they cannot be explained by any reasonable factors (such as the rate of violent crime in the cities or the number of times civilians shoot at the police), then we must conclude that in some cities and at some times, the number of police shootings is wrong. For example, if a city experiences a dramatic decrease in police shootings over a two-year period without any simultaneous changes in the crime rate or the number of officers shot at, then either there were too many shootings in the earlier period or too few in the later. The number of police shootings cannot be just right at both times. If cities A and B differ greatly in the rate of police shootings but do not differ in social composition or crime rates, then one has to suspect that either there are too many shootings in one city or too few in the other.

In their 1973–1974 study, Milton and her colleagues found that the rate (per thousand officers) at which the police shot at civilians in Birmingham was over four times greater than the rate at which officers shot at civilians in Washington, D.C., even though the crime rate in Washington was over twice as high as in Birmingham and Washington had a much larger black population. The shooting rate in Detroit was over twice as high as it was in Oakland, even though the two cities had comparable populations and crime rates. Moreover, police shooting rates declined substantially in Detroit (by 25 percent) and Kansas City (by 38 percent) in the period 1973–1974 even though the rate of violent crime was increasing. (Since this study was completed, policies and shooting rates in many of the cities examined by Milton have changed, and these data should not be read as describing current practice in any of the cities.) These data suggest that departmental policies affect shooting rates.

That suggestion is amply confirmed in a detailed study by Fyfe of changes in shooting rates in New York. In August 1972, the NYPD issued new shooting guidelines and established new shooting review procedures that were more restrictive than those previously in effect. During the year-and-a-half before the new policy went into effect, about eighteen officers per week discharged their firearms; during the three-and-a-half years after it took effect, the weekly average fell to thirteen, a decline of about 30 percent. This decline was net of any accidental discharges, warning shots, suicide attempts, or destruction of animals. The greatest decline involved shooting at fleeing felons. There was no increase during this period in the number of officers shot or stabbed in the line of duty.[32]

In short, police policies make a difference in police shootings. That fact requires us to think hard about what the correct policy ought to be. Unfortunately, that is no easy matter. All departments recognize the right of officers to shoot in self-defense or in the defense of others; many departments prohibit or strongly discourage firing warning shots or shooting at moving vehicles unless the occupants are themselves shooting. The two toughest problems are: first, what standards should be used in deciding that an officer or bystander is in jeopardy? The opponent is armed? Or the threat to life is imminent? Or the officer has reasonable grounds for believing that death or injury is likely? Second, should the police be allowed to shoot to halt a fleeing suspect? If so, what constitutes flight? Should a distinction be made between an adult and a juvenile, or between a person who may have committed (or be about to commit) a violent crime and one who has committed (or is about to commit) a nonviolent one?

The policy of the Federal Bureau of Investigation is often held up as a model. The FBI does not allow its agents to shoot to warn a person or to apprehend a fleeing suspect. But FBI agents typically make their arrests pursuant to a warrant and not at the scene of the crime or because they have probable cause to believe a person they just encountered has committed a felony; by contrast, about half the time city police officers shoot, there is a crime in progress. FBI agents do not respond to domestic disturbance calls; city police officers do, and about one-third of their shootings (and a large fraction of the shots fired at them) occur in these situations.

Devising, implementing, and enforcing a reasonable shooting policy is vital to the creation and maintenance of good police-community relations. This is easier said than done, and no one should suppose that agreement between the police and their critics on the contents of such a policy will be readily obtained. But striving in good faith to do so is important to the establishment of those constructive connections between the police and the community that are vital to all the other purposes of police work, not the least of which is to avoid riots and other demonstrations that are frequently triggered by a lack of confidence (sometimes erroneous) in police policy. Under the best of circumstances, however, any shooting, especially an interracial one, may trigger an outburst. Here, as in so many aspects of law enforcement, heroic efforts can often produce only marginal gains. The ability to accept that fact and proceed nonetheless is a mark of a wise administrator.

Some Nonsolutions

FOR MANY years, some well-meaning but probably mistaken efforts have been made to improve police-community relations by various expedients which have in common the defect of being based on a misconception of the problem. Consider, for example, the effort to find "better" officers, which in practice has meant officers with more education, preferably up through college.

A plausible case can be made for this view. Even if college teaches a man nothing of value in police work, it has two useful side effects: first, it selects from the general population men who have certain qualities (motivation, self-discipline, general intelligence) that are probably quite useful in a police career; second, it inculcates certain characteristics (civility, urbanity, self-control) that might be especially desirable in an officer. It is a measure of our ignorance in these matters that an equally plausible case to the contrary can be made. Recruiting college graduates will reduce substantially (at least for the time being) the chances of adding more blacks and other minority groups to the police forces, for they are underrepresented in college classes. While college may make a person civil (though the campus disturbances of the 1960s suggest that that effect is not quite universal), it also gives him (or reinforces for him) his sense of duty. This has led some college-trained officers to be excessively aggressive and arrest-prone when a gentler hand might be better. Moreover, college graduates may not be able to identify easily with or understand the problems of lower- and working-class persons with whom they must deal. Finally, a police career is most unattractive for a college graduate—the work of a patrol officer is routine, sometimes dull, frequently unpleasant, and occasionally dangerous. One study in New York City showed that patrol officers with a college education displayed a higher degree of cynicism and a greater sense of deprivation than those with less education.[33] In sum, the value of college training is still largely a matter of conjecture.

Better training for men on the force is always recommended. There can be little doubt that the training now received is sometimes perfunctory. But even assuming lengthy preservice training, "human relations" is inevitably that part of the curriculum with the least direct effect on the policemen. The law of arrest, or first aid, or the use of weapons can be taught by lecture and demonstration, but management of personal relations in tense situations is not so easily taught. It is the universal testimony of the officers I have interviewed that training-room discussions of minority groups and police-community relations have little impact, and that such impression as they do produce quickly evaporates when the officer goes on the street and first encounters hostile or suspicious behavior. The officer may remember what he is *not* supposed to do ("don't address blacks with a racially insulting name such as 'boy' "), but he has precious little guidance as to what he *should* do when confronted by a serious verbal challenge to his authority.

If conventional training methods are of little value in this area, is it possible to develop unconventional, more intensive techniques that will work a more profound change in the attitude of the officer? Some departments have experimented with "sensitivity training" designed to produce heightened self-awareness and even significant personality changes. Such methods are based on group discussions, stimulated but not directed by a training leader, in which the participants criticize one another and reexamine themselves in prolonged and often emotional sessions.[34] Sometimes only police officers participate in such sessions; in other experiments, police and community residents participate together. One of the chief purposes of sensitivity training is to change the participants' orientation toward authority and its exercise so that they will engage in cooperative problem solving, rather than struggle to win superiority or maintain personal autonomy.

Unfortunately, the effects on organizational behavior generally of such training (actually, reeducation) methods have not been carefully studied, and the effects on police organization and behavior in particular have scarcely been studied at all. Though there are many enthusiasts for these techniques, and though their enthusiasm may derive from personal experience in seeing people changed, the empirical evidence that desirable change can be induced in organizations as a whole on a lasting basis and without important sacrifices in other values (such as goal attainment, productivity, or equity) is either nonexistent or equivocal.[35] And there are reasons to suppose that police work may be an especially refractory target for these methods. The patrol officer, after all, is not regularly engaged in problem solving with familiar colleagues in a common organization; he is engaging in enforcing the law and settling disputes among strangers, many of whom are fearful or hostile, and some of whom may be dangerous. Conflict is not a figment of either party's imagination; it is real and serious (though either party may exaggerate it and thereby unnecessarily exacerbate it). And the officer typically works alone, or in pairs, and not as part of supportive organizations.

Finally, conventional police-community relations theory assigns a high priority to community organization. In many cities the police have organized a community relations bureau, with officers working out of either headquarters or precinct stations to meet with civic, minority, and neighborhood organizations and to stimulate new activities, especially those involving young people. Some departments have formed neighborhood councils or committees with which senior officers regularly meet to discuss grievances and problems.

The communications strategy is exemplified by the activities of one large midwestern police department. A study of its "district community workshops" discovered that the value of such meetings depended on the character of the neighborhood.[36] In a high-crime-rate area inhabited by both well-to-do whites living in high-rise apartments and lower-income blacks in public housing projects, a workshop meeting was well attended (about two hundred people) by both whites and blacks, but all were adults (there were few young people, especially young blacks, present). There was a cooperative and constructive discussion with the police on how to solve vice and crime problems, especially those in the public housing projects. Plans were announced for assigning officers to "vertical patrols" in the projects. Everyone left feeling that something useful had been accomplished.

In another neighborhood, populated by university students and poor blacks, the workshop meeting was a fiasco. The young *did* attend (about one hundred), mostly to complain about the police handling of a student demonstration. The police refused to answer questions, claiming that the matter was before the courts and thus they were enjoined from speaking about it. The blacks soon became disgusted with the haggling over the demonstration; they cared little about antiwar protest, they said, but cared greatly about the high crime rate in their neighborhood and about the "disrespectful" manner of the police. The three-corner shouting match (students, police, and blacks) broke up in confusion and bitterness.

In a third district, the crime rate was low. Middle- and upper-middle-class whites and blacks lived in a peaceful community and had little interest in police issues. Only thirty persons appeared for the workshop meeting and few raised any crime or police issues. There were complaints, but not ones to which the police could respond, regarding garbage collection, parking regulations, and dogs running loose. Few community leaders were in attendance; most of the audience was composed of chronic complainers, each of whom was irritated by the need to sit through everybody else's account of *his* problem. The meeting ended with little sense of accomplishment.

That the workshop strategy worked well in one district suggests that it is worth doing; that it did not work well in two others indicates that its limits should be clearly recognized. (Some will argue that it is of no value at all if it only reaches middle-class persons, especially adults, but it is hard to understand why the concern of adults for more police protection is any less worthy of being served than the concern of young people for less police abuse.) Efforts to reach the young and those with lower incomes, at least by the communications approach, are exceptionally difficult and perhaps impossible. One first-hand account of such an effort is typical of many. A group of young black "street corner" males was enrolled in a job-preparation program in a west coast city. As the author describes it, the men were "cool"—they spoke in the hip vernacular, wore sunglasses indoors, and dressed in loud (but inexpensive) clothes. Most were school dropouts. Many had police records. They were paid five dollars a day to be in the training program.

Almost daily the men spoke of "police brutality." All wanted to meet a representative of the police. When a sergeant from the community relations bureau finally came, he was almost immediately "put down" with angry questions about "why you cats always kicking cats' asses" and detailed personal horror stories of experiences with the police. The sergeant could not get in a word. The next day a deputy chief appeared to try his hand at improving "communications." He, too, was besieged with stories of alleged brutality. He asked the men if they had filed complaints; none had. The chief asked why not. The men responded that if they did, "we would just get our asses kicked harder by the cop next time." The chief insisted that complaints would be fairly investigated. The men were not satisfied. One asked: "Okay man, you pretty smart. If I smack my buddy here upside the head and he files a complaint, what you gonna do?"

"Arrest you," the chief replied.

"Cool. Now let's say one of your ugly cops smacks *me* upside the head and I file a complaint—what you gonna do?"

"Investigate the complaint," the chief said. If it were true, the police would "take action" and "probably suspend" the officer.

"Well," the black rejoined, "how come *we* get arrested and *you* only get investigated?"

Efforts to distinguish between private resort to violence, for which there is no justification, and official use of violence, for which there may be, were to no avail. The chief was shouted down and finally left.[37]

Better-designed or more protracted efforts might produce more constructive communication between "hip" young black males and the police, but the gains, however worthwhile, are likely to be slight, for the problem is not fundamentally one of "communication." There is genuine conflict between the youths, who want to be left alone, and the police, who regard the young (rightly) as the chief source of crime and disorder, and who seek by various means, some proper and some improper, to control them—often on behalf of older blacks who want "better police protection."

In the 1960s, the issue of "community control" of the police came to the fore. The argument was that both better police protection and better police conduct could only be insured by giving neighborhoods control over their own police. In this way, the police would be responsive to the needs of the local citizens, and the community would develop both policies for the exercise of police discretion and methods for the restraint or correction of police misconduct.

It is difficult to evaluate this policy since, to a great extent, it is a slogan rather than a program. Its adherents believed fervently in it without being able to offer a very clear understanding of what might be involved. And since shifting authority over the police from city hall to the neighborhoods is perhaps the most far-reaching change that could be made in police practice, it is especially important that one examine it closely. "Community control" could vary from having neighborhood groups choose, or consent to the choice of, the police captain assigned to their precincts, to the creation of neighborhood police policy boards that would exercise day-to-day supervision over the policies and actions of officers assigned to a particular locale, and beyond that to organizing the neighborhood so that it could hire, train, and deploy its own independent police force. And the range of control could vary from control over local beat officers (leaving specialized units, such as traffic or even the detectives, centrally managed) to control over all aspects of police work in the area.

Whatever the form of the community control proposals, however, certain questions can be asked that are generally applicable. The first, and perhaps most important, is whether in a period of exceptional tension between whites and blacks living in central cities, the various neighborhoods making up those cities should be given control over their own police forces. If any one neighborhood obtains control over its police, all other neighborhoods will be able to make similar demands. With feelings running high over school integration and busing, the prospects for peace are not likely to be enhanced by Balkanizing the city, equipping each area with its own police force, and letting the disputants, thus armed, settle their differences as best they can.

Second, the question of "community control" assumes that "community" exists and its will can be made effective in police matters. But, as suggested in chapter 2, it is precisely in inner-city areas where community in a meaningful sense is likely to be lacking. It is because of the *absence* of "community" (that is, of shared, spontaneously enforced values) that crime control and police-citizen relations are so difficult. Furthermore, in such neighborhoods the most active and influential factions are often those most inclined to exacerbate and exploit tensions, assert the most extravagant claims, and harass in the rawest manner the employees of whatever government agency operates in that area. Such factions are by no means representative of community opinion, and yet they often tend to dominate discussions and preempt the leading positions. Rank-and-file citizens who have more sober and genuine concerns over crime and police behavior may not be brought to power by "community control"; quite the contrary, their voices may be the ones most likely to be silenced rather than amplified.

Finally, plunging the police into a political arena in which the most emotional and provincial concerns set the tone for decision making is not likely to ease the problem of recruiting and holding able men for the force. A major concern of the patrol officer arises from the inconsistent expectations and contrary authorities that now define his task—his superiors, "politicians," and the public all provide him with various and conflicting definitions of his function, usually (it seems to him) by criticism after the fact. Subordinating him to community councils that regularly and variously debate his role is not likely to increase his sense of confidence or the attractiveness of a police career.[38]

More Promising Prospects

WE ARE only beginning to learn whether there are better changes that could be made. A good deal of thought has been given to ways of identifying men and women who will make good police officers, which is to say persons who can handle the ambiguities of the situations they confront and the various challenges to their personal authority in a reasonable and constructive manner. The chief difficulty has been in specifying, precisely and in advance of recruitment, just what these qualities are. Once we are confident about that, there can be little doubt that ways will be found to screen out recruits who lack these qualities. Analyses carried out in New York City suggest that troublesome recruits can often be identified either before joining the force or during their training and probationary period.[39] Then the problem will become one of finding the administrative and political capacity to insure that poor prospects, once spotted, can be dropped from the force before they achieve what is, thanks to civil service, virtually permanent possession of their jobs.

Once selected, the recruit must be properly trained. Most training programs I have observed emphasize memorization of legal codes and departmental rules more than development of skills at managing social conflict. And familiarization with the law, which is of course important, is done inefficiently (by lectures) rather than efficiently (by programmed, individualized instruction). Furthermore, the precinct or station house socialization process that occurs after the recruit leaves the academy often fails to reinforce the desirable aspects of recruit training, and may in fact lead the recruit to believe that his formal training should be discredited or ignored.

It is easy to misunderstand the problem. What is necessary is *not* to replace training for police work with training for social work, *not* to separate order-maintenance and law-enforcement responsibilities, *not* to substitute "human relations skills" for the ability to make an arrest or take charge of a situation. The debate over the role of the patrolman has tended to obscure the fact that the patrolman does all of these things most of the time—though the law-enforcement, order-maintenance, and service-provision aspects of his task can be analytically distinguished, concretely they are thoroughly intermixed. Even in a routine law-enforcement situation (for example, arresting a fleeing purse snatcher), how the officer deals with the victim and the onlookers at the scene is often as important as how he handles the suspect. The victim and onlookers, after all, are potential witnesses who may have to testify in court; assuring their cooperation is as necessary as catching the person against whom they will testify. The argument about whether "cops" should be turned into "social workers" is a false one, for it implies that society can exercise some meaningful choice over the role the officer should play. Except at the margin, it cannot; what it can do is attempt to prepare them for the complex role they now perform.

The legal code is not irrelevant to performing this role, but neither does it always provide an unambiguous cue as to the correct course of action. And even when it does provide such a cue, the other elements of the situation (for example, challenges to the officer's authority or self-respect) may obscure that cue.

A recruitment program must have the tested capacity to identify persons who can handle calmly challenges to their self-respect and manhood, are able to tolerate ambiguous situations, have the physical capacity to subdue persons, are able to accept responsibility for the consequences of their own actions, can understand and apply legal concepts in concrete situations, and are honest.

A training program should develop each of the above abilities by means of instruction in situations that simulate as far as possible real-world conditions. The object should be to develop an inner sense of competence and self-assurance so that, under conditions of stress, conflict, and uncertainty, the officer is capable of responding flexibly and in a relatively dispassionate manner rather than rigidly, emotionally, or defensively. These objectives will not be attained by simply multiplying courses that, seriatim, take up the law, departmental rules, unarmed combat, and "human relations." There is, of course, a growing awareness of the social and psychological aspects of police work, but lectures on such topics and the scrutiny of texts that urge the reader to become aware of how others perceive him are hardly adequate.

The training conditions must be designed to place officers in situations of stress and conflict in which they must manage their own behavior and that of others in a manner consistent with (but rarely determined by) legal standards. Generating such situations in the classroom is not simple, but the efforts of some departments have shown that it can be done in ways that lead the students involved to experience genuine emotions, lose their tempers, and feel threatened.[40] By observing the behavior of others and by hearing comments on their own behavior in these situations, the recruit can better learn what he can expect from others and (most importantly) from himself in real-life situations. If a way can also be found to continue this process of self-awareness and supervised behavior after being assigned to his first patrol duty, the officer's training can be made continuous rather than (as is now the case) sharply segmented into often inconsistent "academy" and "street" phases.

Finally, the properly recruited and suitably trained officer must be placed into an organizational setting that rewards him for performing well in all aspects of the police function, including working collaboratively with the community. Sometimes we think that police departments are deficient in their community relations because they only reward officers for making arrests, but this is not quite the case. Studies by Brian Forst and others suggest that relatively few officers make a disproportionate share of all arrests and that the rewards officers receive bear little relationship to arrest records. He examined the arrests made in six police departments and found that one-half of all convictions resulted from arrests made by only one-eighth of all officers, and that this difference could not be wholly explained by differences in the officers' duty assignments.[41]

If it is difficult to induce officers to work hard at making good arrests, it will surely be doubly difficult to get them to work diligently and collaboratively at developing community rapport, especially if the community itself is (or appears to be) disorganized, dangerous, and uncooperative. Not only may the officers find such efforts unappealing, their supervisors may find them destructive of the integrity of the chain of command. (An officer who does nothing but respond to radio calls for service is an officer who is continually under the control of that radio and of the supervisor who transmits the calls.) The various "team policing" experiments underway in various cities are the best-known efforts at changing the traditional model of patrol work, but not only are the benefits in either crime control or community relations ambiguous (see chapter 4), some of these efforts, such as the one in Cincinnati, encountered significant resistance from some supervisors.

Properly trained and organized, the police may help evoke a sense of community and a capacity for self-regulation where none is now found. This is the significance, I believe, of the various community security patrols now found in public housing projects and big-city neighborhoods. Not only do they place more eyes and ears on the street and supply escort services for women coming home from supermarkets and bus stops, they can, if both local police and citizen patrols are wisely led, produce a belief that crime control and order maintenance are the joint responsibility of officers and citizens, and that collaborative ventures to this common end are possible.

More attention will have to be given to the costs and benefits of various police methods, such as routine "street stops" to question suspicious pedestrians and drivers. There is no doubt that many of those stopped resent it, though some of the resentment may result from the manner in which it is done rather than the fact of its being done.[42] There is also no doubt that the police frequently find fugitives or contraband by this method. Observers for the crime commission, for example, reported that out of 308 searches by the police, weapons or stolen property were found on about one-fourth of the persons and in over half of the premises.[43] The issue thus becomes one of balancing the gains to law enforcement against the costs to community relations. If, as is likely, some stops under some circumstances are judged to be proper and worthwhile, then a good deal of attention should be given to defining those circumstances and training officers to carry out those stops with civility.

Even under the best of circumstances, however, there are limits to how much can be done. There is a fundamental, and to a degree inescapable, conflict between strategies designed to cut street crime (saturation patrols, close surveillance) and those designed to minimize tensions (avoid "street stops," reduce surveillance, ignore youth groups). Ultimately, the best way to minimize tensions is to find nonpolice methods for reducing street crime. To the extent that better family life, fuller economic opportunities, speedier court dispositions, more effective sentencing decisions, and improved correctional methods can reduce street crime, the burdens on the police and the tensions between police and citizen can be greatly reduced.

PART

III

CRIMINAL JUSTICE

Chapter 7

Penalties and Opportunities

THE AVERAGE CITIZEN hardly needs to be persuaded of the view that crime will be more frequently committed if, other things being equal, crime becomes more profitable compared to other ways of spending one's time. Accordingly, the average citizen thinks it obvious that one major reason why crime has gone up is that people have discovered it is easier to get away with it; by the same token, the average citizen thinks a good way to reduce crime is to make the consequences of crime to the would-be offender more costly (by making penalties swifter, more certain, or more severe), or to make the value of alternatives to crime more attractive (by increasing the availability and pay of legitimate jobs), or both. Such opinions spring naturally to mind among persons who notice, as a fact of everyday life, that people take their hands off hot stoves, shop around to find the best buy, smack their children to teach them not to run out into a busy street, and change jobs when the opportunity arises to earn more money for the same amount of effort.

These citizens may be surprised to learn that social scientists who study crime are deeply divided over the correctness of such views. To some scholars, especially economists, the popular view is also the scientifically correct one—becoming a criminal can be explained in much the same way we explain becoming a carpenter or buying a car. To other scholars, especially sociologists, the popular view is wrong—crime rates do not go up because people discover they can get away with it and will not come down just because society decides to get tough on criminals.

The debate over the effect on crime rates of changing the costs and benefits of crime is usually referred to as a debate over deterrence—a debate, that is, over the efficacy (and perhaps even the propriety) of trying to prevent crime by making would-be offenders more fearful of committing crime. But that is something of a misnomer, because the theory of human nature on which is erected the idea of deterrence (the theory that people respond to the penalties associated with crime) is also the theory of human nature that supports the idea that people will take jobs in preference to crime if the jobs are more attractive. In both cases, we are saying that would-be offenders are reasonably rational and respond to their perception of the costs and benefits attached to alternative courses of action. When we use the word "deterrence," we are calling attention only to the cost side of the equation. There is no word in common scientific usage to call attention to the benefit side of the equation; perhaps "inducement" might serve. To a psychologist, deterring persons from committing crimes or inducing persons to engage in noncriminal activities are but special cases of using "reinforcements" (or rewards) to alter behavior.

The reason there is a debate among scholars about deterrence is that the socially imposed consequences of committing a crime, unlike the market consequences of shopping around for the best price, are characterized by delay, uncertainty, and ignorance. In addition, some scholars contend that a large fraction of crime is committed by persons who are so impulsive, irrational, or abnormal that even if there were no delay, uncertainty, or ignorance attached to the consequences of criminality, we would still have a lot of crime.

Imagine a young man walking down the street at night with nothing on his mind but a desire for good times and high living. Suddenly he sees a little old lady standing alone on a dark corner stuffing the proceeds of her recently cashed social security check into her purse. There is nobody else in view. If the boy steals the purse, he gets the money immediately. That is a powerful incentive, and it is available immediately and without doubt. The costs of taking it are uncertain; the odds are at least fourteen to one that the police will not catch a given robber, and even if he is caught the odds are very good that he will not go to prison, unless he has a long record. On the average, no more than three felonies out of one hundred result in the imprisonment of the offender. In addition to this uncertainty, whatever penalty may come his way will come only after a long delay; in some jurisdictions, it might take a year or more to complete the court disposition of the offender, assuming he is caught in the first place. Moreover, this young man may, in his ignorance of how the world works, think the odds in his favor are even greater and that the delay will be even longer.

Compounding the problems of delay and uncertainty is the fact that society cannot feasibly reduce the uncertainty attached to the chances of being arrested by more than a modest amount (see chapter 4), and though it can to some degree increase the probability and severity of a prison sentence for those who are caught, it cannot do so drastically by, for example, summarily executing all convicted robbers or even by sending all robbers to twenty-year prison terms (see chapter 8). Some scholars add a further complication: the young man may be incapable of assessing the risks of crime. How, they ask, is he to know his chances of being caught and punished? And even if he does know, is he perhaps "driven" by uncontrollable impulses to snatch purses whatever the risks?

As if all this were not bad enough, the principal method by which scholars have attempted to measure the effect on crime of differences in the probability and severity of punishment has involved using data about aggregates of people (entire cities, counties, states, and even nations) rather than about individuals. In a typical study, of which there have been several dozen, the rate at which, say, robbery is committed in each state is "explained" by means of a statistical procedure in which the analyst takes into account both the socioeconomic features of each state that might affect the supply of robbers (for example, the percentage of persons with low incomes, the unemployment rate, or the population density of the big cities) and the operation of the criminal justice system of each state as it attempts to cope with robbery (for example, the probability of being caught and imprisoned for a given robbery and the length of the average prison term for robbery). Most such studies find, after controlling for socioeconomic differences among the states, that the higher the probability of being imprisoned, the lower the robbery rate. Isaac Ehrlich, an economist, produced the best known of such analyses using data on crime in the United States in 1940, 1950, and 1960. To simplify a complex analysis, he found, after controlling for such factors as the income level and age distribution of the population, that the higher the probability of imprisonment for those convicted of robbery, the lower the robbery rate. Thus, differences in the certainty of punishment seem to make a difference in the level of crime. At the same time, Ehrlich did not find that the severity of punishment (the average time served in prison for robbery) had, independently of certainty, an effect on robbery rates in two of the three time periods (1940 and 1960).[1]

But there are some problems associated with studying the effect of sanctions on crime rates using aggregate data of this sort. One is that many of the most important factors are not known with any accuracy. For example, we are dependent on police reports for our measure of the robbery rate, and these undoubtedly vary in accuracy from place to place.

If all police departments were inaccurate to the same degree, this would not be important; unfortunately, some departments are probably much less accurate than others, and this variable error can introduce a serious bias into the statistical estimates of the effect of the criminal justice system.

Moreover, if one omits from the equation some factor that affects the crime rate, then the estimated effect of the factors that are in the equation may be in error because some of the causal power belonging to the omitted factor will be falsely attributed to the included factors. For example, suppose we want to find out whether differences in the number of police-men on patrol among American cities are associated with differences in the rate at which robberies take place in those cities. If we fail to include in our equation a measure of the population density of the city, we may wrongly conclude that the more police there are on the streets, the *higher* the robbery rate and thus give support to the absurd policy proposi-tion that the way to reduce robberies is to fire police officers. Since robberies are more likely to occur in larger, densely settled cities (which also tend to have a higher proportion of police), it would be a grave error to omit such measures of population from the equation. Since we are not certain what causes crime, we always run the risk of inadvertently omitting a key factor from our efforts to see if deterrence works.

Even if we manage to overcome these problems, a final difficulty lies in wait. The observed fact (and it has been observed many times) that states in which the probability of going to prison for robbery is low are also states which have high rates of robbery can be interpreted in one of two ways. It can mean *either* that the higher robbery rates are the results of the lower imprisonment rates (and thus evidence that deterrence works) *or* that the lower imprisonment rates are caused by the higher robbery rates. To see how the latter might be true, imagine a state that is experiencing, for some reason, a rapidly rising robbery rate. It arrests, convicts, and imprisons more and more robbers as more and more robber-ies are committed, but it cannot quite keep up. The robberies are increas-ing so fast that they "swamp" the criminal justice system; prosecutors and judges respond by letting more robbers off without a prison sentence, or perhaps without even a trial, in order to keep the system from becoming hopelessly clogged. As a result, the proportion of arrested robbers who go to prison goes down while the robbery rate goes up. In this case, we ought to conclude, not that prison deters robbers, but that high robbery rates "deter" prosecutors and judges.

The best analysis of these problems in statistical studies of deterrence is to be found in a report of the Panel on Research on Deterrent and Incapacitative Effects, set up by the National Research Council (an arm of the National Academy of Sciences). That panel, chaired by Alfred Blumstein of Carnegie-Mellon University, concluded that the available statistical evidence (as of 1978) did not warrant reaching any strong conclusions about the deterrent effect of existing differences among states or cities in the probability of punishment. The panel (of which I was a member) noted that "the evidence certainly favors a proposition supporting deterrence more than it favors one asserting that deterrence is absent" but urged "scientific caution" in interpreting this evidence.[2]

Subsequently, other criticisms of deterrence research, generally along the same lines as those of the panel, were published by Colin Loftin[3] and by Stephen S. Brier and Stephen E. Feinberg.[4]

Some commentators believe that these criticisms have proved that "deterrence doesn't work" and thus the decks have now been cleared to get on with the task of investing in those programs, such as job creation and income maintenance, that *will* have an effect on crime. Such a conclusion is, to put it mildly, a bit premature.

Rehabilitating Deterrence

PEOPLE are governed in their daily lives by rewards and penalties of every sort. We shop for bargain prices, praise our children for good behavior and scold them for bad, expect lower interest rates to stimulate home building and fear that higher ones will depress it, and conduct ourselves in public in ways that lead our friends and neighbors to form good opinions of us. To assert that "deterrence doesn't work" is tantamount to either denying the plainest facts of everyday life or claiming that would-be criminals are utterly different from the rest of us. They may well be different to some degree—they most likely have a weaker conscience, worry less about their reputation in polite society, and find it harder to postpone gratifying their urges—but these differences of degree do not make them indifferent to the risks and gains of crime. If they were truly indifferent, they would scarcely be able to function at all, for their willingness to take risks would be offset by their indifference to loot. Their lives would consist of little more than the erratic display of animal instincts and fleeting impulses.

The question before us is whether feasible changes in the deferred and uncertain penalties of crime (and, as we shall see, in the deferred and uncertain opportunities for employment) will affect crime rates in ways that can be detected by the data and statistical methods at our disposal.

Though the unreliability of crime data and the limitations of statistical analysis are real enough and are accurately portrayed by the Panel of the National Research Council, there are remedies and rejoinders that, on balance, strengthen the case for the claim that not only does deterrence work (the panel never denied that), it probably works in ways that can be measured, even in the aggregate.

The errors in official statistics about crime rates have been addressed by employing other measures of crime, in particular reports gathered by Census Bureau interviewers from citizens who have been victims of crime. While these victim surveys have problems of their own (such as the forgetfulness of citizens), they are not the same problems as those that affect police reports of crime. Thus, if we obtain essentially the same findings about the effect of sanctions on crime from studies that use victim data as we do from studies using police data, our confidence in these findings is strengthened. Studies of this sort have been done by Itzhak Goldberg at Stanford and by Barbara Boland and myself, and the results are quite consistent with those from research based on police reports.[5] As sanctions become more likely, crime becomes less common.

There is a danger that important factors will be omitted from any statistical study of crime in ways that bias the results, but this problem is no greater in studies of penalties than it is in studies of unemployment rates, voting behavior, or any of a hundred other socially significant topics. Since we can never know with certainty everything that may affect crime (or unemployment, or voting), we must base our conclusions not on any single piece of research, but on the general thrust of a variety of studies analyzing many different causal factors. The Panel of the National Research Council took exactly this position. While noting that "there is the possibility that as yet unknown and so untested" factors may be affecting crime, "this is not a sufficient basis for dismissing" the common finding that crime goes up as sanctions become less certain because "many of the analyses have included some of the more obvious possible third causes and they still find negative associations between sanctions and crimes."[6]

It is possible that rising crime rates "swamp" the criminal justice system so that a negative statistical association between, say, rates of theft and the chances of going to prison for theft may mean not that a decline in imprisonment is causing theft to increase, but rather that a rise in theft is causing imprisonment to become less likely. This might occur particularly with respect to less serious crimes, such as shoplifting or petty larceny; indeed, the proportion of prisoners who are shoplifters or petty thieves has gone down over the last two decades. But it is hard to imagine that the criminal justice system would respond to an increase in murder or armed robbery by letting some murderers or armed robbers off with no punishment. There is no evidence that convicted murderers are any less likely to go to prison today than they were twenty years ago. Moreover, the apparent deterrent effect of prison on serious crimes, such as murder and robbery, was apparently as great in 1940 or 1950, when these crimes were much less common, as it is today, suggesting that swamping has not occurred.[7]

The best studies of deterrence that manage to overcome many of these problems provide evidence that deterrence works. Alfred Blumstein and Daniel Nagin studied the relationship between draft evasion and the penalties imposed for evading the draft. After controlling for the socioeconomic characteristics of the states, they found that the higher the probability of conviction for draft evasion, the lower the evasion rates. This is an especially strong finding because it is largely immune to some of the problems of other research. Draft evasion is more accurately measured than street crime, hence errors arising from poor data are not a problem. And draft evasion cases did not swamp the federal courts in which they were tried, in part because such cases (like murder in state courts) make up only a small fraction of the courts' workload (7 percent in the case of draft evasion) and in part because the attorney general had instructed federal prosecutors to give high priority to these cases. Blumstein and Nagin concluded that draft evasion is deterrable.[8]

Another way of testing whether deterrence works is to look, not at differences among states at one point in time, but at changes in the nation as a whole over a long period of time. Historical data on the criminal justice system in America is so spotty that such research is difficult to do here, but it is not at all difficult in England where the data are excellent. Kenneth I. Wolpin analyzed changes in crime rates and in various parts of the criminal justice system (the chances of being arrested, convicted, and punished) for the period 1894 to 1967, and concluded that changes in the probability of being punished seemed to cause changes in the crime rate. He offers reasons for believing that this causal connection cannot be explained away by the argument that the criminal justice system was being swamped.[9]

Given what we are trying to measure—changes in the behavior of a small number of hard-to-observe persons who are responding to delayed and uncertain penalties—we will never be entirely sure that our statistical manipulations have proved that deterrence works. What is impressive is that so many (but not all) studies using such different methods come to similar conclusions. More such evidence will be found in chapter 10, wherein we shall discover that, though the evidence as to whether capital punishment deters crime is quite ambiguous, most of the studies find that the chances of being imprisoned for murder do seem to affect the murder rate. Even after wading through all this, the skeptical reader may remain unconvinced. Given the difficulties of any aggregate statistical analysis, that is understandable. But if unconvinced, the reader cannot conclude that criticisms of the statistical claims for deterrence have by implication enhanced the statistical claims for job-creation. This is one time when, if you throw out the bath water, you will have to throw out the baby as well.

Evaluating Employment

DETERRENCE and job-creation are not different crime-fighting strategies; they are two sides of the same strategy. The former emphasizes (and tries to increase) the costs of crime; the latter emphasizes (and tries to increase) the benefits of noncrime. Both depend on the assumption that we are dealing with reasonably rational persons who respond to incentives. The principal means used to estimate the effect on crime rates of changes in the benefits of noncrime have been exactly the same as the ones used to evaluate the effect of changes in the costs of crime—the statistical techniques reviewed by the National Research Council Panel.

To make this clear, let us return to our original example. The young man who was trying to decide whether to mug a little old lady is still yearning for the money necessary to enjoy some high living. Let us assume that he considers, as a way of getting money, finding a job. He knows he will have to look for one, and this will take time. Even if he gets a job, he will have to wait to obtain his first paycheck. Moreover, he knows that young men have difficulty finding their first jobs, especially in inner-city neighborhoods such as his, and there is a great deal of uncertainty attached to even the delayed benefits of legitimate employment. Thus, he cannot be certain that the job he might get would provide benefits that exceed the costs. Working forty hours a week as a messenger, a dishwasher, or a busboy might not be worth the sacrifice in time, effort, and reputation on the street corner that it entails. The young man may be wrong about all this, but if he is ignorant of the true risks of crime, he is probably just as ignorant of the true benefits of noncrime.

In addition to the problems of delay, uncertainty, and ignorance is the fact that society cannot make more than modest changes in the employment prospects of young men. Job creation takes a long time when it can be done at all, and many of the jobs created will go to the "wrong" (that is, not criminally inclined) persons; thus, youth unemployment rates will not vary greatly among states and will change only slowly over time. And if we are to detect the effects of existing differences in unemployment rates (or income levels) on crime, we must estimate those effects by exactly the same statistical techniques that are used to estimate the effects of criminal justice sanctions. Indeed, they involve the very same equations (remember, to measure the effects of sanctions, we first had to hold constant the effects of socioeconomic variables; now, to measure the effects of the latter, we must first hold constant the former).

The problem of measurement error arises because we do not know with much accuracy the teenage or youthful unemployment rate by city or state. Much depends on who is looking for work and how hard, how we count students who are looking for only part-time jobs, and whether we can distinguish between people out of work for long periods and those who happen to be between jobs at the moment. Again, since inaccuracies in these data vary from place to place, we will obtain biased results.

The problem of omitted factors is also real, as is evident in a frequently cited study done in 1976 by Harvey Brenner of Johns Hopkins University.[10] He claimed to find that, between 1940 and 1973, increases in the unemployment rate led to increases in the homicide rate. But he omitted from his analysis any measures of changes in the certainty or the severity of sentences for murder, factors that other scholars have found to have a strong effect on homicide.[11]

Finally, there is probably a complex, not a simple, relationship between crime and unemployment (or poverty), just as there may be a complex relationship between imprisonment and crime. For example, suppose in a statistical study that managed to overcome the problems already mentioned, we discover that as unemployment rates go up, crime rates go up. One's natural instinct is to interpret this as meaning that rising unemployment causes rising crime. It is just as possible that rising crime causes rising unemployment. This could be the case if young men examining the world about them concluded that crime pays more than jobs (for instance, that stealing cars is more profitable than washing them). They might then leave their jobs in favor of crime. That this happens is no mere conjecture; it lies at the heart of some unknown but probably large fraction of the growing "underground economy."[12] Some young men find dealing in drugs or other rackets much more attractive than nine-to-five jobs, but technically they are "unemployed." Or it may be the case that both crime and unemployment are the results of some common underlying cause. In 1964, the unemployment rate for black men aged twenty to twenty-four was 10 percent; by 1978 it was 23 percent. During the same period, crime rates, in particular those involving young black men, went up. Among the several possible explanations are the changes that have occurred in the inner parts of large cities where so many young blacks live. As I suggested in chapter 2, there has been a movement out of the inner cities of both jobs and the social infrastructure that is manned by adult members of the middle class. The departure of the jobs led to increased unemployment, the departure of the middle class to lessened social control and hence to more crime. If we knew more than we now know, we would probably discover that all three relationships are working simultaneously—for some persons, unemployment leads to crime, for others crime leads to unemployment, and for still others social disintegration or personal inadequacies leads to both crime and unemployment.

That several of these relationships are in fact at work is suggested by the previously mentioned study of Brenner's. Even if the effect of unemployment on homicide persisted after taking into account changes in penalties (which it probably does not), Brenner himself noted that the murder rate also went up with increases in per capita income and (sometimes) inflation as well as with a rise in joblessness.[13] But if the stress of joblessness leads to more murders, what is it about increases in average income (or in inflation) that also lead to more murders? And if society attempts to reduce the murder rate by reducing unemployment, how can it do this without at the same time increasing the murder rate because, as a result of lessened unemployment, it has managed to increase per capita incomes or stimulate inflation?

I do not say this to explain away the studies purporting to show that unemployment or poverty causes crime, for in fact (contrary to what many people assert) there are very few decent pieces of research that in fact show a relationship between economic factors and crime. Robert W. Gillespie reviewed studies available as of 1975 and was able to find three that asserted the existence of a significant relationship between unemployment and crime but seven which did not.[14] Thomas Orsagh and Ann Dryden Witte in 1981 reviewed the studies that had appeared since 1975 and found very little statistically strong or consistent evidence to support the existence of a connection. The evidence linking income (or poverty) and crime is similarly inconclusive, and probably for the same reasons: there are grave methodological problems confronting anyone trying to find the relationship, and the relationship, to the extent it exists, is probably quite complex (some people may turn to crime because they are poor, some people may be poor because they have turned to crime but are not very good at it, and still other persons may have been made both poor and criminal because of some common underlying factor). To quote Orsagh and Witte: "Research using aggregate data provides only weak support for the simple proposition that unemployment causes crime . . . [and] does not provide convincing tests of the relationship between low income and crime."[15]

Back to Square One: Studying Individuals

WE SEEM to be at a dead end. But we are not. Whenever we are trying to discover a relationship between hard-to-measure factors that operate deep inside a complex social structure, we are well advised not to rely on any single method of analysis and particularly well advised not to rely on statistical studies using aggregate data. We should attack the same problem from a number of angles, using different kinds of data and various methodologies. Above all, we should look at what happens to individuals (rather than to cities or states) and what happens when a new program is tried (rather than measuring the natural variation found in the world as it is).

Ideally, we would like to know how the probability or severity of a possible punishment will affect the behavior of persons who *might* commit a serious crime. Such persons probably constitute only a small fraction of the total population, but they are an important fraction. Most of us would not commit a serious crime because of the operation of internal controls on our behavior, reinforced by the fear of embarrassment should our misconduct be detected. A few of us may commit serious crimes with only small regard to the risks, unless those risks can be made great and immediate. For example, most men would never dream of killing their wives, and a few men might kill them (perhaps in an alcoholic rage) unless a police officer were standing right next to them. But for a certain fraction of men, the idea of doing away with their wives is strongly conditioned by their perception of the risks. Wives, and in particular feminist organizations, concede this when they demand, as they have with increasing vigor, the strict enforcement of laws against wife-abuse. (Not long ago, the New York Police Department was obliged to promise in writing to arrest and prosecute wife-beating men who previously had been handled in a more conciliatory fashion.)

I mention wife-abuse and murder because some people think of such actions as inevitably the result of a deranged or irrational mind, and thus of one insensitive to the risks attendant on such actions. Sometimes this may be so, but more often it is not, as is evident by the fact that the arrival of a police officer usually results in the end of the fight, at least in its physical phase. Even when no officer is there, people pay attention to some costs when engaged in even the most emotional behavior. As my colleague Richard Herrnstein likes to point out, when husbands and wives start throwing dishes at each other, they are more likely to throw the everyday crockery rather than the fine china. I can imagine getting drunk enough or mad enough to challenge somebody in a bar to a fight, but I cannot imagine getting drunk or mad enough to challenge that somebody if his name happens to be Sugar Ray Leonard or Mean Joe Greene.

If the consequences of even emotional and impulsive acts are given some weight by most people, then the consequences of less emotional acts (such as shoplifting, auto theft, robbery, and burglary) are likely to play an even larger role in affecting the willingness of people to engage in them. What we would like to know is how changes in the prospective costs of crime and the prospective benefits of pursuing legitimate alternatives to crime affect, at the margin, the behavior of those individuals who are "at risk."

Persons who are "at risk" are those who lack strong, internalized inhibitions against misconduct, who value highly the excitement and thrills of breaking the law, who have a low stake in conformity, who are willing to take greater chances than the rest of us, and who greatly value quick access to ready cash. Such persons tend, disproportionately, to be young males. As Philip J. Cook has argued, it is not necessary for those would-be offenders to be entirely rational or fully informed for the criminal justice system (or the legitimate labor market) to have an effect on them.[16] It is only necessary that they attach some value to the consequences of their actions (since we know they attach a positive value to the loot, it is reasonable to suppose they also attach some value—a negative one, that is—to the chances of being caught) and that they operate on the basis of at least a crude rule of thumb about how great or small those risks are, a rule of thumb that can be affected by society.

Most of us are probably not very well informed about the true costs of crime; being law-abiding, we probably imagine that the chances of being caught are higher than in fact they are and that the severity of the sentence (measured in years in prison) is greater than it really is. But most of us depend for our information on newspaper stories, detective programs on television, and our own deep fear of being exposed as a disreputable person. But persons at risk (young men hanging around on street corners and thieves who associate with other thieves) have quite different sources of information. These are the accounts of other young men and other thieves who have had a run-in with the police or the courts and who therefore can supply to their colleagues a crudely accurate rule of thumb: "the heat is on" or "the heat is off," Judge Bruce MacDonald* is either "Maximum Mac" or "Turn 'Em Loose Bruce," the prosecutor will let you "cop out" to a burglary charge so that it gets marked down to a misde-

---

*A fictional name.

meanor larceny or will "throw the book at you" and demand "felony time."

It is the behavior of these persons, thus informed, that we wish to observe. But how? As we have seen, we cannot easily do it with aggregate statistical studies in which the behavior of these persons is often buried in the "noise" generated by the behavior of the majority of people who do not commit crimes whatever the advantages. There have in fact been only a few efforts to measure the deterrent effect of the sanctions of the criminal justice system on individuals, as opposed to cities or states (though as we shall see in chapter 9, some of the studies of rehabilitation can be reinterpreted as studies of deterrence). One such effort was made by Ann Witte, who followed for about three years the activities of 641 men released from prison in North Carolina. She gathered information not only about their subsequent brushes with the law (80 percent were rearrested) but also about their experiences with the law before being imprisoned (their prior risk of being arrested, convicted, and imprisoned), the time it took them to find a job after release and the amount it paid in wages, and such aspects of their life style as their involvement with alcohol and drugs.

Witte could not find out directly how these ex-convicts evaluated their chances of being caught if they broke the law in the future, but she could observe how frequently in the past (that is, before being imprisoned the last time) their arrests had led to a conviction and their convictions had led to imprisonment. Her assumption was that these men might be influenced in their future conduct by their past experience with the criminal justice system. The results of her analysis based on this assumption were complex and not entirely consistent, but in general she found that "deterrence works"—the higher the probability of being punished in the past, the lower the number of arrests per month free on the street in the future. She also found that deterrence works differently for different kinds of offenders. For persons who engaged in violent offenses or drug use, the severity of the prior sentence seemed to have the greatest effect, whereas for persons who engaged in less serious property offenses the certainty of imprisonment seemed to be most significant. Deterrence may not work, judging from her data, for thieves who were also drug addicts. The availability of jobs had no consistent effect on subsequent criminality.[17]

There are some obvious limitations to this study. One is that, as Witte notes, it is a study of "losers"—older men (the average age was thirty-two) who had already been in prison, often many times. What we would prefer knowing is whether differences in sanctions or job availability affect the behavior of persons not yet involved in crime or young men involved for the first time. Because her group consisted of older, ex-cons, it is quite possible her findings understate the true effect of either sanctions or jobs.

A comparable study was carried out in Cook County, Illinois, and this was aimed at the young offender. Charles A. Murray and Louis A. Cox, Jr. followed the criminal careers (measured by the number of times they were arrested per month free on the street) of 317 Chicago boys who had been incarcerated for the first time by the Illinois Department of Corrections. Though young (their average age was sixteen), they were scarcely novices at crime: they had been arrested an average of thirteen times each before receiving this, their first prison sentence. Nor were their offenses trivial: as a group, they had been charged with fourteen homicides, twenty-three rapes, over three hundred assaults and a like number of auto thefts, nearly two hundred armed robberies, and over seven hundred burglaries. The patience of the court finally exhausted, they were sent off to a correctional institution, where they served an average sentence of ten months. Murray and Cox followed them for (on the average) seventeen months after their release. During this period, the frequency with which they were arrested (that is, arrests per month per one hundred boys) declined by about two-thirds. To be exact, the members of this group of hard-core delinquents were arrested 6.3 times each during the year before being sent away but only 2.9 times each during the seventeen months on the street after release.[18]

Murray and Cox refer to this as the "suppression effect"; namely, the tendency of the first exposure to prison to suppress the rate at which delinquents are arrested and, presumably, the rate at which they actually were committing crimes.* In chapter 9, we shall consider some additional implications of this study as well as some of the objections that have been raised to it.

The Murray and Cox study, one of the few of its kind that has been carried out, adds some support to the deterrence theory. But it still focuses on persons who have already committed crimes; we remain uncertain about the effect of changes in the criminal justice system on would-be offenders. It is almost impossible to study behavior that does not occur except to ask, as some scholars have done, various persons, often students,

---

*Another study of individual responses to sanctions was carried out among shoplifters caught by store detectives in a large California department store. Of the 371 individuals caught shoplifting during one year, only 3 were caught again during the year in any of the department stores in that region, even though the majority who were caught were not taken to court. The authors interpret this as evidence of the deterrent effect of apprehension, though the lack of any control group (persons shoplifting but not caught) render this conclusion somewhat speculative. Lawrence E. Cohen and Rodney Stark, "Discriminatory Labeling and the Five-Finger Discount: An Empirical Analysis of Differential Shoplifting Dispositions," *Journal of Research in Crime and Delinquency* 11 (1974): 25–39. For a similar conclusion, see also Mary Owen Cameron, *The Booster and the Snitch* (New York: Free Press, 1964), pp. 159–170.

whether they would commit or have committed a crime when they perceived the penalties to be of a given severity and a given probability. One such study was done among students at an eastern college,[19] and another among high school students in Arizona.[20] Both found that the students who believed there was a high probability of being punished for a particular criminal act were less likely to report (anonymously) having committed the act than were students who thought there was a low probability of being punished. Both studies are broadly consistent with the view that deterrence works, but both are also difficult to interpret. It is hard to be confident that the number of offenses the students reported bears any relationship to the number they actually committed. More important, the studies raise the possibility that what actually deters these students (very few of whom commit any serious acts with any frequency) is not what they guess to be the chances of being caught, but the moral opprobrium with which such acts are viewed. As will be discussed in chapter 12, for most people in most circumstances, the moral nature of the act and the internalized inhibitions on misconduct arising out of that moral code are probably the major deterrents to crime. Interviewing students may highlight that fact, but it cannot tell us what happens, at the margin, when society alters the certainty or severity of punishment for a given offense. And for purposes of public policy, that is exactly what we want to know.

Experimenting with Changing the Costs of Crime

THE BEST WAY to find out the circumstances under which punishing or helping people will affect the likelihood of such persons committing crimes is to try it. Unfortunately, learning from experience is harder than acquiring experience, because many things that are tried as ways of reducing crime, including both alterations in the penalties for crime and in the opportunities for avoiding crime, are never evaluated in any serious way. As a result, the study of public policy toward crime is cluttered with unsupported assertions and reinvented wheels.

There have been some efforts to make changes under conditions permitting a serious and competent evaluation, and we can report the results. A few were designed from the first as true experiments (one of them, the Kansas City Preventive Patrol project, was described in chapter 4), others have been "quasi-experiments"—changes in policy that were accompanied by efforts to find out what happened (such as the assignment of more officers to the New York City subways, also described in chapter 4).

Most experiments in deterrence have involved changes in police behavior rather than changes in the behavior of judges and prosecutors. As we saw in chapter 4, the result of those changes seem to indicate that the more focused and aggressive the police effort, the greater the chance of it making a difference. Changes in the level of random preventive patrol in marked cars seemed to make little difference in crime rates in Kansas City, but changes in the number of officers riding New York subway cars and changes in the aggressiveness with which San Diego police stopped and interrogated persons on the streets did seem to make a difference.* Comparable results come from a study of drunk driving in Great Britain. The police began a program to use a breathalyzer to catch inebriated motorists in hopes of reducing traffic accidents, especially fatal ones. A careful study by H. Laurence Ross clearly indicates that these hopes were born out: "the Road Safety Act caused a reduction in casualties" by as much as two-thirds during weekend evenings when drunk driving is likely to be most common.[21] Unhappily, the police did not like to enforce this law, which could lead to the mandatory revocation of the driving license of a motorist whose blood alcohol level exceeded .08 percent. In time, the authorities made a highly publicized effort to get the police to make random stops and administer breathalyzer tests, and once again accidents declined.[22]

Perhaps the most dramatic evidence of the operation of deterrence—dramatic because it involved a true experiment on individuals in the real world—comes from an effort in Minneapolis to find out how the police can best handle incidents of spouse assault. The conventional wisdom had been that if one or both parties to such an assault were handled by the officer informally—by mediation or referral to a social work agency—the parties would be better off than if the assaulter were arrested. And the police themselves often preferred not to make an arrest because it took time and effort and often led to no prosecution when the victim refused to press charges. With the advice of the Police Foundation, a group of Minneapolis officers began handling their misdemeanor spouse-assault

---

*A study by Barbara Boland and myself involving a complex statistical analysis of the relationship between police behavior and robbery rates in thirty-five large American cities seems to confirm these experimental findings. The number of police officers on the street and the aggressiveness with which they patrolled had, independently, effects on the reported rate of robberies. The study employed methods (estimating simultaneous equations using two-stage least squares) and assumptions designed to eliminate the risk that the finding of a deterrent effect would be spurious owing to the reciprocal relationship between crime and the number and behavior of police officers. In particular, it was designed to overcome the problems mentioned earlier in this chapter and in the report of the National Research Council Panel on Deterrence arising from the fact that the number of robberies may affect the number of police and the rate at which they make arrests just as the number of police and the arrest rate may affect the number of robberies. James Q. Wilson and Barbara Boland, "The Effect of the Police on Crime," *Law and Society Review* 12 (Spring 1978): 367–390, and "The Effects of the Police on Crime: A Rejoinder," *Law and Society Review* 16 (1981–1982): 163–169.

cases by randomly assigning the assaulter to one of three dispositions: arresting him, advising him, or sending him out of the house to cool off. Over 250 cases were treated in this experimental fashion and followed up for six months. The assaulters who were arrested were less likely to be reported to the police for a subsequent assault than were those advised and much less likely than those sent out of the house. And this was true even though the arrested person, in the vast majority of cases, spent no more than a week in jail.[23]

These police experiments and quasi-experiments support the concept of deterrence, but they are not an especially hard test of it. The police are the persons closest to a potential offender, and if they suddenly act in a more conspicuous or aggressive manner, these changes are often quickly noticed by would-be offenders who then alter their behavior accordingly. Moreover, the kinds of offenses most worrisome to citizens are often those, such as burglary, street robbery, and assault, that are difficult for the police to detect or intercept. The deterrent effect of policing is likely to be greatest when the police can act in a visible way in a closed system (such as a subway or in a school building) or when they can take action on their own initiative without first waiting for a report that a crime has occurred (as in stopping motorists and administering breathalyzer tests or questioning suspicious teenagers on a street corner). The deterrent value of the police is likely to be least when the crime to be deterred involves stealth (such as burglary).

A tougher and, for policy purposes, more useful test of deterrence would be to alter the sentences a person gets without altering police conduct. We have surprisingly few careful studies of the results of doing that even though sentences are regularly altered. Many states have passed mandatory minimum sentences for certain offenses and some have tried to eliminate plea bargaining or, at least, to insure that serious offenders cannot have the charges against them reduced simply to induce a guilty plea. Unfortunately, most of these changes were made under circumstances that rendered any serious evaluation of their effect difficult, if not impossible.

The two best-known changes in sentencing practices that have been studied were the so-called Rockefeller drug laws in New York and the Bartley-Fox gun law in Massachusetts. In 1973, New York State revised its criminal statutes relating to drug trafficking in an attempt to make more severe and more certain the penalties for the sale and possession of heroin (the law affecting other drugs was changed as well, but the focus of the effort, and the most severe penalties, were reserved for heroin). The major pushers—those who sold an ounce or more of heroin—would be liable for a minimum prison term of at least fifteen years and the possibility of life imprisonment. There were some loopholes. An ounce dealer could plea bargain the charges against him down, but to no lower a charge than would entail a mandatory one-year minimum prison sentence. Police informants could get probation instead of prison, and persons under the age of sixteen were exempt from the mandatory sentences. Persons ages sixteen to eighteen might be exempted from the law, a provision that was made explicit by amendments passed in 1975. A group was formed to evaluate the effect of this law. Its report, issued in 1977, concluded that there was no evidence the law had reduced either the availability of heroin on the streets of New York City or the kinds of property crime often committed by drug users. Of course, it is almost impossible to measure directly the amount of an illegal drug in circulation or to observe the illicit transactions between dealers and users, but a good deal of circumstantial evidence, gathered by the study group, suggests that no large changes occurred. There were no marked shifts in deaths from narcotics overdoses, in admissions to drug treatment programs, in the incidence of serum hepatitis (a disease frequently contracted by junkies who use dirty needles), or in the price and purity of heroin available for sale on the street (as inferred from undercover buys of heroin made by narcotics agents).

The explanation for this disappointing experience, in the opinion of the study group, was that difficulties in administering the law weakened its deterrent power, with the result that most offenders and would-be offenders did not experience a significantly higher risk of apprehension and punishment. There was no increase (or decrease, for that matter) in the number of arrests, no increase in the number of indictments, and a slight decline in the proportion of indictments resulting in conviction. Offsetting this was a higher probability that a person convicted would go to prison. The net effect of these offsetting trends—fewer indictments but a higher risk of imprisonment if indicted and convicted—was that the probability of imprisonment for arrested drug dealers did not change as a result of the law: it was about one imprisonment per nine arrests before the law, and about one in nine afterward. On the other hand, the sentences received by those who did go to prison became more severe. Before the law was passed, only 3 percent of persons imprisoned for drug offenses received a sentence of three years or more. After the law went into effect, 22 percent received such sentences. Perhaps because sentences became more severe, more accused persons demanded trials instead of pleading guilty and, as a result, the time it took to dispose of the average drug case nearly doubled.

Does the experience under the Rockefeller law disprove the claim that deterrence works? Not at all. If we mean by "deterrence" changing behavior by increasing either the certainty or the swiftness of punishment, then the Rockefeller law, as it was administered, could not have deterred behavior because it made no change in the certainty of punishment and actually reduced the swiftness of it. If, on the other hand, we define "deterrence" as changing behavior by increasing the severity of punishment, then deterrence did not work in this case. What we would like to know is whether heroin trafficking would have been reduced *if* the penalties associated with it could have been made swifter or more certain.

It is possible that severity is the enemy of certainty and speed. As penalties get tougher, defendants and their lawyers have a greater incentive to slow down the process, and those prosecutors and judges who oppose heavy sentences for drug dealing may use their discretionary powers to decline indictment, accept plea bargains, grant continuances, and modify penalties in ways that reduce the certainty and the celerity of punishment. The group that evaluated the Rockefeller law suggests that reducing severity in favor of certainty might create the only real possibility of testing the deterrent effect of changes in sentences.[24]

The Bartley-Fox gun law in Massachusetts was administered and evaluated in ways that avoided some of the problems of interpreting the results of the Rockefeller drug laws. In 1974, the Massachusetts legislature amended the law that had long required persons carrying a handgun to have a license by stipulating that a violation of this law would now entail a mandatory penalty of one year in prison, which may not be reduced by probation, parole, or judicial finagling. When the law went into effect in April 1975, various efforts were made to evaluate both the compliance of the criminal justice system with it and the law's impact on crimes involving handguns. James A. Beha traced the application of the law for two years and concluded that, despite widespread predictions to the contrary, the police, prosecutors, and judges were not evading the law. As in New York, more persons asked for trials, and delays in disposition apparently increased, but unlike in New York the probability of punishment increased for those arrested. Beha estimated in 1977 (at a time when not all the early arrests had yet worked their way through the system) that prison sentences were being imposed four times more frequently on persons arrested for illegally carrying firearms than had been true before the law was passed. Owing to some combination of the heavy publicity given to the Bartley-Fox law and to the real increase in the risk of imprisonment facing persons arrested while carrying a firearm without a license, the casual carrying of firearms in Massachusetts seems to have decreased. This was the view expressed to interviewers by participants in the system, including persons being held in jail, and it was buttressed by the fact that there was a sharp drop in the proportion of drug dealers arrested by the

Boston police who, at the time of their arrest, were found to be carrying firearms.[25]

Three studies were made of the impact of the law on serious crime. They used slightly different methods, but in general came to the same conclusion; namely, that there was a measurable decline in the kinds of crimes that involve the casual use of firearms. More exactly, there appeared to be a decline in the proportion of assaults, robberies, and homicides in which a gun was used even though the total number of assaults and robberies in Boston was going up and the number of murders was constant. Moreover, the proportion of assaults and robberies in which guns were used did not go down in other large cities in the United States during this time.[26] In sum, the Bartley-Fox law, as applied, seems, at least during the years in which its effect was studied, to have increased the risk associated with carrying a gun, reduced the frequency with which guns were casually carried, and thereby reduced the rate at which certain gun-related crimes were committed.

An effort to achieve the same results in Michigan did not work out as well, in large measure because the judges there (in particular the judges in Wayne County, which includes Detroit) refused to apply the law. The Michigan Felony Firearm Law, which went into effect in 1977, required the imposition of a two-year prison sentence for possessing a firearm while committing a felony, and the two-year firearm sentence was to be added on to whatever sentence was imposed for the other felony. There was no general change in either the certainty or the severity of sentences issued to gun-carrying felons. To avoid adding on the two-year term required by the Felony Firearm Law, many judges would reduce the sentence given for the original felony (say, assault or robbery) in order to compensate for the add-on. In other cases, the judge would dismiss the gun count or the defendant would be allowed to plea to a less serious charge.[27] Given this evasion, it is not surprising to learn that there was little effect of the law on the rate at which gun-related crimes were committed.[28]

Several states have recently altered the legal minimum drinking age; because of the effect of teenage drinking on highway fatalities, these changes have been closely studied. Between 1970 and 1973, twenty-five states lowered their legal drinking age. Shortly thereafter, Allan F. Williams and his associates examined the effect of these age reductions on highway accidents and concluded that the changes in the laws had contributed to an increase in fatal motor vehicle accidents.[29] Reacting to the implications of such findings, at least fourteen states, beginning in 1976, raised their minimum drinking ages from eighteen or nineteen to twenty or twenty-one. Williams and associates studied these changes in nine states and concluded that making it illegal for young persons (typically, those eighteen and under) to buy alcoholic beverages led to a reduction in fatal auto accidents occurring at night (when most drink-related accidents take place).[30] Alexander C. Wagenaar looked closely at one state, Michigan, and came to the same conclusion. When the legal drinking age there was lowered to eighteen, the number of persons ages eighteen to twenty involved in accidents who reportedly had been drinking began to rise; when the drinking age was raised to twenty-one, the number of such persons in crashes began to decrease.[31] Comparable conclusions were reached from a study of the consequences of altering the legal drinking age in Maine.[32] In his evaluation of laws governing drunk driving around the world, H. Laurence Ross concluded that increasing the certainty of punishment reduces the level of drunk driving.[33] By contrast, decriminalizing abortions in Hawaii did not seem to affect the estimated number of abortions performed.[34]

In sum, the evidence from these quasi-experiments is that changes in the probability of being punished can lead to changes in behavior, though this may not happen when the legal changes exist only on paper and not in practice or when the benefits to be had from violating the law are so great as to make would-be perpetrators indifferent to the slight alteration in the risks facing them. For example, when the prospective gains from heroin trafficking or obtaining (and supplying) illegal abortions are very large, these gains can swamp the effect of modest changes in the costs of these actions, especially when (as with the New York drug law and the Michigan firearms law) the criminal justice system does not in practice impose greater risks. When the prospective benefits from violating the law are small (as with teenage drinking or perhaps with carrying an unlicensed gun), small changes in the risks can have significant effects on behavior.

All this means that it is difficult, but not impossible, to achieve increased deterrent effects through changes in the law. To obtain these effects, society must walk a narrow line—the penalties to be imposed must be sufficiently great to offset, at the margin, the benefits of the illegal act but not so great as to generate resistance in the criminal justice system to their prompt imposition.

Experiments with Changing the Benefits of Noncrime

THE HOPE, widespread in the 1960s, that job-creation and job-training programs would solve many social problems, including crime, led to countless efforts both to prevent crime by supplying jobs to crime-prone youth and to reduce crime among convicted offenders by supplying them with better job opportunities after their release from prison. One preventive program was the Neighborhood Youth Corps that gave jobs to poor young persons during the afternoons and evenings and all days during the summer. Gerald D. Robins evaluated the results of such programs among poor blacks in Cincinnati and Detroit. He found no evidence that participation in the Youth Corps had any effect on the proportion of enrollees who came into contact with the police.[35] Essentially the same gloomy conclusion was reached by the authors of a survey of some ninety-six delinquency prevention programs, though there were a few glimmers of hope that certain programs might provide some benefits to some persons.[36] For example, persons who had gone through a Job Corps program that featured intensive remedial education and job training in a residential camp were apparently less likely to be arrested six months after finishing their training than a control group.[37]

Though preventing crime and delinquency by job programs of the sort developed by the "Great Society" seemed a lost hope, there was, initially at least, more success reported from efforts to reduce crime among ex-offenders. Philip Cook followed 325 men who had been released from Massachusetts prisons in 1959 and found that those parolees who were able to find "satisfactory" jobs (not just any job) were less likely to have their parole revoked because they committed a new crime during an eighteen-month follow-up period. This was true even after controlling for the personal attributes of the parolees, such as race, intelligence, marital status, education, prior occupation, and military service.[38]

Findings such as Cook's may have reinforced the belief of policy makers that if only we could reintegrate the ex-offender into the labor market, we could cut crime and at the same time save money through reduced prison populations. By the early 1970s, forty-two states had adopted some variety of "work-release" programs for prisoners by which convicts nearing the end of their prison terms were released into the community in order to work at various jobs during the day, returning to prison at night or on weekends. Gordon P. Waldo and Theodore G. Chiricos evaluated the results of work-release in Florida, and did so on the basis of a particularly sophisticated research design. Eligible inmates were *randomly* assigned to either a work-release or a nonrelease group, to insure that there were no differences between those enrolled in the program and those not enrolled. And many different measures of recidivism were calculated, not just whether the offender was later arrested (as I suggest in chapter 9, this is a common flaw in most experiments on rehabilitation), but also the *rate* of arrests per month free. Waldo and Chiricos found no differences whatsoever in the rearrest rate (or in any measure of recidivism) between persons in work-release and persons not.[39] An equally unpromising result was found by Ann Witte in North Carolina, though there work-release may have led offenders to commit somewhat less serious offenses.[40]

If work-release seems not to reduce crime rates, perhaps it is because it focuses on work rather than wealth. Perhaps if ex-offenders had more money, especially during the crucial few months after their release, they would not need to steal in order to support themselves. Some preliminary evidence gives credence to this view. In Baltimore, about four hundred ex-convicts had been randomly assigned to one of four groups: those receiving nothing, those receiving employment assistance, those receiving financial aid, and those receiving both job placement services and financial aid. After two years, it was clear that getting employment counseling made no difference in the chances of being rearrested but that getting financial aid ($60 a week for thirteen weeks) did make a small difference (about 8 percent). There were a host of problems with this finding, however. For one thing, recidivism was defined as whether or not the person was rearrested, not the *rate* at which he was rearrested (thus possibly obscuring changes in the frequency with which persons committed crimes). Moreover, the study excluded first offenders, alcoholics, heroin users, and persons who had not committed property offenses.[41]

A fuller test of the combined effects of employment and wealth on criminal behavior was made in Georgia and Texas. Called TARP (Transitional Aid Research Program), it involved randomly assigning about two thousand ex-convicts in each state to groups that on release from prison received financial aid, job placement services, or nothing. This experiment was not only much larger than the one in Baltimore, it did not exclude certain categories of offenders, and it used the number of arrests (and not simply whether or not arrested even once) as the measure of the outcome. It also arranged for the financial aid that ex-convicts received to be reduced, dollar for dollar, by any income they received from jobs—a more realistic assumption than operated in Baltimore, where the ex-convicts got to keep their financial aid whether or not they worked.

The ex-convicts receiving financial aid and/or employment counseling had about the same arrest rate after release as did the group not receiving the aid or the counseling. Moreover, individuals receiving TARP financial aid worked less than those who did not, so the money could be said to have discouraged, rather than encouraged, employment. The authors of the evaluation, however, were not discouraged by these findings. A complex statistical analysis led them to claim that *if* the financial aid had not induced the ex-convicts to reduce the amount of time they worked, then the payments might have reduced the ex-cons' tendency to commit crimes. That speculation, weak at best, has been challenged by critics.

What is not in dispute is that, as administered, the TARP payments did not reduce crime.[42]

The reader who has followed this far a somewhat confusing array of findings should conclude, I think, something like this: there is some experimental evidence (the Cook study, TARP) that unemployment among ex-convicts tends to contribute to crime, but it is by no means easy to find ways of decreasing that unemployment (the work-release evaluation), and unemployment can be artificially increased by paying people not to work (TARP).

The best and most recent effort to master the link between employment and crime was the "supported work" program of the Manpower Demonstration Research Corporation (MDRC). In ten locations around the country, MDRC randomly assigned four kinds of people with employment problems to special workshops or to control groups. The four kinds of problem persons were long-term welfare (Aid to Families of Dependent Children) recipients, youthful school dropouts, former drug addicts, and ex-convicts. The workshops provided employment in unskilled jobs supplemented by training in job-related personal skills. The unique feature of the program was that all the participants in a given work setting were drawn from the people with problems so as to minimize the usual difficulties experienced by persons with chronic unemployment problems when they find themselves competing with persons who are successful job seekers and job holders. Moreover, the workshops were led by sympathetic supervisors (often themselves ex-addicts or ex-convicts) who gradually increased the level of expected performance until, after a year or so, the trainees were able to go out into the regular job market on their own. This government-subsidized work in a supportive environment, coupled with training in personal skills, was the most ambitious effort of all we have examined to get persons with chronic problems into the labor force. Unlike vocational training in prison, supported work provided real jobs in the civilian world and training directly related to what the recipient was paid to do. Unlike work-release programs, supported work did not leave the ex-convict to sink or swim on his own in the competitive civilian job market.

Welfare recipients and ex-addicts benefited from supported work, but ex-convicts and youthful school dropouts did not. Over a twenty-seven-month observation period, the school dropouts in the project were arrested as frequently as the similar dropouts in the control group, and the ex-offenders in the project actually were arrested more frequently (seventeen more arrests per hundred persons) than the ex-offenders in the control group.[43]

Some individuals did benefit, and they are exactly the ones we would predict would have benefited given what we know about the criminal career. School dropouts who had not been arrested before they joined the program were less likely to be arrested later on than similar dropouts in the control group; on the other hand, youths with a prior arrest record did not benefit at all from the program. As we shall see in chapter 9, this is consistent with what we have learned from various efforts at rehabilitation; namely, young persons inexperienced in crime are much easier to change than young persons who have committed several crimes. By the same token, the older (over age thirty-five) ex-convicts seemed to benefit more from the program than the younger ex-offenders.[44] This is consistent with the well-known tendency of many persons to "mature out of crime" in their thirties; the supported work program probably gave these people a little extra push in this direction.

The clear implication, I think, of the supported work project—and of all the studies to which I have referred—is that unemployment and other economic factors may well be connected with criminality, but the connection is not a simple one. If, as some persons often assume, "unemployment causes crime," then simply providing jobs to would-be criminals or to convicted criminals would reduce their crime rates. There is very little evidence that this is true, at least for the kinds of persons helped by MDRC. Whether the crime rate would go down if dropouts and ex-convicts held on to their jobs, we cannot say, because, as the supported work project clearly showed, within a year-and-a-half after entering the program, the dropouts and ex-convicts were no more likely to be employed than those who had never entered the program at all, despite the great and compassionate efforts made on their behalf.[45] There are some persons for whom help, training, and jobs will make a difference—the young and criminally inexperienced dropout, the older "burned-out" ex-addict, the more mature (over age thirty-five) ex-convict. But ex-addicts, middle-aged ex-cons, and inexperienced youths do not commit most of the crimes that worry us. These are committed by the young, chronic offender.

Recall what we learned in chapter 1 from Marvin Wolfgang and his colleagues at the University of Pennsylvania. By following the criminal careers of about ten thousand boys born in Philadelphia in 1945, these scholars found that about one-third of the boys were arrested, but for about half of these, their criminal "careers" stopped with their first arrest. However, once a juvenile had been arrested three times, the chances that he would be arrested again were over 70 percent.[46] These findings are consistent with the view that, for novice offenders (to say nothing of nonoffenders), some combination of informal social control, the deterrent effect of punishment, and the desire for normal entry into the world of work served to restrain the growth of criminality. It is among this group that we should look for evidence of the effects of changes in the probability and severity of punishment and of changes in job availability. At the other end of the scale, 6 percent of the Philadelphia boys committed five or more crimes before they were eighteen, accounting for over half of all the recorded delinquencies of the entire ten thousand boys and about two-thirds of all the violent crimes committed by the entire cohort.[47] The evidence from MDRC is consistent with the view that job programs are not likely to be effective with these repeat offenders. Since we have only a few studies of the effect of deterrence on individuals (as opposed to large aggregates of people), we cannot be confident that increasing the certainty or severity of punishment would affect this group of hard-core, high-rate offenders, but there is some evidence in the Witte and Murray and Cox studies that it may.

Conclusions

THE RELATIONSHIP between crime on the one hand and the rewards and penalties at the disposal of society on the other is complicated. It is not complicated, however, in the way some people imagine. It is not the case (except for a tiny handful of pathological personalities) that criminals are so unlike the rest of us as to be indifferent to the costs and benefits of the opportunities open to them. Nor is it the case that criminals have no opportunities. In the TARP study, for example, about half the convicts were employed just prior to being imprisoned. And in the Cook study, it was clear that ex-convicts can find jobs of a sort, though often not very attractive ones.

It is better to think of both people and social controls as arrayed on a continuum. People differ by degrees in the extent to which they are governed by internal restraints on criminal behavior and in the stake they have in conformity;[48] they also differ by degrees in the extent to which they can find, hold, and benefit from a job. Similarly, sanctions and opportunities are changeable only within modest limits. We want to find out to what extent feasible changes in the certainty, swiftness, or severity of penalties will make a difference in the behavior of those "at the margin"—those, that is, who are neither so innocent nor so depraved as to be prepared to ignore small changes (which are, in fact, the only feasible changes) in the prospects of punishment. By the same token, we want to know what feasible (and again, inevitably small) changes in the availability of jobs will affect those at the margin of the labor market—those, that is, who are neither so eager for a good job or so contemptuous of "jerks" who take "straight jobs" as to ignore modest changes in job opportunities. I am aware of no evidence supporting the conventional liberal view that while the number of persons who will be affected by changing penalties is very small, the number who will be affected by increasing jobs is very large; nor am I aware of any evidence supporting the conventional conservative view, which is the opposite of this.

I believe that the weight of the evidence—aggregate statistical analyses, evaluations of experiments and quasi-experiments, and studies of individual behavior—supports the view that the rate of crime is influenced by its costs. This influence is greater—or easier to observe—for some crimes and persons than for others. It is possible to lower the crime rate by increasing the certainty of sanctions, but inducing the criminal justice system to make those changes is difficult, especially if committing the offense confers substantial benefits on the perpetrator, if apprehending and punishing the offender does not provide substantial rewards to members of the criminal justice system, or if the crime itself lacks the strong moral condemnation of society. In theory, the rate of crime should also be sensitive to the benefits of noncrime—for example, the value and availability of jobs—but thus far efforts to show that relationship have led to inconclusive results.[49] Moreover, the nature of the connection between crime and legitimate opportunities is complex: unemployment (and prosperity!) can cause crime, crime can cause unemployment (but probably not prosperity), and both crime and unemployment may be caused by common third factors. Economic factors probably have the greatest influence on the behavior of low-rate, novice offenders and the least on high-rate, experienced ones. Despite the uncertainty that attaches to the connection between the economy and crime, I believe the wisest course of action for society is to try simultaneously to increase both the benefits of noncrime and the costs of crime, all the while bearing in mind that no feasible changes in either part of the equation is likely to produce big changes in crime rates.

Some may grant my argument that it makes sense to continue to try to make those marginal gains that are possible by simultaneously changing in desirable directions both the costs of crime and benefits of noncrime, but they may still feel that it is better to spend more heavily on one side or the other of the cost-benefit equation. I have attended numerous scholarly gatherings where I have heard learned persons subject to the most searching scrutiny any evidence purporting to show the deterrent effect of sanctions but accept with scarcely a blink the theory that crime is caused by a "lack of opportunities."[50] Perhaps what they mean is that since the evidence on both propositions is equivocal, then it does less harm to believe in—and invest in—the "benign" (that is, job-creation) program. If so, they are surely wrong. If we try to make the penalties for crime swifter and more certain, and it should turn out that deterrence does not work, then all we have done is increase the risks facing persons who commit a crime. If we fail to increase the certainty and swiftness of penalties, and it should turn out that deterrence *does* work, then we have needlessly increased the risk of innocent persons being victimized.

There is one objection to this line of analysis with which I do agree. If we try to improve on deterrence by sharply increasing the severity of sentences, and we are wrong, then we may spend a great deal of money and unnecessarily blight the lives of offenders who could safely be punished for much shorter periods of time. Reaching a sound judgment about how severe penalties should be is a much more difficult matter than deciding how certain they should be; indeed, one cannot reach such a judgment at all on purely empirical grounds. The problem of severity is inextricably bound up with the problem of justice. However, we can say some things, on scientific grounds, about what the crime-reduction effect of prison sentences of varying lengths may be, regardless of whether anybody is deterred by the prospect of such a sentence. This is the question of incapacitation, to which we now turn.

Chapter 8

Incapacitation

WHEN CRIMINALS are deprived of their liberty, as by imprisonment (or banishment, or very tight control in the community), their ability to commit offenses against citizens is ended. We say these persons have been "incapacitated," and we try to estimate the amount by which crime is reduced by this incapacitation.

Incapacitation cannot be the sole purpose of the criminal justice system; if it were, we would put everybody who has committed one or two offenses in prison until they were too old to commit another. And if we thought prison too costly, we would simply cut off their hands or their heads. Justice, humanity, and proportionality, among other goals, must also be served by the courts.

But there is one great advantage to incapacitation as a crime control strategy—namely, it does not require us to make any assumptions about human nature. By contrast, deterrence works only if people take into account the costs and benefits of alternative courses of action and choose that which confers the largest net benefit (or the smallest net cost). Though people almost surely do take such matters into account, it is difficult to be certain by how much such considerations affect their behavior and what change, if any, in crime rates will result from a given, feasible change in either the costs of crime or the benefits of not committing a crime. Rehabilitation works only if the values, preferences, or time-horizon of criminals can be altered by plan. There is not much evidence that we can make these alterations for large numbers of persons, though there is some evidence that it can be done for a few under certain circumstances.

Incapacitation, on the other hand, works by definition: its effects result from the physical restraint placed upon the offender and not from his subjective state. More accurately, it works provided at least three conditions are met: some offenders must be repeaters, offenders taken off the streets must not be immediately and completely replaced by new recruits, and prison must not increase the post-release criminal activity of those who have been incarcerated sufficiently to offset the crimes prevented by their stay in prison.

The first condition is surely true. Every study of prison inmates shows that a large fraction (recently, about two-thirds) of them had prior criminal records before their current incarceration; every study of ex-convicts shows that a significant fraction (estimates vary from a quarter to a half) are rearrested for new offenses within a relatively brief period.[1] In short, the great majority of persons in prison are repeat offenders, and thus prison, whatever else it may do, protects society from the offenses these persons would commit if they were free.

The second condition—that incarcerating one robber does not lead automatically to the recruitment of a new robber to replace him—seems plausible. Although some persons, such as Ernest van den Haag, have argued that new offenders will step forward to take the place vacated by the imprisoned offenders, they have presented no evidence that this is the case, except, perhaps, for certain crimes (such as narcotics trafficking or prostitution), which are organized along business lines.[2] For the kinds of predatory street crimes with which we are concerned—robbery, burglary, auto theft, larceny—there are no barriers to entry and no scarcity of criminal opportunities. No one need wait for a "vacancy" to appear before he can find an opportunity to become a criminal. The supply of robbers is not affected by the number of robbers practicing, because existing robbers have no way of excluding new robbers and because the opportunity for robbing (if you wish, the "demand" for robbery) is much larger than the existing number of robberies. In general, the earnings of street criminals are not affected by how many "competitors" they have.

The third condition that must be met if incapacitation is to work is that prisons must not be such successful "schools for crime" that the crimes prevented by incarceration are outnumbered by the increased crimes committed after release attributable to what was learned in prison. It is doubtless the case that for some offenders prison is a school; it is also doubtless that for other offenders prison is a deterrent. The former group will commit more, or more skillful, crimes after release; the latter will commit fewer crimes after release. The question, therefore, is whether the net effect of these two offsetting tendencies is positive or negative. The evidence presented in chapter 9 bears directly on this issue. All studies of the extent to which prisons reform offenders are also, in effect, studies of whether they *de*form them. In other words, when we compare the post-release crime rates of persons who have gone to prison with the crime rates of similar persons who have not, we can ask whether prison has made them better off (that is, rehabilitated them) or made them worse off (that is, served as a "school for crime"). In general, there is no evidence that the prison experience makes offenders as a whole more criminal, and there is some evidence that certain kinds of offenders (especially certain younger ones) may be deterred by a prison experience. Moreover, interviews with prisoners reveal no relationship between the number of crimes committed and whether the offenders had served a prior prison term.[3] Though there are many qualifications that should be made to this bald summary, there is no evidence that the net effect of prison is to increase the crime rates of ex-convicts sufficiently to cancel out the gains to society resulting from incapacitation.

In short, the three conditions that must be met for incapacitation to reduce crime are in fact met. What remains is to find out how much crime is reduced by sending offenders to prison and then to ask whether those gains in crime reduction are worth the cost in prison space and (possibly) in justice.

In Search of Individual Offense Rates

TO determine the amount of crime that is prevented by incarcerating a given number of offenders for a given length of time, the key estimate we must make is the number of offenses a criminal commits per year free on the street.* If a community experiences one thousand robberies a year, it obviously makes a great deal of difference whether these robberies are the work of ten robbers, each of whom commits one hundred robberies per year, or the work of one thousand robbers, each of whom commits only one robbery per year. In the first case, locking up only five robbers will cut the number of robberies in half; in the second case, locking up one hundred robbers will only reduce the number of robberies by 10 percent.

In the first edition of this book, I reported, in the concluding chapter, on the work that had just been completed by Shlomo and Reuel Shinnar in which they produced an elegant mathematical formula for estimating the crime-reduction potential of incapacitation under various assump-

---

*Scholars who study incapacitation call the number of crimes committed per offender per year free "lambda," or λ. To avoid technical terminology, I will refer to it as the "individual offense rate."

tions. Their key assumption was that the average rate of offending—that is, the number of crimes committed by the average criminal per year free —was ten. On the basis of this assumption and others, they estimated that the street robbery rate in New York State would be only one-fifth what it was in 1970 if every person convicted of such a crime spent five years in prison.[4]

About the time the Shinnars published this argument, other scholars were appearing in print with estimates of the individual offense rate that were much lower than ten. David Greenberg, using various methods, estimated that the average offender commits something on the order of two serious* offenses per year.[5] Based on this estimate, Greenberg concluded that if society were to increase the length of the average prison sentence by one year (it is now two years), we would cut the rate of serious crime by only about 4 percent.[6] Stevens Clarke undertook to calculate the incapacitative effect of prison on juvenile offenders (Greenberg had been concerned with adults) and decided that, at least in Philadelphia, the proportion of all serious crimes averted by the present sentences given to young offenders was no more than 4 percent.[7] Stephan Van Dine and his colleagues at the Academy for Contemporary Problems made an estimate of the crime-reduction effects of imposing a five-year prison term on all persons convicted of a felony in one county in Ohio, and concluded that this stringent policy would reduce violent crime by only 4 percent.[8] Since so many different critics were arriving at similar low estimates of what incapacitation might produce, many persons began questioning the large crime-reduction effects claimed by the Shinnars.

At this point, the matter was taken up by a panel of experts appointed by the National Research Council (a part of the National Academy of Sciences), the same panel that analyzed the academic controversy over deterrence described in chapter 7. Jacqueline Cohen of Carnegie-Mellon University prepared, at the invitation of the panel, a careful analysis of the competing claims of various scholars. She concluded that Greenberg and Clarke both "underestimate the individual crime rate."[9] Reexamining Clarke's data under more reasonable assumptions, Cohen decided that the proportion of serious crimes averted by present imprisonment rates for juveniles was two to three times larger than that estimated by Clarke and, by implication, the number of crimes that could be prevented by increasing the use of prison would also be much higher.[10] Similarly, Greenberg made some questionable assumptions, as well as an error in his calculations, that rendered his

---

*By "serious," Greenberg meant one of the seven "index" crimes as classified by the FBI— murder, aggravated assault, forcible rape, robbery, burglary, larceny, and auto theft.

estimates of dubious value, but there was no easy way to revise his calculations to provide a better estimate.[11]

Though the panel did not deal with the Van Dine estimates, other scholars did. Three separate articles were published pointing to a fundamental error in the Van Dine calculations.[12] In their rejoinder, the Van Dine group, in effect, conceded the correctness of the criticism and in subsequent published work revised their estimate of the incapacitation effect upward.[13] What they had originally done was to assume that the persons arrested in Ohio had committed only the crimes for which they were charged and that the only additional crimes that would be averted by sending them away to prison for long terms would have been those other crimes for which they had previously been arrested. They assumed, in short, that these offenders never committed any crimes that did not lead to an arrest. Since this was obviously untrue, their original, very low estimate of the crime-reduction effect of incapacitation had to be in error.

Cohen and the panel concluded in 1978 that the most important research task confronting persons interested in incapacitation was to obtain better estimates of individual offense rates.[14] A major step in that direction was taken the following year with the publication of a new estimate, the most sophisticated to date, of those rates. Working with individual adult criminal records of all those persons arrested in Washington, D.C., during 1973 for any one of six major crimes (over five thousand persons in all), Alfred Blumstein and Jacqueline Cohen suggested that the individual offense rate varied significantly for different kinds of offenders. For example, it was highest for larceny and lowest for aggravated assault. But they also found, as had other scholars before them, that there was not a great deal of specialization among criminals—a person arrested today for robbery might be arrested next time for burglary. The major contribution of their study was the ingenious method they developed for converting the number of times persons were arrested into an estimate of the number of crimes they actually committed, a method that took into account the fact that many crimes are not reported to the police, that most crimes known to the police do not result in an arrest, and that some crimes are likely to be committed by groups of persons rather than by single offenders. Combining all the individual crime rates, the offenders in this study (a group of adults who had been arrested at least twice in Washington, D.C.) committed between nine and seventeen serious offenses per year free.[15]

This number was strikingly similar to the original estimates used by the Shinnars that had provoked so much criticism. And confidence in the Blumstein-Cohen estimates was increased when the results of a major study at the Rand Corporation became known. Researchers there had been interviewing prisoners (first in California, then in other states) to find out directly from known offenders how much crime they were committing while free. No one can be certain, of course, that the reports of the convicts constitute an accurate record of their crimes, undetected as well as detected, but the Rand researchers cross-checked the information against arrest records and looked for evidence of internal consistency in the self-reports. Moreover, the inmates volunteered information about crimes they had committed but for which they had not been arrested. Still, it is quite possible that the self-reports were somewhat inaccurate. However, it is reasonable to assume that inmates would be more likely to conceal crimes they did commit rather than admit to crimes they did not commit. Thus, any errors in these self-reports probably lead to an underestimate of the true rate of criminality of these persons.

The Rand group found that the average California prisoner had committed about fourteen serious crimes per year during each of the three years he was free.[16] This number falls squarely within the range estimated, using very different methods, by Blumstein and Cohen and, again, is comparable to the original estimate of the Shinnars. To state the California findings in slightly different terms, if no one was confined in state prison, the number of armed robberies in California would be about 22 percent higher than it now is.[17]

After their initial survey of 624 incarcerated male felons in California, the Rand group enlarged their study to include about 2,200 inmates in the states of California, Michigan, and Texas. Again, they gathered self-reports on crimes committed while free. This larger survey produced even higher estimates of individual offense rates. A person serving time in California for robbery, for example, would on the average admit to committing fifty-three robberies per year free; in Michigan, the number was seventy-seven. Those who were active burglars reported committing ninety burglaries per year in California. Interestingly, the offense rates of Texas inmates were much lower—on the average, robbers committed nine robberies a year and burglars committed twenty-four burglaries.[18] This apparently was because Texas sent to prison so much larger a fraction of its convicted robbers and burglars that many inmates were low-rate offenders; in California and Michigan, where sentencing policies seem more lenient, a smaller proportion of low-rate offenders wind up in prison.

But the Rand group learned something else which would turn out to be even more important. The "average" individual offense rate was virtually a meaningless term because the inmates they interviewed differed so sharply in how many crimes they committed. A large number of offenders committed a small number of offenses while free and a small number of offenders committed a very large number of offenses. In statistical language, the distribution of offenses was highly skewed. For example, the median number of burglaries committed by the inmates in the three states was about 5 a year, but the 10 percent of the inmates who were the highest-rate offenders committed an average of 232 burglaries a year. The median number of robberies was also about 5 a year, but the top 10 percent of offenders committed an average of 87 a year. As Peter W. Greenwood, one of the members of the Rand group, put it, incarcerating one robber who was among the top 10 percent in offense rates would prevent more robberies than incarcerating eighteen offenders who were at or below the median.[19]

Not long after the Rand group began publishing its findings, Brian Forst and his colleagues at the Institute for Law and Social Research (INSLAW) in Washington, D.C., began to release data from their survey of 1,700 federal offenders whose criminal careers they had followed from 1970 through 1976. These persons also had high individual offense rates, nearly eight nondrug crimes per year free. And they also had a highly skewed distribution of offenses—over half were not known to have committed even one crime after being released from prison, but the other half committed at least nineteen per person per year.[20] Once again, more evidence that incapacitation makes a difference to society, at least if it is directed at the right offenders.

"Selective" Versus "Collective" Incapacitation

THE initial response to the view of the Shinnars was not only that they exaggerated the number of crimes being committed by active, serious offenders, but that they neglected the great cost of reducing the crime rate by locking up a larger fraction of these offenders or by keeping those already inside locked up for longer periods of time. The argument that the Shinnars had greatly exaggerated individual crime rates was eventually disproved, as we have seen. But the argument about cost remained. Even the Shinnars admitted that if New York State were to follow their recommendations and send every convicted mugger and robber to prison for five years, the state would have to find prison space for an estimated forty to sixty thousand persons convicted of these "safety" crimes.[21] But as of 1970, only five years before the Shinnars published their study, New York State was incarcerating only nine thousand persons for having committed a violent crime or burglary and was holding in prison only a little over twelve thousand persons for all felonies combined.[22] Thus, to accommodate the Shinnars' plan, the space available for persons convicted of violent crimes and burglary would have to be increased (at a minimum) four-fold.

Joan Petersilia and Peter Greenwood, both members of the Rand group, also came to the conclusion that reducing crime by a significant amount through longer prison terms would be very costly. They analyzed the arrest records of 625 persons convicted in Denver, Colorado, of serious crimes between 1968 and 1970. Instead of estimating the effect of differing sentencing policies on a large group of offenders whose individual behavior was unknown, they looked at the actual arrest record of each person individually and asked whether a particular sentencing policy (say, a three-year mandatory minimum) would have led to the imprisonment of the offender for his last offense and thereby have prevented the offense from being committed. Knowing this, they could then calculate how many additional persons would have to be sent to prison. Their analysis suggested that incapacitation works, but at a price. If every person convicted of a felony received a five-year prison term, the number of felonies committed would drop by 45 percent but the size of the prison population would increase by 450 percent. If the mandatory five-year term were reserved for repeat offenders, such as convicted felons who had previously been convicted of a felony, then the crime rate would drop by 18 percent and the prison population would increase by 190 percent.[23]

These conclusions about the cost of achieving large crime reductions through incapacitation were sobering, but one finding was also puzzling. The Petersilia-Greenwood data clearly indicated that reserving the mandatory minimum sentence for repeat offenders would be no more advantageous—in terms of crimes prevented for a given increase in prison population—than if it were imposed on all convicted persons, including first-time offenders. At first blush, this seemed contrary to common sense. If recidivists commit a disproportionately large share of all serious crime, how can it be that locking them up for five years would cut the crime rate by a smaller fraction than would be achieved by locking up first-time offenders?

One explanation for the puzzle, suggested by Petersilia and Greenwood, was that most repeat offenders are already given prison terms by judges and so there is not much more to be gained by insuring that every repeat offender gets a long term.[24] But another possible explanation became clear to the Rand group as they studied the self-reports of prison inmates in three states. They learned from their survey that a small number of offenders have very high offense rates. Suppose that judges, in sentencing criminals, *do not know who the high rate offenders are* and thus give the longest sentences to persons who may not be the most serious criminals. Judges, we know, give the longest sentences to persons who are convicted for the most serious crimes and who have a long prior record.[25] That seems reasonable until one asks whether a person convicted of, say, robbery who has a prior conviction for a felony is any more likely to be a high-rate offender (that is, a frequent recidivist) than a person convicted of robbery who does not have a prior record.

It would seem plausible to assume that high-rate offenders have longer rap sheets than low-rate offenders. After all, a person who has committed a dozen robberies is more likely to get arrested and prosecuted than one who has committed his first stick-up. Judges make this assumption when they give longer sentences to a robber who has a prior conviction than to one who has been convicted for the first time. But we cannot be certain this assumption is correct, and researchers at Rand have found evidence that should make us question it.[26] In their study of California prison inmates, they learned that judges are more likely to send low-rate burglars to jail than to prison. Since jail terms ordinarily cannot exceed one year, this means that the low-rate burglars who wind up in jail will usually be serving shorter sentences than the high-rate ones who wind up in prison. So far, so good. But the match between rate of offending and the choice between jail or prison is not very close. For example, of the high-rate burglars, over half went to jail rather than to prison. Not only do most low-rate burglars get a break, so also do most high-rate ones. And if we look just at those offenders who are in prison, we find that the time they serve there bears little relationship to the rate at which they are offending while free on the street. In California, imprisoned low-rate robbers and imprisoned high-rate robbers serve almost identical sentences—about fifty months. Indeed, imprisoned low-rate burglars actually serve longer sentences (thirty months) than do imprisoned high-rate burglars (twenty months).[27]

The California study is one of the few of its kind, and we cannot be certain that the poor match it discovers between rate of offending and length of prison term would be true if the study looked at all robbers and burglars (and not just at those in prison) or looked more closely at the exact nature of the robberies and burglaries these persons committed (and not just at the number). But at the very least, the Rand data should force us to take a hard look at the relationship between official records (such as rap sheets) and actual offense rates.

Whatever the exact nature of that relationship, all the evidence we have implies that, for crime-reduction purposes, the most rational way to use the incapacitative powers of our prisons would be to do so selectively. Instead of longer sentences for everyone, or for persons who have prior records, or for persons whose present crime is especially grave, longer sentences would be given primarily to those who, when free, commit the most crimes. Exactly the same conclusion was reached by Brian Forst and his colleagues who studied the careers of criminals in the federal system.[28]

But how do we know who these high-rate, repeat criminals are? Knowing the nature of the present offense is not a good clue. The reason for this is quite simple—most street criminals do not specialize. Today's robber can be tomorrow's burglar and the next day's car thief.[29] When the police happen to arrest him, the crime for which he is arrested is determined by a kind of lottery—he happened to be caught red-handed, or as the result of a tip, committing a particular crime that may or may not be the same as either his previous crime or his next one. If judges give sentences based entirely on the gravity of the present offense, then a high-rate offender may get off lightly because on this occasion he happened to be caught snatching a purse. The low-rate offender may get a long sentence because he was unlucky enough to be caught robbing a liquor store with a gun.

Prosecutors have an understandable tendency to throw the book at persons caught committing a serious crime, especially if they have been caught before. To a certain extent, we want to encourage that tendency. After all, we not only want to reduce crime, we want to see criminals get their just deserts. Society would not, and should not, tolerate a system in which a prosecutor throws the book at purse snatchers and lets armed robbers off with a suspended sentence. But while society's legitimate desire for retribution must set the outer bounds of any sentencing policy, there is still room for flexibility within those bounds. We can, for example, act so that all robbers are punished with prison terms, but give, within certain relatively narrow ranges, longer sentences to those robbers who commit the most crimes.

If knowing the nature of the present offense and even knowing the prior record of the offender are not accurate guides to identifying high-rate offenders, what is? Obviously, we cannot ask the offenders. They may cooperate with researchers once in jail, but they have little incentive to cooperate with prosecutors before they go to jail, especially if the price of cooperation is to get a tougher sentence. But we can see what legally admissible, objective attributes, of the offenders best predict who is and who is not a high-rate offender. In the Rand study, Greenwood and his colleagues discovered, by trial and error, that the following seven factors, taken together, were highly predictive of a convicted person being a high-rate offender: he (1) was convicted of a crime while a juvenile (that is, before age sixteen), (2) used illegal drugs as a juvenile, (3) used illegal drugs during the previous two years, (4) was employed less than 50 percent of the time during the previous two years, (5) served time in a juvenile facility, (6) was incarcerated in prison more than 50 percent of the previous two years, and (7) was previously convicted for the present offense.

Using this scale, Greenwood found that 82 percent of those predicted to be low-rate offenders in fact were, and 82 percent of those predicted to be medium- or high-rate offenders also were. To understand how big these differences are, the median California prison inmate who is predicted to be a low-rate offender will in fact commit slightly more than one burglary and slightly less than one robbery per year free. By contrast, the median California inmate who is predicted to be a high-rate offender will commit ninety-three burglaries and thirteen robberies per year free. In other states, this prediction scale may be more or less accurate.

A similar, though not identical, scale was developed by Brian Forst and William Rhodes at INSLAW and was based on their study of federal offenders. High-rate offenders (what they call "career criminals") are likely to be those who are young, who use heroin sometimes and who use alcohol heavily, who have a long criminal career (and thus who started in crime at an early age), who have served a long prison term, and whose present offense involves violence. Applying this scale to federal offenders whom they followed for five years, Forst and his associates found that 85 percent of those predicted to be career criminals were in fact rearrested, most of them within twelve months; only 36 percent of those not predicted to be high-rate offenders were rearrested.[30]

Opinions differ as to the effect on the crime rate and prison population of making sentences for high-rate offenders longer than those for low-rate ones. Greenwood applied his scale to California and found that if all low-rate robbers received two-year prison terms (most now receive longer ones) and all high-rate robbers received seven-year terms (most now receive shorter ones), the number of robberies committed in the state would drop by an estimated 20 percent with no increase in the prison population.[31] In a state such as Texas, which already has a tough sentencing policy, the gain from shifting to this more selective approach would be less.

Even at Rand, colleagues of Greenwood disagree about the policy implications of the fact, which they do not dispute, that a handful of high-rate offenders is responsible for much crime. Jan and Marcia Chaiken argue that while the factors Greenwood uses enable him to identify that *group* of offenders who are especially dangerous, they will lead to substantial errors when they are used to identify any *individual* as a high-rate offender, especially if the identification must rely only on that information currently available in official records.[32] In a forthcoming review of this and related issues, a group at Harvard headed by Susan Estrich, Mark H. Moore, and Daniel McGillis argues that it would be better to improve the ability of police and prosecutors to identify and arrest high-rate offenders than to improve the ability of judges to sentence convicted offenders; indeed, if we solved more crimes, the judges would have more reliable official information about who the dangerous offenders really are and therefore could more effectively apply their existing rules of thumb in choosing sentences. I am skeptical that we can much improve our ability to solve crimes and so I doubt that this strategy will make sentencing decisions any easier. Judges now incarcerate selectively and always will; the central question is whether we can improve on the basis for that selectivity. Further research may well overcome some of the problems in the Greenwood scale. And in the meantime, Greenwood and the Chaikens agree that we can now identify the low-rate offenders with substantial accuracy. At a minimum, we can do a better job of keeping sentences for these persons short so as not to consume scarce prison space needed for those persons whose behavior is morally more repugnant or statistically more risky.

Some Policy Issues

OBVIOUSLY, a policy of reducing crime by selective incapacitation (that is, by adjusting prison terms to reflect predicted individual offense rates) raises a number of issues. Though these issues are important, one must bear in mind that they cannot be resolved by comparing selective incapacitation to some ideal system of criminal justice in which everyone receives exactly his just deserts. No such system exists or ever will. One must compare instead the proposed policy with what exists now, with all its imperfections, and ask whether the gains in crime reduction are worth the risks entailed when we try to make predictions about human behavior.

The first issue is whether it is permissible to allow crime-control to be an objective of sentencing policy. Some persons, such as Andrew von Hirsch, claim that only retribution—what he calls "just deserts"—can be a legitimate basis for sentencing.[33] To some extent, he is undoubtedly correct. Even if we were absolutely certain that a convicted murderer would never murder again, we would still feel obliged to impose a relatively severe sentence in order to vindicate the principle that life is dear and may not be unlawfully taken without paying a price. Moreover, the sentences given low-rate offenders must reflect society's judgment as to the moral blame such behavior deserves, and the sentences given high-rate offenders ought not exceed what society feels is the highest sentence appropriate to the crime for which the offenders were convicted. And low-rate offenders should get a sufficiently severe sentence to help persuade them, and others like them, not to become high-rate offenders. Still, after allowing for all of these considerations, there will inevitably remain a range of possible sentences within which the goal of incapacitation can be served. The range will exist in part because there is no objective way to convert a desire for retribution into a precise sentence for a given offense and in part because legislatures will almost invariably act so as to preserve some judicial discretion so that the circumstances of a case which can not be anticipated in advance may affect the sentence. Among those circumstances is a concern for protecting society from the threat that a given offender represents.

The second issue is whether our prediction methods are good enough to allow them to influence sentence length. The answer to that question depends on what one will accept as "good enough." Absolute certainty will never be attainable. Moreover, criminal justice *now,* at almost every stage, operates by trying to predict future behavior. When a prosecutor decides how much plea bargaining he will allow, he is trying to predict how a judge or jury will react to his evidence, and he is often trying to guess how dangerous an offender he has in his grasp. When a judge sets bail, he is always making a prediction about the likelihood of a person out on bail showing up for his trial and is frequently trying to predict whether the person, if out on bail, will commit another crime while free. When a defense attorney argues in favor of his client being released on his own recognizance, without bail, he is trying to persuade the judge to accept his prediction that the accused will not skip town. When the judge passes a sentence, he is trying, at least in part, to predict whether the convicted person represents a future threat to society. When a parole board considers a convict's application for early release, it tries to predict—often on the basis of a quantitative system, called a "base expectancy table"— whether the person will become a recidivist if released. Virtually every member of the criminal justice system is routinely engaged in predicting behavior, often on the basis of very scant knowledge and quite dubious rules of thumb. The question, therefore, is this: are the kinds of predictions that scholars such as Greenwood and Forst make about future criminality better (more accurate) and thus fairer than the predictions prosecutors and judges now make?

A third issue is tougher. Is it fair for a low-rate offender who is caught committing a serious crime to serve a shorter sentence (because he is not much of a threat to society) than a high-rate offender who gets caught committing a relatively minor offense? Probably not. Sentences would have to have legal boundaries set so that the use of selective incapacitation could not lead to perverse sentences—armed robbers getting one year, purse-snatchers getting five. Since, to the best of my knowledge, selective incapacitation has never been made the explicit basis of a state sentencing policy, we cannot be certain how manageable this problem of reconciling justice and crime control will be.

Finally, there is bound to be a debate about the legal and even ethical propriety of using certain facts as the basis for making predictions. Everyone would agree that race should not be a factor; everyone would probably agree that prior record should be a factor. I certainly believe that it is proper to take into account an offender's juvenile as well as his adult record, but I am aware that some people disagree. But can one take into account alcohol or drug use? Suppose the person claims to be cured of his drinking or his drug problem; do we believe him? And if we do, do we wipe the slate clean of information about these matters? And should we penalize more heavily persons who are chronically unemployed, even if unemployment is a good predictor of recidivism? Some people will argue that this is tantamount to making unemployment a crime, though I think that overstates the matter. After all, advocates of pretrial release of arrested persons, lenient bail policies, and diverting offenders away from jail do not hesitate to claim that having a good employment record should be counted in the accused's favor. If employment counts in favor of some, then obviously unemployment may be counted against others. Since advocates of "bail reform" are also frequent opponents of incapacitation, selective or collective, it is incumbent on them to straighten out their own thinking on how we make use of employment records. Nonetheless, this important issue deserves thoughtful attention.

On one matter, critics of prison may take heart. If Greenwood and the others are correct, then an advantage of selective incapacitation is that it can be accomplished without great increases (or perhaps any increases) in the use of prisons. It is a way of allocating more rationally the existing stock of prison cells to produce, within the constraints of just deserts, greater crime-control benefits. Many offenders—indeed most offenders—would probably have their sentences shortened, and the space thereby freed would be allocated to the small number of high-rate offenders whom even the most determined opponents of prison would probably concede should be behind bars.

They ought to take heart, but not too much heart. The estimates of the crime-reduction effect of selective incapacitation are based on a static world—a fixed number of criminals committing a predictable number of crimes. But crime rates have been increasing since the early 1960s and no sharp, lasting downward trend is yet in evidence. Moreover, states such as California, though they have experienced greatly increased prison populations, still make much less use of prison than does, say, Texas, so that in California a significant number of offenders, perhaps serious ones, are not confined at all.

Even if the recent modest decline in crime rates were to continue, the number of persons in prison would probably increase for the next several years. This is because a decline in crime rates would likely reflect, at least in part, a decline in the number of young males in the population. But young males are less likely to go to prison than older males, in large measure because of the tendency of judges to defer a sentence to prison until the offender has acquired a lengthy criminal record—which means until he has become older. This tendency is especially marked in those places where judges in adult courts do not see, or are not influenced by, the juvenile record of adult offenders. Thus, the peak in commitments to prison will occur some years after the peak in crime rates. Moreover, the size of prison populations is determined not only by the number of new commitments, but by the length of the sentence of persons in prison. Those sentences have not been getting shorter of late. (Ironically, they have not got much longer, either, despite the fact that a growing fraction of the persons in prison have committed violent or other serious offenses.[34]) Combining all these factors, Alfred Blumstein and his colleagues at Carnegie-Mellon University, using Pennsylvania data, predict that prison populations in that state will not reach their peak until 1990, and perhaps later.[35]

If one adds to all this the extreme level of overcrowding now characteristic of many state prisons, the case for prison construction becomes very strong. One can moderate this need to a degree by shortening some of the very longest sentences, but no one has yet calculated how large a gain in prison space such sentence shortening would produce. And if one believes that deterrence works (see chapter 7), then one may wish to see a larger fraction of convicted offenders get some prison term, even if just a short one. None of this is to deny that real opportunities exist for exploiting nonprison methods of handling the nonviolent, less serious offender—restitution, community service, intensive probation, halfway houses, and the like. But even after making the largest possible allowance for such commendable methods, it is hard to escape the realization that, however selectively we set the sentences for robbers and burglars, the need to accommodate a rising level of new commitments and to relieve present overcrowding and the bestiality that so often accompanies it, new facilities will be needed.

Some persons find prison construction undesirable because they think prisons are deplorable. Such sentiments are sometimes organized into movements designed to place a moratorium on prison construction. It is never clear what alternative such persons would suggest. As of November, 1979, well over half (58 percent) of all state inmates were imprisoned for a violent offense, 14 percent for murder alone. Only 7 percent were in prison because of drug offenses. Of the one-third who were serving time for nonviolent property crimes, over half were burglars.[36] Who among these prisoners should be released to relieve overcrowding and accommodate new commitments? And the number who would have to be released to eliminate overcrowding is very large, as can be inferred from the fact that, if one uses 60 square feet per prisoner as the standard, then 58 percent of all one-person cells and 90 percent of all two-person cells are overcrowded.[37] Vague talk about "alternatives to incarceration" is no substitute for a clear, quantitative estimate of how many persons can be diverted, safely, from prison and where these diverted persons are to go.

Indeed, much of the debate about incapacitation is not about its crime-reduction potential or the relationship between imprisonment and a social concern for appropriate retribution; it is rather about a set of diversionary arguments designed to make American penal policy look as bad as possible while sidestepping any serious confrontation with the hard policy choices.

One such argument is: "The United States already imprisons a larger proportion of its population than any other civilized nation, or at least any civilized nation outside the Soviet bloc." This is like disproving the need for hospitals by saying that the United States already hospitalizes a larger fraction of its population than any other nation. It implies that we are sending people to prison without any regard to the number of crimes committed (or sending them to hospitals without regard to whether they are sick). The proper question is whether we imprison a higher fraction of those arrested, prosecuted, and convicted than do other nations. No comprehensive international data exist on this subject, but such comparisons as do exist suggest that the argument that this country overimprisons is, to say the least, questionable. Kenneth I. Wolpin at Yale compared the probability of being convicted and imprisoned for various offenses in England and the United States. In the period 1961–1967, persons who were prosecuted for robbery in England were much more likely to be convicted than those prosecuted for that crime in the United States (about 79 percent were convicted in England, only 42 percent in this country). Of those convicted of robbery, a higher percentage (48 percent) were imprisoned in England than in the United States (31 percent). On the other hand, sentences for robbery tended to be longer in the United States.[38]

A second argument is: "Sending a person to prison costs more than sending a person to Harvard." God knows, Harvard is expensive enough. I am relieved to hear that something else costs more. But I assume that most parents send their children to college rather than to prison for reasons other than its being cheaper. Similarly, society sends criminals to prison rather than college, despite the fact that it costs more, because society believes it is getting something for its money from prison that it could not get from college: greater safety (temporarily), some prospect of deterrence, and the satisfaction of its desire for lawful retribution. I wish persons who point to the costs of prison as if that were a conclusive argument would apply that view consistently. For example: "It costs more to send children to Harvard than it would cost to send them to work in the coal mines." Or, "We cannot afford to send sick people to hospitals because it costs $50,000 (or whatever) per bed to build a hospital."

A third argument: "If we build more prisons, we will fill them up whether we need to or not."[39] Or put in other words, the size of our prison population is determined, not by the crime rate, but by the capacity of our prisons. A much-heralded study by Abt Associates in 1981 seemed to provide evidence to confirm this view. On the average, it claimed, new additions to prison capacity are filled to overflowing within two years after completion and filled past the level of overcrowding within five years.[40] The Panel on Sentencing Research of the National Research Council took a close look at the Abt findings and concluded that they were seriously in error. To use the council's words, the Abt study "provides no valid support for the capacity model."[41] Among the errors it discovered were computational mistakes, implausible assumptions, and a failure to look at the very different experiences of individual states (fifteen of which actually experienced decreases in their prison populations between 1971 and 1975).[42]

The problem of how best to manage our prison populations cannot, obviously, be left to such sloganeering. Neither can it be left to the whims of state legislators who find it politically irresistible to vote for tougher penalties for certain crimes but politically awkward to vote for the money to pay for the necessary additions to prisons or to allow new prisons to be built in their districts. It is possible to think sensibly about the uses of prison by asking what kinds of offenders should be sent to what kinds of facilities and for how long, by estimating carefully both the prison-capacity and crime-reduction implications of any proposed sentencing policy, and by avoiding the tendency to think that the best way to handle crime is always to impose the longest possible sentences.

Chapter 9

Rehabilitation

THE FIRST EDITION of this book appeared in 1975 on the heels of an article by the late Robert Martinson in which he reviewed the results of well over two hundred separate efforts to measure the effects of programs designed to rehabilitate the convicted offender. Martinson's article[1] was a summary of what he, with Douglas Lipton and Judith Wilks, had published in a massive volume that had initially been commissioned by the New York State Governor's Committee on Criminal Offenders.[2] That volume systematically examined virtually all of the studies available in print between 1945 and 1967 that met various modest tests of methodological adequacy. The major conclusion of that review as stated in Martinson's article soon became familiar to almost everyone even casually interested in crime-control programs: "With few and isolated exceptions, the rehabilitative efforts that have been reported so far have had no appreciable effect on recidivism."[3]

It did not seem to matter what form of treatment in the correctional system was attempted—whether vocational training or academic education; whether counseling inmates individually, in groups, or not at all; whether therapy was administered by social workers or psychiatrists; whether the institutional context of the treatment was custodial or benign; whether the sentences were short or long; whether the person was placed on probation or released on parole; or whether the treatment took place in the community or in institutions. Indeed, some forms of treatment (notably a few experiments with psychotherapy) actually produced an *increase* in the rate of recidivism.

The Martinson review was unique in its comprehensiveness but not in its findings. R. G. Hood came to much the same conclusion in a review published in 1967;[4] Walter C. Bailey, after examining one hundred studies of the efficacy of treatment and especially the fifty or so that claimed positive results, concluded in 1966 that the "evidence supporting the efficacy of correctional treatment is slight, inconsistent, and of questionable reliability";[5] Leslie T. Wilkins observed in 1969 that "the major achievement of research in the field of social psychology and treatment has been negative and has resulted in the undermining of nearly all the current mythology regarding the effectiveness of treatment in any form."[6]

In retrospect, little of this should have been surprising. It requires not merely optimistic but heroic assumptions about the nature of man to lead one to suppose that a person, finally sentenced after (in most cases) many brushes with the law, and having devoted a good part of his youth and young adulthood to misbehavior of every sort, should, by either the solemnity of prison or the skillfulness of a counselor, come to see the error of his ways and to experience a transformation of his character. Today we smile in amusement at the naïveté of those early prison reformers who imagined that religious instruction while in solitary confinement would lead to moral regeneration. How they would now smile at us at our presumption that conversations with a psychiatrist or a return to the community could achieve the same end. We have learned how difficult it is by governmental means to improve the educational attainments of children or to restore stability and affection to the family, and in these cases we are often working with willing subjects in moments of admitted need. Criminal rehabilitation requires producing equivalent changes in unwilling subjects under conditions of duress or indifference.

By the end of the 1970s, politicians and scholars alike had by and large learned the same message—"nothing works." In fact, that is not quite an accurate summary of what Martinson and the others found or said. His article and their book contained many hints that *some* reductions in criminality for *some* kinds of offenders under *some* circumstances were possible. But the exaggeration contained in the popular conclusion was pardonable, for even giving the most generous possible interpretation to the hints of success here and there did not allow one to find any clear and consistent rehabilitative effect on which a public policy might be based.

And it would take strong evidence of such an effect to ease the growing philosophical doubts that many persons were beginning to entertain about criminal court sentences that depended on the presumption of rehabilitation for their justification. If rehabilitation is the goal, and persons differ in their capacity to be rehabilitated, then two persons who have committed precisely the same crime under precisely the same circumstances might receive very different sentences, thereby violating the offenders' and our sense of justice. The indeterminate sentence, widely used in many states, is expressive of the rehabilitation ideal: a convict will be released from an institution, not at the end of a fixed period, but when someone (a parole board, a sentencing board) decides he is "ready" to be released. Rigorously applied on the basis of existing evidence about what factors are associated with recidivism, this theory would mean that if two persons together rob a liquor store, the one who is a young black male from a broken family, with little education and a record of drug abuse, will be kept in prison indefinitely, while an older white male from an intact family, with a high school diploma, and no drug experience, will be released almost immediately. Not only the young black male, but most fair-minded observers, would regard that outcome as profoundly unjust.

In practice, the system does not work as its theory implies. But neither does it work well. The decision when to release a prison inmate is, in many states, given over to a parole board from which few if any appeals are possible. In New York State, for example, the twelve members of the board of parole, who in the early 1970s had jurisdiction over all prisoners serving more than ninety days (a total well in excess of twenty thousand), could, among other things, decide when to release a prisoner who was serving an indeterminate sentence. Supposedly the board examined all aspects of the prisoner's life and behavior to decide if he is "ready" for release. If it were capable of and had the time for such profound judgments, it might well behave in the way described in the aforementioned liquor store example. But of course no board can make profound judgments about the thousands of cases it hears every year, with the result that it adopts instead a rule of thumb: if a prisoner is thought to be "rehabilitated," he will be released when he has served one-third of his sentence or three years, whichever is less. The board decided who is rehabilitated and who is not by reviewing a file of reports and questioning the inmate for ten or fifteen minutes at an interview. If parole was denied, the inmate was not told the reason; if he objected, there was no appeal.

The Citizen's Inquiry on Parole and Criminal Justice in New York City prepared in 1974 a study of the results of this parole system. For a four-year period, the percentage of prisoners returned to prison within one year was calculated for those who were granted parole and those who, by being denied parole, were required to serve their full sentence. Overall, there was no statistically significant difference between the return to prison rates of those paroled and those not—about 10 or 11 percent of each group went back to prison within the year.[7] Clearly, the parole board was unable to guess who had been rehabilitated and who had not.

As the scientific basis for the possibility of rehabilitation was shown wanting, the philosophical rationale for making it the chief goal of sentencing began collapsing. By the latter part of the 1970s, there appeared a revival of interest in the deterrent, incapacitative, and retributive functions of the criminal justice system.

But not everyone was convinced that rehabilitation had failed. During the 1960s, there had developed in California a remarkable concentration of talent and energy devoted to finding and testing rehabilitation programs, especially ones designed to treat delinquents in the community. Marguerite Q. Warren, Ted Palmer, and others not only used advanced psychological testing to classify delinquents by personality type and employed skilled counselors to provide intensive community supervision, they randomly assigned delinquents to the treatment and control groups in order to insure the best possible scientific evaluation of the results.

At first, these results were encouraging, so much so that the President's Commission on Law Enforcement and Administration of Justice, in its 1967 report to Lyndon Johnson, endorsed the Community Treatment Program (CTP) of the California Youth Authority, describing it as having reduced delinquency (as measured by parole revocation) from 52 percent among youth who were incarcerated before release to 28 percent among those given intensive counseling in the community.[8]

The Martinson article was particularly critical of these claims. In their reanalysis of the California data, Lipton, Martinson, and Wilks concluded that Warren and her colleagues had substantially undercounted the number of offenses committed by the youth in the experimental community program. Apparently, probation officers assigned to these delinquents developed such close relations with their charges, and were so eager to see their program succeed, that they failed to report to the authorities a number of offenses committed by the experimentals, whereas youth assigned to the control groups had their offenses reported in the normal way by probation and parole authorities.

Given the resources devoted to the California project and the publicity it had received, it is hardly surprising that its leaders counterattacked. Ted Palmer published in 1975 a rebuttal to the Martinson article, claiming that it overlooked or downplayed a number of success stories in the rehabilitation literature and that in particular it misrepresented the CTP. Palmer conceded that the youth in the experimental program had a number of offenses overlooked by counselors, but argued that these were largely minor or technical violations, many of which were detected simply because the youth were under closer observation and some of which involved merely the failure to participate regularly in the intensive supervision program. Moreover, the Martinson review ended in 1967; if it had continued through 1973, Palmer said, the differences between experimentals and controls, at least for serious offenses, would have been clear.[9]

Martinson responded vigorously to this challenge, and the battle was joined.[10] In the midst of the verbal pyrotechnics of Palmer and Martinson —they were nothing if not spirited adversaries—a new and, as it turned out, more weighty voice was heard. Paul Lerman, a Rutgers sociologist, published a book-length evaluation of the CTP (as well as of the California probation subsidy program) in which he concluded, after a painstaking analysis of the published data, that "the CTP did not have an impact on youth behavior that differed significantly from the impact of the control program."[11] Moreover, the "community" focus of the experimental program turned out to be somewhat exaggerated—in fact, the great majority of experimental youth were placed in detention at least once and many were detained repeatedly in order to maintain control over them. Indeed, the youth in the experimental "community" program were *more* likely to be sent to detention centers than the control group supervised by regular parole officers. Finally, Lerman found strong evidence that, though the CTP had tried to match experimental and control groups by randomly assigning youth to each, over the many years the program operated the two groups began to differ markedly in their characteristics as persons dropped out of the program for one reason or another. In particular, the experimental group came to be composed disproportionately of persons who were older, had higher IQ's, and were diagnosed as "neurotic" (rather than as "power-oriented"). This intriguing finding, largely buried in an appendix to the Lerman book, raises issues to which we shall return presently.

Lerman had made many of these points earlier in a 1968 article; he made them more elaborately in the 1975 book. Curiously, Palmer, who continued to protest against the Martinson article, appears to have taken little notice, at least publicly, of the Lerman criticisms. Palmer's book-length attack on Martinson and his reassertion of the claims of the CTP appeared in 1978; there is no mention of Lerman in it.[12]

While the debate in correctional journals raged, the public view, insofar as one can assess it from editorials, political speeches, and legislative initiatives, was that Martinson was right. Because of this widespread belief that "nothing works," the National Research Council, the applied research arm of the prestigious National Academy of Sciences, created in 1977 a Panel on Research on Rehabilitative Techniques, chaired by Professor Lee Sechrest, then of the Department of Psychology of Florida State University. The panel was charged with reviewing existing evaluations of rehabilitative efforts to see if they provided a basis for drawing any conclusions about the effectiveness of these efforts. Its first report— on efforts to rehabilitate in correctional institutions—was issued in 1979; a second report, on how to design better efforts, appeared two years later.[13]

Owing to the importance in the public debate of the review by Lipton, Martinson, and Wilks (LMW), that book was made the focus of the panel's attention. In addition, the report examined reviews that analyzed studies appearing after 1968, the cutoff date for the LMW review. Among the papers commissioned by the panel was a detailed reanalysis of a sample of the studies analyzed by LMW, carried out by two scholars not identified with the ongoing debate, Stephen Fienberg and Patricia Grambsch.

The conclusion of the panel is easily stated: by and large, Martinson and his colleagues were right. More exactly, "The Panel concludes that Lipton, Martinson, and Wilks were reasonably accurate and fair in their appraisal of the rehabilitation literature."[14] If they erred at all, it was in being overly generous. They were sometimes guilty of an excessively lenient assessment of the methodology of a given study. Moreover, the evaluations published since 1968 provide little evidence to reverse this verdict. For example, David F. Greenberg's 1977 review of the more recent studies comes to essentially the same conclusion as Martinson.[15] S. R. Brody's survey in England on the institutional treatment of juvenile offenders agrees.[16]

The panel looked in particular at Palmer's argument that nearly half the studies cited by Martinson showed a rehabilitative effect. The panel was not persuaded: "Palmer's optimistic view cannot be supported, in large part because his assessment accepts at face value the claim of the original authors about effects they detected, and in too many instances those claims were wrong or were overinterpretations of data. . . . " In any event, "we find little support for the charge that positive findings were overlooked."[17]

The conclusion that Martinson was right does not mean that he or anyone else has proved that "nothing works," only that nobody has proved that "something works." There is always the chance, as the panel noted, that rehabilitative methods now in use but not tested would, if tested, show a beneficial effect and that new methods yet to be tried will prove efficacious. (One such method will be discussed later in this chapter.)

Are Some Offenders Amenable to Treatment?

ONE unresolved issue is whether certain kinds of offenders are more amenable to rehabilitation than others. If this is the case, and if the amenable subjects are mixed together in a treatment group with nonamenable ones, then any reductions in criminality among the former might be masked by increases in criminality among the latter; the average (and misleading) result would be "no change."

This view has been vigorously advanced by Daniel Glaser, among others. Writing in 1973, a year before the Martinson article appeared, he pointed to evidence from a variety of evaluative studies suggesting that certain kinds of offenders were especially amenable to rehabilitation. They tended to be persons who could easily communicate, who had not found their prior criminal career to be especially rewarding, and who had not been greatly disappointed by their efforts to find legitimate alternatives to crime. The CTP, for example, made explicit use of a psychological classification scheme designed to differentiate among delinquents on the basis of their "interpersonal maturity level" and their particular mode of behavior. One such group was classified as having a relatively high level of maturity, by which is meant the members had an internalized set of standards and some regard for the opinions of others, but displayed as well neurotic tendencies, either feelings of guilt and anxiety or a proclivity to "acting-out." The interpretation of the CTP data by Glaser, Palmer, and others was that these anxious, neurotic, guilt-stricken delinquents benefited substantially from intensive counseling. Recognizing the criticisms already leveled by Lerman (in his 1968 article) at the CTP, Glaser felt that even allowing for counselor bias the neurotics did substantially better in the treatment groups than they did when left alone in the control groups. Moreover, Glaser has argued that Lerman himself neglected the long-term effects of treatment on different types of delinquents.[18]

If this is true, then those studies which show no change among treated offenders may include not only some "amenables" who commit less crime but some nonamendables who actually commit more crimes as a result of the treatment. And this is exactly what Palmer believed he found in the CTP data. In his 1978 book, he showed the monthly arrest rates for two kinds of offenders: the "conflicted" (by which he apparently means "neurotic") and the "power-oriented" (by which he seems to mean those delinquents who lack an internalized set of conventional standards and either manipulate others or identify with the norms of a deviant group). Neurotic delinquents in the treatment group had a lower monthly arrest rate than neurotics in the control group, both during the early stages of the program and four years after discharge. "Power-oriented" offenders in the treatment groups, on the other hand, had a *higher* arrest rate than the power-oriented controls four years after discharge. Glaser had surmised that this increase in criminality among power-oriented delinquents in the treatment program arises because they learn from it how to manipulate their counselors, obtain favors, win early release, and generally "con" the system. "Treating" such persons (at least by means of verbal therapy) apparently makes society worse off.

An earlier study by Stuart Adams provides some confirmation for this point of view. In 1961 he described the "Pilot Intensive Counseling Organizations" (PICO) in California, aimed at reducing delinquency among older juvenile offenders. The eligible youth were first classified as "amenable" or "nonamenable" by the persons running the project. (Exactly how they reached these judgments is not clear.) Once classified, they were then randomly assigned to either a treatment or control group. (The treatment consisted of individual counseling sessions, once or twice a week for about nine months, carried on inside a correctional institution.) After nearly three years of observation, Adams discovered that the amenable delinquents who had been treated were much less likely than amenable delinquents who had not been treated to be returned to custody. On the other hand, delinquents judged nonamenable who were given counseling did much worse—indeed, they were more likely to be returned to jail than the nonamenables who had not been treated. In short, if you are amenable, treatment may make you less criminal; if you are not, treatment can make you more criminal. Adams found that the delinquents judged to be amenable were "bright, verbal, and anxious." These characteristics are similar to those of the neurotics in the CTP.[19]

This conclusion is consistent with a good deal of evidence about the effects of psychotherapy generally. Changing delinquents is not fundamentally different from changing law-abiding people: "crime," after all, is not a unique form of behavior; it is simply behavior that is against the law. The illegality of the behavior is no trivial matter, but illegality alone does not differentiate one action from many similar actions. For example, many (perhaps most) offenders tend to do poorly in school, to have emotional problems, to find it difficult to get along with parents and friends, and to drink a good deal of alcohol. They are generally a mess. But poor school work, strained peer relations, emotional stress, and drinking liquor are not illegal.

Psychologists have long argued over whether any form of therapy will help any kind of problem. H. J. Eysenck, in a famous pair of articles published in 1952 and 1965, claimed that there was little evidence that therapy did anybody much good.[20] He was (and is) the Robert Martinson of psychotherapy. Of late, psychologists have questioned the sweeping nature of Eysenck's claim. Mary Lee Smith and Gene V. Glass published in 1977 a comprehensive review of nearly four hundred controlled evaluations of therapy and counseling and concluded that the client was often better off being treated than not. However, they noted that the improvements were generally with respect to such matters as fear and self-esteem and much less often with respect to such matters as "adjustment" (under which heading, of course, one finds most criminal behavior). Smith and Glass also tried to measure what factors made some subjects more amenable to therapy than others. They were able to identify two statistically significant ones: the resemblance of the therapist to the client, and the IQ of the client. Brighter clients did better than duller ones.[21]

Similarly, if we are to believe Lerman, the brighter (and more neurotic) delinquents remained in the CTP program longer than those with the opposite characteristics; thus, any improvement measured by Palmer in their law-abidingness may result either from their greater receptivity to therapy, or from their tendency over time to outnumber the more delinquent-prone youth, or both.

The possibility that some persons are amenable to criminal rehabilitation is intriguing, but it is not yet clear how much to make of it. The National Research Council Panel took note of the issue but remains skeptical that we have any clear understanding of it. The CTP, the major source of claims about amenability, is methodologically flawed. The PICO project did not define amenability with any rigor. Classifying a criminal as "amenable" may only mean that a therapist has a good hunch as to who will cooperate with the program. But if the therapist cannot communicate to others the basis for that hunch or provide a clear explanation of its rationale, it is hard to see how it can be used routinely as the basis for classifying and treating offenders. Moreover, some difficult legal and ethical issues arise. Suppose we are able to differentiate, accurately, amenable from nonamenable offenders. Suppose further that the treatment from which the amenables will benefit is less restrictive, more benign, and shorter in duration than the conventional punishment to which nonamenables will be assigned. Should we allow the criminal justice system to be "nicer" to "amenable" offenders than to nonamenable ones, even though their offenses and prior records may be identical? (Of course, it may also turn out that the rehabilitative program is felt by the recipients to be more onerous than doing "straight time"; the issue, however, remains the same.)

Nevertheless, the possibility of identifying amenable subjects and aiming at them programs that work is sufficiently attractive as to merit intensive new research. Someone has even coined a shorthand term to describe what we now suspect are the amenable subjects of therapy: YAVIN (young, anxious, verbal, intelligent, neurotic).

Recidivism, Rates, and Restrictiveness

THE MOST dramatic new argument in the continuing debate over rehabilitation, however, comes from two authors who do not, at first glance, appear to be writing about rehabilitation at all. Charles A. Murray and Louis A. Cox, Jr., members of a private research organization, were retained to find out what happens to chronic delinquents in Chicago who are confronted by sanctions of varying degrees of restrictiveness.[22]

The Chicago authorities wanted to know if any of the programs offered in that city (ranging from commitment to a conventional juvenile reformatory, to newer programs that left the delinquent in the community or sent him to a wilderness program) changed the rate at which delinquents committed offenses. Such studies have been done many times, usually with the negative results reported by Martinson. But Murray and Cox redefined the outcome measure in a way that seems to make a striking difference. Until now, almost all students of recidivism "rates" or rehabilitation outcomes have measured the success or failure of a person by whether or not he was arrested for a new offense (or was convicted of a new offense, or had his parole revoked) after leaving the institution or completing the therapeutic program. "Success" was an either-or proposition: if you did not (within a stated time period) get into trouble again, you were a success; if you did get into trouble—*even once*—you were a "failure." Though the evaluators of rehabilitation programs typically speak of "recidivism rates," in fact they do not mean "rate" at all; they mean "percent who fail." More accurately, they use "rate" in the sense of "proportion," as in the "birth rate" or the "tax rate." But there is a different meaning of rate: the *frequency* of behavior per unit of time. Even a cursory glance through the studies reviewed by Lipton, Martinson, and Wilks reveals that almost all of them use "recidivism rate" to mean "the proportion who fail."

It was Murray's and Cox's happy thought to use rate in the sense of frequency and to calculate how many arrests per month were charged against a given group of delinquents before and after being exposed to Chicago juvenile treatment programs, and to do so separately for each kind of program involved. They examined three groups of youth.

The first was composed of 317 serious delinquents. They had been arrested an average of 13 times prior to being sent to the Department of Corrections, which was when Murray and Cox first started to track them. They were young (the average age was sixteen) but active: they had been charged with 14 homicides, 23 rapes, over 300 assaults and 300 auto thefts, nearly 200 armed robberies, and over 700 burglaries. The boys entered the study by having been sentenced by the court to a state correctional institution where they served an average of about ten months. Murray and Cox followed them for (on the average) seventeen months after their release.

By the conventional measure of recidivism, the results were typically discouraging—82 percent were rearrested. But the *frequency* with which they were arrested during the follow-up period fell dramatically—the monthly arrest rate (that is, arrests per month per 100 boys) declined by about *two-thirds*. To be exact, the members of this group of hard-core delinquents were arrested 6.3 times each during the year before being sent away but only 2.9 times each during the seventeen months on the street after release.

The second group consisted of 266 delinquents who were eligible to go to a state reformatory but who instead were diverted to one of several less custodial programs run by the Unified Delinquency Intervention Services (UDIS), a Cook County (Chicago) agency created to make available in a coordinated fashion noninstitutional, community-based programs for serious delinquents. Though chosen for these presumably more therapeutic programs, the UDIS delinquents had criminal records almost as severe as those sent to the regular reformatories—an average of over 13 arrests per boy, of which 8 were for "index" (that is, serious) offenses, including 9 homicides, over 500 burglaries, and over 100 armed robberies. Nonetheless, since these youths were specially selected for the community-based programs, one would expect that in the opinion of probation officers, and probably in fact, they represented somewhat less dangerous, perhaps more amenable delinquents.

Despite the fact the UDIS group may have been thought more amenable to treatment, the reduction in their monthly arrest rates was *less* than it had been for the group sent to the reformatories (about 17 percent less). In general, UDIS did not do as well as the regular Department of Corrections. Even more interesting, Murray and Cox found that the more restrictive the degree of supervision practiced by UDIS, the greater the reduction in arrest rates. Youths left in their homes or sent to wilderness camps showed the least reduction (though some reduction nonetheless); those placed in group homes in the community showed a greater reduction; and those put into out-of-town group homes, intensive-care residential programs, or sent to regular reformatories showed the greatest reduction. If this is true, it implies that how strictly the youth were supervised, rather than what therapeutic programs were available, had the greatest effect on the recidivism rate.

Ordinarily, we do not refer to the crime-reduction effects of confinement as "rehabilitation." Technically, they are called the results of "special deterrence" ("special" in the sense that the person deterred is the specific individual who is the object of the intervention, and not the general delinquent population). "Rehabilitation" usually refers to interventions that are "nice," benevolent, or well intended, or that involve the provision of special services. A psychologist might say that rehabilitation involves "positive reinforcements" (such as counseling) rather than "negative reinforcements" (such as incarceration). Indeed, the National Research Council Panel defines rehabilitation as the result of "any planned intervention" that reduces further criminal activity, "whether that reduction is mediated by personality, behavior, abilities, attitudes, values, or other factors," provided only that one excludes the effects of fear or intimidation, the latter being regarded as sources of special deterrence.

Although the distinction has a certain emotional appeal, it makes little sense either scientifically or behaviorally. Scientifically, there is no difference between a positive and negative inducement; behavioral psychologists long ago established that the two kinds of reinforcements have comparable effects. (It is not generally true that rewards will change behavior more than punishments, or vice versa.) Behaviorally, it is not clear that a criminal can tell the difference between rehabilitation and special deterrence if each involves a comparable degree of restriction. Rehabilitation can (and usually does) involve a substantial degree of coercion, even of intimidation ("be nice or you won't get out," "talk to the counselor or stay in your cell," "join the group discussion or run the risk of being locked up"). Behavior-modification therapy can involve the simultaneous use of positive reinforcers ("follow the rules and earn a token") and negative ones ("break the rules and lose a token"). It might help the discussion of offender-oriented programs if the distinction between rehabilitation and special deterrence were collapsed.

The real issue raised by the Murray-Cox study is not, however, what to call the effect they observe, but whether they have actually observed any effect at all. A number of criticisms have been made of it, but two are of special importance. First, does the decline in arrests indicate a decline in actual criminality or merely an increase in skill at avoiding apprehension? Second, if there is an actual decline in criminality, might this not be explained by the maturation of youth, that is, growing out of crime as they become older? Michael D. Maltz, Andrew C. Gordon, and their colleagues made these and other criticisms in response to a preliminary report of the Murray-Cox findings.[23] In their later, book-length treatment of the Chicago project, Murray and Cox responded.

The second criticism seems the easiest to answer. Murray and Cox were able to show that the decline in rearrest rates existed for all incarcerated serious delinquents regardless of age. As an additional check, the authors examined a third group—nearly 1,500 youth born in Chicago in 1960 and arrested at least once by the Chicago Police Department before their seventeenth birthdays. Since this group was chosen at random from all arrested youth of the same age, it naturally is made up primarily of less serious offenders. Indeed, only 3 percent of this group was ever referred to UDIS or the Department of Corrections. When the monthly arrest rates for this group were examined, the data showed a more or less steady increase throughout the teenage years. Being arrested or being placed on probation had no apparent effect on subsequent delinquency. By all the tests they used, therefore, the decline in arrest rates for those delinquents given strict supervision cannot be explained by the fact that they were simply getting older.

The other criticism is harder to answer. Strictly speaking, it is impossible to know whether arrest data are a reasonable approximation of the true crime rate. No one argues, of course, that every crime results in an arrest. All that is at issue is whether a more or less constant fraction of all crimes result in arrests. There are two possibilities: either having been arrested before draws police attention to the boy (he is "stigmatized" or "labeled"), thus making him *more* likely to be arrested for subsequent crimes; or the arrest and subsequent punishment increases his skills at avoiding detection (the system has served as a "school for criminals"), thus making him *less* likely to be arrested for a given offense.

Now it is obvious that the first of these two possibilities—the "labeling" effect of being arrested—cannot be true, for as we have seen, delinquents who are placed under supervision have their subsequent arrest rates *decline*. If the police "pick on" previously arrested youth, either they do so without making an arrest (by keeping an eye on "troublemakers," for example) or they try harder to arrest them but find the youth are not committing as many crimes as before.

The other possibility—that boys become skilled at avoiding arrest—is impossible to disprove, but Murray and Cox raise some serious questions as to whether this gain in skills, if it occurs at all, could explain the decline in arrest rates. Perhaps their most telling argument is this: one must not only believe that correctional institutions are "schools of crime," one must believe they are such excellent schools that they produce a two-thirds gain in arrest-avoiding skills. This would make reformatories and group homes the most competent educational institutions in the country, since no one has yet shown that conventional schools, with the best available educational technology, can produce comparable gains in learning noncriminal skills. And all this must be accomplished within the ten-month period that is the average length of detention. It is still possible, of course, that the "schools of crime" hypothesis is true, but it requires one to make some heroic assumptions in order to sustain it: that large numbers of boys learn more during ten months in a reformatory than they learn in ten years on the street; that the great majority, despite their statements to the contrary made to interviewers, increase their commitment to crime as a way of life (rather than as an occasionally profitable activity) as a result of incarceration; and that the object of their efforts when back on the street is to employ their sharpened skills at avoiding apprehension while committing relatively unprofitable crimes rather than attacking more profitable (and riskier) targets.

Though Murray and Cox make a persuasive case for the validity of their findings, it cannot be taken as a conclusive study. For one thing, we would like to know what happens to these delinquents over a much longer period. Most studies of rehabilitation suggest that any favorable effects tend to be extinguished by the passage of time (though such extinction usually appears within the first year). We would also like to know more about the kinds of offenses for which these persons were arrested, before and after court intervention (perhaps they change the form of their criminal behavior in important ways). And above all, we would like to see such a study repeated in other settings by other scholars. It may even be possible to do this retrospectively, with data already in existence but never before analyzed using frequency of offending (rather than proportion of failures) as the measure of outcome.

In fact, long before the Murray-Cox study, LaMar T. Empey and Maynard L. Erickson had reported on the Provo Experiment in Utah, an effort to reduce delinquency that was evaluated by arrest rates before and after treatment—the same outcome measure used by Murray and Cox (indeed, the latters' book contains a foreword by Empey). The Provo Experiment was, in principle at least, an even better test of changing recidivism rates than the Chicago project because the former, unlike the latter, randomly assigned delinquent boys to either treatment or control groups and kept detailed records (in addition to before-and-after measures) of what actually happened to the boys in the treatment programs. The experimental program was community-based, but, unlike conventional probation or even group homes, involved an intensive level of participation in a supervised group discussion program, absence from which was promptly penalized by being locked up. The program was in time killed by community opposition (many persons thought it excessively punitive, others quarreled over who should pay for it). The four years worth of data which could be gathered, however, indicate that there have been substantial reductions in arrest rates that cannot be explained by maturation or social class differences for all boys. This was true of both those incarcerated and those left in the community, with the greatest reductions occurring among boys in the experimental programs.[24] Though open to criticism, the Provo data provide some support for the view that, if one measures offense *frequency*, some kinds of programs involving fairly high degrees of restrictiveness and supervision may make some difference.

The Murray-Cox and the Empey-Erickson studies are important, not only because they employ rates rather than proportions as the outcome measure or even because they suggest that something might work, but also because they suggest that the study of deterrence and the study of rehabilitation must be merged—that, at least for a given individual, they are the same thing. Until now, the two issues have been kept separate. It is not hard to understand why: welfare and probation agencies administer "rehabilitation," the police and wardens administer "deterrence"; advocates of rehabilitation think of themselves as "tender-minded," advocates of deterrence see themselves as "tough-minded"; rehabilitation supposedly cures the "causes" of crime, while deterrence deals only with the temptations to crime; psychologists study rehabilitation, economists study deterrence. If Murray-Cox and Empey-Erickson are correct, these distinctions are artificial, if not entirely empty.

The common core of both perspectives is, or ideally ought to be, an interest in explaining individual differences in the propensity to commit crime, or changes in a single individual's propensity over time. The stimuli confronting an individual can rarely be partitioned neatly into things tending to produce pain and those likely to produce pleasure; most situations in which we place persons, including criminals, contain elements of both. If explaining individual differences is our object, then studying individuals should be our method. Studies that try to measure the effect on whole societies of marginal changes in aggregate factors (such as the probability of being imprisoned, or the unemployment rate) are probably nearing the end of the line—even the formidable statistical methodologies now available are unlikely to overcome the gross deficiencies in data that we shall always face.

Policy makers need not embrace the substantive conclusions of Murray and Cox (though it is hard to see how they could reasonably be ignored) to appreciate the need to encourage local jurisdictions to look at the effect of a given program on the rate of behavior of a given set of offenders. If they do, they may well discover, as Murray and Cox feel they discovered in Chicago, that for the serious, chronic delinquent, the strategy of minimal intervention (probation, or loosely supervised life in the community) fails to produce any desirable changes (whether one calls those changes deterrence or rehabilitation), whereas tighter, more restrictive forms of supervision (whether in the community or in an institution) may produce some of these desired changes, or at the very least not produce worse delinquency through "labeling" or "stigmatization." It is hard to imagine a reason for not pursuing this line of inquiry.

Chapter 10

The Death Penalty

WHATEVER else may be said about the death penalty, it is certain that it incapacitates (dead murderers only murder again in our nightmares) and it does not rehabilitate (save, perhaps, in an afterlife). Everything else is uncertain. We do not know whether, as it has been applied in this country, executions deter murderers more than the prospect of imprisonment. We do not know whether, in recent years, sentences of death have been imposed capriciously or in a discriminatory fashion. And we disagree about whether the penalty of death is a morally fitting or a morally repugnant form of retribution.

I have chosen my words carefully, and in view of the great passions that capital punishment arouses in so many of us, they ought to be read carefully. We do not know whether the death penalty *as it has been imposed in this country* deters murderers. There can be little doubt, I think, that under some circumstances the death penalty almost surely alters behavior. If every murderer were executed on the spot, without delay or error, it is inconceivable that there would not be fewer murders. Indeed, if people who sneezed on subway trains were executed, we would find a lot less sneezing, even though we often think of sneezing as an involuntary act (just as we sometimes think of murder as an impassioned one). The Nazis certainly believed in the power of capital punishment to alter behavior, and no one can doubt that they were right, given the wholesale and ruthless use they made of this penalty. The Mafia also believes in the deterrent power of executions. Law enforcement officers who have tried to recruit informants among the Mafia will testify to the accuracy of that belief, even though organized gangsters make rather selective and sparing use of this ultimate sanction. The question for makers of public policy, however, is not whether under some circumstances the death penalty deters, but whether it deters as it has been imposed in a free society in the past or is likely to be imposed in the future. Moreover, we need to know, not whether the prospect of an execution deters, but whether it deters *more than the prospect of other penalties*, chiefly long prison terms. We are interested, to put the matter technically, in the marginal deterrent effect of executions. As I hope to show, it is quite unlikely that we shall ever be able to find out what that effect, if any, is.

We are uncertain about whether there is any racial bias in death sentences imposed *in recent years*. There are good grounds for believing that such bias existed in decades past, particularly in the South, notably for crimes in which black men raped white women. But we cannot judge contemporary behavior by an evaluation derived from past behavior, though we are entitled to use the evidence of past behavior as good grounds for being especially suspicious and thus for inquiring into this matter with the greatest care. While persons condemned to death are today* (as in the past) found disproportionately in the South, and while blacks are overrepresented among those now on death row, neither the greater use of the death penalty by the South nor the overrepresentation of blacks, taken by themselves, is evidence of discrimination.

There is disagreement about the moral propriety of capital punishment. But because there is disagreement about a matter of morality does not mean that nothing serious, interesting, and persuasive can be said about the subject. Disagreement about moral values is not evidence of the arbitrary nature of any statement about values. When I wrote the first edition of this book, the debate about capital punishment was almost entirely about its deterrent effect, and I chided my colleagues for neglecting the (to me) far more important question of the moral arguments that could be made for or against it. Since that time (though no doubt for reasons having little to do with my chiding), the quality and seriousness of the philosophical debate has markedly improved. One can now read serious philosophical arguments in favor of executions (as by Ernest van den Haag and Walter Berns) and serious philosophical arguments against executions (as by Richard O. Lempert and Charles L. Black).[1]

Important things can be said about the moral propriety of capital punishment, but the purpose of this chapter is more limited: to assess the

---

*As of the end of 1981, thirty-six states had a death penalty law under the terms of which 838 persons had been condemned to death. Of these, 827 were males and 605 (72 percent of the total) were in one of the fifteen southern states having a capital punishment law. The states without such a law were, as of December 1981: Maine, Massachusetts, Rhode Island, New Jersey, Michigan, Wisconsin, Minnesota, Iowa, North Dakota, Kansas, West Virginia, Oregon, Alaska, and Hawaii.

social science evidence by which the usefulness and fairness of the death penalty might be judged. Though this will fall well short of a full consideration of the role, if any, that capital punishment ought to play in our society, a discussion of the (possible) deterrent effect and the (possible) discriminatory application of executions has tended to dominate all public debates on the subject.

It is not entirely clear to me why the debate should be so preoccupied with the alleged usefulness of executions. It is not enough to say that it is because capital punishment, if it can be shown to have a deterrent effect, will be an important weapon in the fight against crime. It is inconceivable that capital punishment will ever be imposed on more than a small handful of offenders, and then only for having committed especially heinous crimes. In the period 1930–1960, when there were scarcely any constitutional barriers to the use of the death penalty, the number of executions never exceeded two hundred in any single year and in most years was closer to one hundred. During this same period, there were at least seven thousand homicides committed in every year but two, and in most years there were over eight thousand. For any given murderer, thus, execution was a relatively unlikely event. Of course, if we knew (which we do not) what proportion of all homicides involved murder in the first degree (that is, premeditated murder), the risk of execution may have been much greater. But even if murder was significantly deterred by the death penalty, there is no reason to suppose that this would have much of an effect on the number of robberies. I estimate that the average citizen is at least forty times as likely to be a victim of a robbery than of a homicide. The crimes that victimize and frighten us the most are not likely to change in number whether or not some murderers are executed. If the death penalty does deter murder, then perhaps some robbers would be less likely to employ life-threatening force against their victims, which would, of course, be a gain for all of us. But we cannot be certain of this.

Perhaps the popular debate over the death penalty is dominated by the issue of deterrence because as citizens we tend to believe (or at least hope) that facts can settle philosophical quarrels. We despair of making our opponent give up by using against him an especially telling philosophical argument; we suspect that he will merely shrug it off, misinterpret it, or deny it any conclusive force. But if we can confront him with a hard fact, then, we suppose, he will be forced to yield. Proponents cannot imagine a reasonable person opposing capital punishment if in fact it does prevent murders, and opponents cannot imagine a reasonable person favoring it if it does not.

But in fact neither proponents nor opponents need change their minds just because the facts about deterrence—supposing for the moment we can discover them—are against them. We might well want capital punishment even if we were certain it had no marginal crime-reduction effect, because we think it to be the morally necessary punishment for certain heinous crimes. Conversely, we might oppose capital punishment even if we were certain that it did have a deterrent effect because we think it morally wrong for the state to take human lives. I suspect, however, that there is a certain asymmetry here. It is easier to defend executions that have no deterrent effect than to oppose executions that do have such an effect. In the first instance, we cause harm only to the guilty person (provided, of course, we are confident he is guilty), whereas in the second case we knowingly countenance the murder of one or more innocent persons in order to spare ourselves the spectacle of a state-ordered death. If deterrence works, that fact will probably make opponents of the death penalty a bit more uncomfortable than proponents would be if it could be shown that deterrence does not work, but not, I think, so uncomfortable that they will change their minds.

But we need not speculate about such possibilities, because the facts are not clear and, in my judgment, are not likely ever to become clear.

Deterrence

PERHAPS the first serious effort in this country to assess the deterrent effect of the death penalty was that of Thorsten Sellin, an opponent of capital punishment. In his first study, he did four things.[2] First, he compared homicide rates between adjacent states with and without the death penalty. The crude rates for homicide in these groups of states appeared to be about the same and to change in the same ways, regardless of whether a state did or did not have the death penalty on the books. Second, he compared homicide rates within states before and after they abolished or restored the death penalty. The rates did not change significantly after the legal status of the penalties changed. Third, he examined homicide rates in those cities where executions occurred and were presumed to have been publicized. There was no difference in the homicide rates in those cities where executions occurred and were presumed to have been publicized. There was no difference in the homicide rate before and after the executions. (Similar studies, with similar results, were done by Robert Dann, Leonard D. Savitz, and William Graves.[3] Graves even uncovered evidence in California that led him to speculate that there was an increase in the number of homicides on the days immediately preceding an execution.) Finally, Sellin sought to discover whether law-enforcement officers were safer from murderous attacks in states with the death penalty than in those without it. He found that the rate at which police officers were shot and killed in states that had abolished capital punishment was the same as the rate in states that had retained the death penalty. Donald R. Campion reached the same conclusion after studying the deaths of state police officers.[4]

It is sometimes argued in rejoinder to these findings that while executions may not deter murderers generally, they will help protect prison guards and other inmates from fatal assaults by convicts who "have nothing else to lose." Sellin compiled a list of fifty-nine persons who committed murders in state and federal prisons in 1965. He concluded that it is "visionary" to believe that the death penalty could reduce the "hazards of life in prison." Eleven of the prison murders were found in states without capital punishment and forty-three were in states with it. (The other five were in federal prisons.)

All these studies have serious methodological weaknesses. One problem is the degree of comparability of states with and without the death penalty. Sellin tried to "match" states by taking contiguous ones (for example, Michigan, Indiana, and Ohio), but of course such states are not really matched at all—they differ not only in the penalty for murder but in many other respects as well, and these other differences may offset any differences resulting from the form of punishment.

Another problem lies in the definition of a capital crime. What should be studied is the rate of crimes for which capital punishment is legally possible. I am not aware of any data on "murder rates" that distinguish between those homicides (like first-degree murder) for which death may be a penalty and those (like second-degree murder or nonnegligent manslaughter) for which it may not. Sellin's studies compare homicide rates, but no one knows what fraction of those homicides are first-degree murders for which execution is possible, even in the states that retain capital punishment.

Finally, and perhaps most important, it is not clear from many of these studies what is meant by "the death penalty." If what is meant is simply the legal possibility of execution, then "the death penalty" may be more fiction than fact. In many states that had the death penalty on the books, no executions were in fact carried out for many years. The majority members of a legislative commission in Massachusetts, for example, reported in 1968 that the death penalty is no deterrent to crime, but the minority members pointed out that no one had been executed in the state since 1947, and therefore no one could say whether the legal possibility of execution was or was not a deterrent. Indeed, in 1960 there were only fifty-six executions in the entire country, more than half of these occurring in the South; in 1965 there were only seven; between 1968 and 1976 there were no executions; since 1977 there have been (as of mid-1982) four.

In the same vein as Sellin's work was a study by Hans Zeisel analyzing the effects, if any, of the unofficial moratorium on executions that occurred in this country between 1968 and 1976. Zeisel argued that if executions in fact deter murders, then those states that during the late 1960s stopped executing murderers would have experienced a greater growth in the murder rate than those states that had never executed anyone for many decades. He concluded that those states that had recently stopped executions experienced less of an increase in the murder rate than did those states that had abolished capital punishment long ago. His argument was that the failure of the sudden ending of capital punishment to unleash a disproportionate increase in the murder rate was evidence that the death penalty in fact did not deter murder.[5]

The weakness in this argument is much the same as the weakness in the similar argument made earlier by Sellin: the states that suddenly stopped executions were very different from those that had abolished it long ago. The states that stopped in the 1960s were mostly southern states; the states that had stopped decades earlier were mostly northern states. Moreover, as Arnold Barnett has observed, massive population shifts were occurring at the same time as the changes in the death penalty, with northerners moving to the South and southerners moving to the North. These shifts may well have affected murder rates in ways that offset whatever effect the ending of capital punishment had. Finally, the states that stopped executing in the 1960s were not making much of a change in their policies, because for many years preceding the moratorium they scarcely executed anyone. Between 1960 and 1967, when they stopped, the sixteen southern states together were executing about twenty persons a year; a few individual states, such as Georgia, Florida, and Mississippi, were executing as many as two a year; most other southern states were executing virtually no one.[6] Thus, it is by no means clear that the "change" that occurred in 1967 was significant enough to warrant a comparison between states that did and did not make it.

In short, state-by-state comparisons are not likely to tell us much about the effect of capital punishment because the states differ in so many ways in addition to their willingness to execute. There are two statistical techniques by which this problem can be addressed. One is to compare states at one point in time in ways that hold constant those social and economic factors that might influence the murder rate; the other is to analyze changes over time in the murder rate in one or more states or the nation as a whole. The first method is called "cross-sectional" analysis, the latter "longitudinal" analysis.

There have been several cross-sectional studies. One by Isaac Ehrlich, comparing states as of 1940, found that (other things being equal) executions deter homicides, and another, by Dale Cloninger, comparing states as of 1960, agreed.[7] But other cross-sectional studies have found no deterrent effect. These include one by Peter Passell that compared states in both 1950 and 1960 and one by Brian Forst that analyzed changes across states between 1960 and 1970.[8] There have been some lively exchanges among the authors of these studies, and a number of critics have pointed out what they believe are flaws in both the studies finding and those not finding a deterrent effect of the death penalty.[9]

There are many reasons why these cross-sectional studies are in conflict. They often use data from different years (1940, 1950, and 1960), and it is possible the death penalty was a deterrent in some periods but not in others. They control, statistically, for somewhat different factors, and this affects the reliability with which the effect of executions is estimated. For example, Cloninger, who found that executions deter homicides, omitted from his analysis the probability of being convicted for homicide and the length of the prison terms to which nonexecuted murderers were sentenced. It is possible that some of the deterrent effect Cloninger ascribed to differences in the number of executions were in fact attributable to differences among the states in the chances of being convicted and the length of time those convicted served in prison.

The best-known studies attempting to discover whether executions deter murders are the longitudinal ones. Their fame rests in part on the fact that one of them, that by Isaac Ehrlich, was introduced in evidence by the Department of Justice when its lawyers were arguing in favor of the death penalty before the Supreme Court. Ehrlich's study, the first sophisticated longitudinal analysis of the death penalty, was an effort to discover what effect year-to-year changes in the number of persons executed in the United States as a whole may have had on the number of homicides committed in the nation between 1933 and 1969. He held constant changes in such social factors as the unemployment rate, labor force participation, income, and the racial and age composition of the population. He also inserted into his equation variables designed to measure the probability of a murderer being arrested and the probability of an arrested murderer being convicted. He found that changes in the probability of being executed did have an independent effect on the murder rate, as follows: every additional execution per year resulted in seven or eight fewer murders.[10]

Kenneth I. Wolpin performed a similar analysis for England and Wales between 1929 and 1968. He concluded that, provided certain assumptions are satisfied, executing an additional murderer in a given year would produce about four fewer murder victims.[11]

Both studies, but especially Ehrlich's, have been criticized. One criticism has to do with the assumed independence of a jury's decision to convict a charged murderer and a judge's willingness to sentence him to death. Both Ehrlich and Wolpin discovered that the higher the probability of being convicted for murder, other things being equal, the lower the murder rate, whether or not the person was executed. The implication is that convicting an alleged murderer has some deterrent effect on would-be murderers, as does executing murderers. Both propositions support the general theory of deterrence. But in the case of capital murder, they may well confound one another. Suppose a jury knew that if it found a person guilty, the chances of his being executed were very high. Common sense tells us that this knowledge would make many juries reluctant to convict some persons of first-degree murder. As a result, a greater use of executions for murder might have the effect of producing fewer convictions for murder, so that the deterrent effect of both convictions and executions would be lost. This is no mere speculative possibility. In Great Britain, where judges had less discretion in imposing death sentences than did American judges, the number of murderers found to be insane, and thus spared the gallows, dropped sharply after the death penalty was abolished in 1965. It is hard to attribute this change to a sudden improvement in the mental health of English criminals. What apparently happened was that the high probability of execution before 1965 had produced an artificially low rate of "conviction" during that period, with the insanity plea being used to avoid conviction.

Ehrlich's own data, in the opinion of some, support the conclusion that an increase in the use of the death penalty would decrease the chances of an accused murderer being convicted by about 17 percent.[12] Such a decrease might well nullify the deterrent effect of the death penalty. Wolpin in his analysis of the English data makes it clear that in order to draw any policy conclusions from the statistical relationship between executions and murderers, one must first be confident that changing the execution rate will not change the conviction rate.

A second criticism has to do with the time period covered by the analysis. Ehrlich's study covered the years 1933 through 1969. Between 1962 and 1969, the number of executions dropped sharply, from forty-seven in 1962 to two in 1967 and zero in 1968 and 1969. And during the 1960s, crime rates, including the murder rate, were going up sharply. Suppose we omit from Ehrlich's analysis these last four years and recalculate his equations for the period 1933–1962, the period during which executions were still being used with some frequency. When Peter Passell and John B. Taylor did this, they discovered that the death penalty lost its deterrent effect, or more precisely that the statistically significant negative correlation between murders and executions disappeared.[13] This suggests that executions were not a deterrent when they were relatively commonplace (that is, between 1933 and 1962), and the murder rate was relatively steady, but appeared to become a deterrent only after 1962, when executions decreased sharply and the murder rate rose dramatically.

But so many things were happening during the 1960s not captured in the Ehrlich equation—the increase in the private ownership of handguns, the rise in racial tensions, the growth in all forms of crime, the spread of the ethos of individual self-expression—that we cannot be confident that a finding that executions deter murder only during such unusual and brief periods warrants much confidence.

One thing in particular that was changing during the 1960s was the decline in the use of prisons and the shortening of prison sentences. While the crime rate was going up, the prison population was going down. Indeed, at all points, the criminal justice system was becoming less effective so that the chances of a given felon evading arrest, prosecution, and punishment steadily improved. These changes, more than changes in the probability of being executed (which, by 1965, was an exceedingly unlikely event in any case), may have contributed to an increase in all forms of crime, including murder.

Ehrlich did not include in his study a measure of the length of a prison sentence for murder for the very good reason that these data did not exist. But there is reason to believe that sentences were getting shorter during the 1960s. In 1960, 47 percent of the murderers released from prison had served five years or more; by 1970, only 36 percent had served terms of at least five years.[14] If we wanted to determine the marginal deterrent effect of the death penalty, we would first find out what the effect on the murder rate would have been if prison terms had been getting longer (rather than shorter); we would then ask whether the death penalty added anything to the deterrent effect of prison.

Wolpin's study avoids some of these problems, but not all. In particular, the apparent deterrent effect of capital punishment in England and Wales, unlike that in the United States, is more or less steady over the entire period studied (1929–1968). Even though executions in England became much less common after 1957 (they were abolished a decade later), Wolpin's data suggest that the deterrent effect of executions can be detected in both the pre–1957 and post–1957 periods. On the other hand, Wolpin is not able to rule out the possibility that some of the increase in homicides that occurred, especially after World War II, was the result of a decline in the length of time served in prison by those murderers who were not executed (the English records contain no information on time served).[15]

That the length of the prison term awarded to nonexecuted murderers may be important is suggested by Kenneth L. Avio's study of the effect of the death penalty in Canada. Using methods similar to those of Ehrlich, but applying them to Canadian data for the period 1929–1960, Avio concluded that there was no significant relationship between changes in the chances of being executed and changes in the homicide rate. He did observe, however, an effect on the homicide rate of changes in the length of time spent in prison by murderers who are not executed—the longer the stay, the fewer the murders. (Since the death penalty was mandatory in Canada for convicted murderers during this period, those murderers who served prison terms were those who had their sentences commuted. On the average, 64 percent of the murderers were executed; the remainder served a prison term that averaged just under fourteen years.[16]) If comparable data on the length of prison terms had been available to Ehrlich and Wolpin, it is possible that the results of their analyses may have changed.

It is also possible, of course, that executions deter murders in England but not in the United States. That might be true because, before the use of the death penalty was first restricted and then abolished, a convicted murderer faced in England a much greater risk of execution than he did in this country. Indeed, before 1957, death was the mandatory penalty for murder in England, although murderers could be found insane and a sentence of death could be commuted to life imprisonment by the Crown. Even with these loopholes, however, about one-half of all convicted murderers in England were in fact executed between 1900 and 1955 (after 1957, only one-tenth were).[17]

But it is even more possible that no statistical study, however carefully done, can shed much light on the deterrent effect of the death penalty, at least in nations that will make, at most, sparing and highly selective use of it.

Arnold Barnett has performed some calculations to show just how difficult shedding this light may be. He reviewed both cross-sectional studies finding a deterrent effect (Ehrlich) and those not finding it (Passell and Forst) and concluded that all three studies had a common problem: there was so much statistical "noise" in the analyses that it would be almost impossible to get any reliable estimates of deterrence out of them. The source of this noise is not entirely clear, but its effect is that the equations used to explain the number of executions in each state in a given year produce so many errors (that is, the difference between the predicted number of executions and the actual number occurring is so great) that the effect on murder of a rare event such as an execution could literally be swamped by the errors. For example, Passell's study led to an estimate of the total number of homicides in forty-three states in 1960 that was wrong by 1,635. If we assume that each execution might prevent five murders and since we know there were forty-four persons executed for murder in 1960, there might have been 220 murders prevented. But 220 is less than 14 percent of the 1,635 errors produced by the Passell equation. As a result, if there were a deterrent effect, Passell probably could not have found it.[18]

Matters get worse when we recall that the vast majority of murderers would not be eligible for capital punishment in any event. Most people, I suspect, would restrict the death penalty to "cold-blooded" killers and not extend it to persons who commit crimes of passion or otherwise act impulsively. In most people's view cold-blooded killers probably include persons who deliberately murder for material gain, terrorists who kill innocent people for some political purpose, wanton murderers who derive pleasure from the act of killing, and possibly also those robbers and arsonists who carry out crimes in ways knowingly designed to cause the death of innocent bystanders. We do not know how many such murderers there are, but they undoubtedly account for only a minority, perhaps a small minority, of all homicides. For all the reasons mentioned, there will probably never be any evidence to show whether the death penalty does or does not affect the frequency with which such persons kill. If the public and elected officials are to make decisions in this matter, they will have to rely on their own best judgment. "Best judgment" means two things: a guess as to how a small number of potential offenders will react to the risk of death, and sober reflection on whether such a penalty is fair and just. Social science can contribute little to these judgments except to make clear that there is no systematic, accepted evidence that, lumping all murders together in the nation (or a state) as a whole, a change in the (small and delayed) risk of execution has a demonstrable effect on the rate at which these murders occur.

Discrimination

EVEN if the death penalty deters crime, the public still might not wish to impose it if the public were convinced that it would be imposed in a capricious or discriminatory manner. It was just this suspicion of capriciousness that led the Supreme Court, by a five-to-four vote, to declare capital punishment to be unconstitutional in 1972.[19] Justices William Brennan and Thurgood Marshall stated that they thought that executions were cruel and unusual punishment under any circumstances and thus inherently unconstitutional; the other three justices in the majority, though they obviously had misgivings about the death penalty, were only prepared to say it was unconstitutionally cruel and unusual if it was imposed in a capricious or discriminatory manner.

The evidence available to the Court at that time certainly seemed to support such concerns, especially in the South. Marvin Wolfgang and Anthony Amersterdam examined more than three thousand rape convictions in eleven southern states between 1945 and 1965. They found that though blacks convicted of rape were not likely to be executed (only 13 percent were), they were almost seven times as likely to be executed as whites convicted of the same crime. And if the black had raped a white woman, he was eighteen times as likely to be executed as all other racial combinations of criminals and victims. These findings could not be explained away by any other circumstances of the crime.[20] The evidence was less clearcut in the North. Wolfgang had earlier published a study of 439 persons sentenced to death for murder in Philadelphia between 1914 and 1958. They were divided into two categories: those for whom the sentence was commuted and those who were actually executed. Blacks were somewhat more likely than whites to be executed, but the difference, while statistically significant, was not large (88 percent of the blacks and 80 percent of the whites were executed). Among those charged with felony murder (that is, with having caused a death that occurs in the course of committing another kind of crime, such as robbery, rape, or burglary), whites were three times as likely as blacks to have their sentences commuted.[21]

To meet the concerns expressed by the Court, thirty-five states passed new capital punishment statutes between 1972 and 1976, at which time the Court ruled again. By a seven-to-two vote (Brennan and Marshall dissenting), the Court in *Gregg* v. *Georgia* held that the death penalty "does not invariably violate the Constitution" provided there are "suitable" limits to and guidelines for its use.[22] In a series of cases decided at the same time, the Court upheld death penalty statutes in Florida, Georgia, and Texas that allowed the court to consider information about the defendant and in particular any mitigating circumstances surrounding his offense, that supplied reasonably clear standards to guide the judge and jury in deciding whether to impose the death penalty, and that required that every death sentence be reviewed by a higher state court. One of these approved statutes was typical of several in providing for a two-stage trial—the first on the guilt or innocence of the accused, the second on the penalty to be imposed on the convicted defendant. States that did not have these procedures or that made the death penalty mandatory (as was the case at the time in Louisiana) had their capital punishment statutes overturned on constitutional grounds. (In passing, the Court stated that the social science evidence on the deterrent effect of the death penalty was "inconclusive" but that this sanction was "undoubtedly a significant deterrent" in some cases.)

By 1981, 838 prisoners were on death row under sentence of death (4 were executed). About 40 percent of the death-row population was black (all 4 of the executed men were white). However, though the Supreme Court had approved certain death penalty statutes as procedurally fair, some persons worried that blacks were still being unfairly selected for execution.

The most thorough review of the studies of discrimination in the use of the death penalty is that by Gary Kleck. He analyzed seventeen studies, twelve dealing with murder and five with rape, and concluded that they did not provide reliable evidence of racial discrimination in murder cases but did provide some such evidence in rape cases.[23] Though most of the studies purported to discover a discriminatory application of the death penalty, the great majority were methodologically defective in important ways. The most serious fault was the failure of the analysts to take into account the prior record of the offender. We would expect persons with more serious prior records to be more likely to receive the death penalty for a given offense than persons with no prior record or only a modest one. Only one study examined prior record, that by Charles Judson, and it found no evidence of racial bias.[24] If black murderers are more likely to have a long prior record than white ones, the failure to take this into account would lead to spurious results.

A second problem is the failure of several studies to take into account the severity of the offense. Naturally, all homicides are serious matters, but some are more serious than others: a gangland slaying differs in its blameworthiness from a fatal barroom fight, the killing of innocent bystanders from the shooting of a stubborn robbery victim, and a killing spree with many victims from the murder of a criminal accomplice.

What one learns from examining the nature of the offense as well as the prior record of the offender is evident in a recent study of 350 murder cases presented to the grand jury of Dade County (Miami), Florida, between 1973 and 1976. Of the 350 cases, 81 (23 percent) resulted in convictions for first-degree murder and of these 10 (3 percent) resulted in death sentences. Nine of the ten death sentences were imposed on persons who killed during the course of a robbery. In one, a husband and wife were kidnapped and then executed. In another, two persons were kidnapped and one of them, a pregnant woman, was strangled and shot. In a third, a restaurant employee was kidnapped, beaten over the head with a tire iron, and shot. Indeed, most of the death-penalty cases involved "execution-style" murders, usually following a kidnapping or involving innocent bystanders at the crime scene. The author of this analysis compared the ten death-penalty murders to the other forty-four convictions for felony murder (that is, murder committed in the course of another felony, such as a robbery) that resulted in life imprisonment rather than death sentences. He concluded that thirty-eight of the forty-four could be distinguished, on reasonable legal grounds applied to the facts of the case, from the ten death-penalty cases; six could not. All in all, the circumstances of the case, not the race of the defendants, explained the differences in penalties; where the differences could not be explained, it seemed to be because some judges simply refused to impose the death penalty in certain cases. There was "no conclusive evidence of racial discrimination."[25]

That racial bias may not be present does not mean that death penalty decisions are not arbitrary. There may be elements of caprice having nothing to do with race. We saw this in the six unexplained Dade County cases, and Franklin Zimring and his co-workers found similar evidence of hard-to-defend distinctions being made in murder cases in Philadelphia.[26] The procedural standards imposed on state courts by the Supreme Court have apparently narrowed the amount of disparity, but they clearly have not eliminated it.

Recently, a new and much-discussed study of racial bias in death penalty cases appeared that seemed to show that there was marked discrimination against blacks who had been sentenced to death since 1973 in Florida, Georgia, Ohio, and Texas. This finding rests primarily on evidence that blacks who kill white victims are much more likely than any other racial combination of offender and victim (white kills white, black kills black, or white kills black) to be sentenced to death. The authors, William J. Bowers and Glenn L. Pierce, found that the greater risk of blacks being condemned to death when they kill whites persists after one controls for whether or not the crime was a felony murder.[27] Unfortunately, this study suffers from the same defects of almost all other studies in this genre—it tells us nothing about the prior record of the defendant and almost nothing about the exact circumstances of the crime (except whether or not it was a felony murder). As we saw in the Dade County study, these circumstances, when known, permit one to explain differences in outcome in ways having little to do with race; as we saw in Judson's study of California, knowing the prior record (and other facts) about the defendant also reduced the effect of race to a minimum. Since it is relatively rare for blacks to kill whites, one wants especially to know the circumstances surrounding these crimes to see if, as in Dade County, these unusual events have unusual (and unusually heinous) attributes. Bowers and Pierce may have such evidence, though they have not presented it. It is possible that when such case attributes are fully known, bias, perhaps substantial bias, will appear. But as yet, it has not.

Unlike murder cases, the evidence finding racial discrimination in rape cases is quite strong. Kleck's review of the leading studies persuades him that, though these studies are methodologically as crude as are many of the earlier murder studies, it is doubtful that the introduction of facts concerning the prior record of the defendants or the exact circumstances of the offense would eliminate the gross disparity in sentences imposed on whites and blacks, to the disadvantage of the latter. But capital punishment for rape is for all practical purposes a thing of the past. The last men executed for rape died in 1964 (three whites, three blacks). Between then and 1980, only one person was sentenced to death for rape (actually, for "sexual battery") and he was white. It is unlikely there will be many more, if any, such cases. In only two states (Florida and Mississippi) is any sexual offense punishable by death, and in both instances the statutes restrict the penalty to adult males who rape or sexually abuse female children under the age of twelve. In a 1977 decision, the Supreme Court held that the rape of an adult woman was not a sufficiently grave offense to warrant the death penalty.[28] In short, though the evidence on racial bias in rape sentences is strong, it is no longer relevant to a contemporary evaluation of the death penalty.

The fact that the studies of the use of the death penalty in murder cases reveal no strong evidence of racial bias does not mean, of course, that no such bias operates. It may operate but in ways hard to detect, or in some places but not others. At one time, it probably operated with a vengeance in certain parts of the country. Proving this by means of studies of who is given what sentence is feasible, but difficult. As I hope is clear, any effort to discover whether improper considerations, such as race, affect a sentence must first discover the extent to which that sentence can be explained by reference to proper factors, such as the exact nature of the offense and the prior record of the offender.

Another way to approach the matter is to ignore sentencing studies and ask instead whether the rate at which whites and blacks are sentenced to death or executed is the same as the rate at which whites and blacks actually commit murders. We know the latter with some accuracy because the overwhelming majority of all murders are intraracial—blacks killing blacks, whites killing whites. Interracial murder occurs in less than 10 percent of the cases. Therefore, we can assume that by counting murder victims by race we are, in effect, counting murderers by race. Kleck calculated the rate at which blacks and whites were sentenced to death during 1967–1978 and the rate at which they were actually executed for murder for the period 1930–1967. For the modern period (1967–1978, the only period for which race-specific sentencing data are available), blacks were less likely to be sentenced to death for murder than whites. For the longer period (1930–1967), black murders were slightly less likely to result in the execution of blacks than were white murders to result in the execution of whites, though the pattern shifted from year to year.[29]

None of these statistics proves the absence of discrimination. Judges and juries in some places could discriminate sharply against blacks and in other places discriminate in their favor, giving a net effect of zero. That this may have been the case is shown by Kleck's analysis of execution rates by region. From 1930 through 1949, blacks were more likely than whites to be executed in the South and less likely than whites to be executed in the North. During the most recent period (1950–1967), however, these regional differences by and large vanished so that the rates in each region became almost identical. What these studies do suggest is that, like the studies of sentencing decisions, it is hard to find strong evidence of clear, systematic discrimination by race in murder cases, especially in the contemporary period. This is entirely consistent with what we know about sentencing generally, in noncapital as well as capital cases. A recent study by a panel of the National Academy of Sciences concluded that the primary determinants of sentences are the seriousness of the offense and the offender's prior record and that "factors other than racial discrimination in sentencing account for most of the disproportionate representation of blacks in prison."[30]

The last word is not in on these matters, as we have only begun to gather information on capital sentencing under the rules and guidelines in effect since the *Gregg* decision in 1976. In gathering that evidence I hope we will abandon the double standard that has governed so much thinking about the death penalty. We must insist that persons claiming to find racial bias meet the same severe tests of methodological rigor that we demand of persons claiming to find a deterrent effect in capital punishment. At one conference on the death penalty which I attended, studies purporting to show a deterrent effect were subjected to the most searching criticisms; no flaw went undetected or undeplored. That is as it should be. But many of the same people at this conference embraced without a moment's hesitation the flimsiest possible evidence of racial bias in capital cases, even though the methodological sins of almost all these studies were far graver than those to be found in recent studies of deterrence.[31] That is not as it should be.

For better or worse, the Supreme Court of the United States has launched this country on a large and risky experiment, testing whether our most severe—and the only irreversible—penalty can be applied in ways that meet reasonable standards of fairness. The scholarly community ought to evaluate that test by the best possible research that looks closely at the kinds of cases that do and do not lead to capital sentences. Understandably, but unfortunately, most of the past research on discrimination has been done by persons who were determined opponents of the death penalty. Though that is not an unworthy motive, it is one that may lead to carelessness when the most easily obtainable facts seem to support one's darkest suspicions. I have learned that it is precisely when the facts seem to confirm most abundantly one's preconceptions that one ought to dig deeper and work harder.

The Court may also suppose that it has created an opportunity to find out whether the death penalty deters. I doubt that, even with the best efforts, we will learn the answer to that question. I may be wrong, but I suspect that we will never know whether the delayed application of a rare sanction (the death penalty) to behavior we cannot count accurately (heinous first-degree murders) makes a significant difference in the rate of that behavior.

In the meantime, I hope that persons running for public office will stop acting as if we knew the answer to the deterrent effect of capital punishment, or failing that, will at least spend less time talking about the usefulness of a sanction that cannot have an effect on most of the crime we find frightening. If the death penalty is to be an issue, it should be seen as an issue of justice, not of utility. We should debate whether death is the proper and fitting penalty for crimes that we abhor. In our culture, we seem to be uncomfortable about making these arguments; in this reluctance, we implicitly deny our capacity for serious philosophical discourse while exaggerating our capacity for scientific knowledge.

Chapter 11

Heroin

I T HAS BEEN widely believed that much of the increase in predatory crime is the result of heroin addicts supporting their habits; that heroin use has become a middle-class white as well as lower-class black phenomenon of alarming proportions; and that conventional law-enforcement efforts to reduce heroin use have not only failed but may in fact be contributing to the problem by increasing the cost of the drug for the user, leading thereby to the commission of even more crimes and the corruption of even more police officers.* These generally held opinions have led to an intense debate over new policy initiatives to deal with heroin, an argument usually described as one between advocates of a "law-enforcement" policy (which includes shutting off overseas opium supplies and heroin-manufacturing laboratories, arresting more heroin dealers in the United States, and using civil commitment procedures, detoxification centers, and methadone maintenance programs) and partisans of a "decriminalization" policy (which includes legalization of the use or possession of heroin, at least for adults, and distribution of heroin to addicts at low cost, or zero cost, through government-controlled clinics).

The intensity of the debate tends to obscure the fact that most of the widely accepted opinions on heroin use are not supported by much evidence; that the very concept of "addict" is ambiguous and somewhat misleading; and that many of the apparently reasonable assumptions about heroin use and crime—such as the assumption that the legalization of heroin would dramatically reduce the rate of predatory crime, or that intensified law enforcement drives the price of heroin up, or that oral

---

*Original version of this chapter written with Mark H. Moore and I. David Wheat, Jr.

methadone is a universal substitute for heroin, or that heroin use spreads because of the activities of "pushers" who can be identified as such—turn out on closer inspection to be unreasonable, unwarranted, or at least open to more than one interpretation.

"Punitive" versus "Medical" Approaches

MOST IMPORTANT, the current debate has failed to make explicit, or at least to clarify, the philosophical principles underlying the competing positions. Those positions are sometimes described as the "punitive" versus the "medical" approaches, but these labels are of little help. For one thing, they are far from precise: putting an addict in jail is certainly "punitive," but putting him in a treatment program, however benevolent its intentions, may be seen by him as no less "punitive." Shifting an addict from heroin to methadone may be "medical" if he makes the choice voluntarily—but is it so if the alternative to methadone maintenance is a criminal conviction for heroin possession? And while maintaining an addict on heroin (as is done in Great Britain and as has been proposed for the United States) is not "punitive" in any legal sense, neither is it therapeutic in any medical sense. Indeed, there seem to be no forms of therapy that will "cure" addicts in any large numbers of their dependence on heroin. Various forms of intensive psychotherapy and group-based "personality restructuring" may be of great value to certain drug users, but by definition they can reach only very small numbers of persons, and perhaps only for limited periods of time.

But the fundamental problem with these and other labels is that they avoid the central question: does society have only the right to protect itself (or its members) from the harmful acts of heroin users, or does it have in addition the responsibility (and thus the right) to improve the well-being (somehow defined) of heroin users themselves? In one view, the purpose of the law is to insure the maximum amount of liberty for everyone, and an action of one person is properly constrained by society if, and only if, it has harmful consequences for another person. This is the utilitarian conception of the public interest and, when applied to heroin use, it leads such otherwise unlike men as Milton Friedman, Herbert Packer, and Thomas Szasz to oppose the use of criminal sanctions for heroin users. The late Professor Packer, for example, wrote that a desirable aspect of liberalism is that it allows people "to choose their own roads to hell if that is where they want to go."

In another view, however, society has an obligation to enhance the well-being of each of its citizens even with respect to those aspects of their lives that do not directly impinge on other people's lives. In this conception of the public good, all citizens of a society are bound to be affected —indirectly but perhaps profoundly and permanently—if a significant number are permitted to go to hell in their own way. A society is therefore unworthy if it permits, or is indifferent to, any activity that renders its members inhuman or deprives them of their essential (or "natural") capacities to judge, choose, and act. If heroin use is such an activity, then its use should be proscribed. Whether that proscription is enforced by mere punishment or by obligatory therapy is a separate question.

The alternative philosophical principles do not necessarily lead to diametrically opposed policies. A utilitarian might conclude, for example, that heroin use is so destructive of family life that society has an interest in proscribing it (though he is more likely, if experience is any guide, to allow the use of heroin and then deal with its effect on family life by advocating social services to "help problem families"). And a moralist might decide that though heroin should be illegal, any serious effort to enforce that law against users would be so costly in terms of other social values (privacy, freedom, the integrity of officialdom) as not to be worth it, and he thus might allow the level of enforcement to fall to a point just short of that at which the tutelary power of the law would be jeopardized. Still, even if principles do not determine policies uniquely, thinking clearly about the former is essential to making good judgments about the latter. And to think clearly about the former, it is as important to ascertain the effects of heroin on the user as it is to discover the behavior of a user toward society.

The User

THERE IS no single kind of heroin user. Some persons may try it once, find it unpleasant, and never use it again; others may "dabble" with it on occasion but, though they find it pleasurable, will have no trouble stopping; still others may use it on a regular basis but in a way that does not interfere with their work. But some persons, who comprise a large (if unknown) percentage of all those who experiment with heroin, develop a relentless and unmanageable craving for the drug such that their life becomes organized around searching for it, using it, enjoying it, and searching for more. Authorities differ on whether all such persons (whom

I shall call "addicts," though the term is not well defined and its scientific status is questionable) are invariably physiologically dependent on the drug, as evidenced by painful "withdrawal" symptoms that occur whenever they cease using it. Some persons may crave the drug without being dependent, others may be dependent without craving it. We need not resolve these definitional and medical issues, however, to recognize that many (but not all) heroin users are addicts in the popular sense of the term.

No one knows how many users of various kinds there are, at what rate they have been increasing in number, or what happens to them at the end of their "run." That they increased in number during the 1960s is revealed, not only by the testimony of police and narcotics officers, but by figures on deaths attributed to heroin. Between 1967 and 1971, the number of deaths in Los Angeles County attributed to heroin use more than tripled, and although improved diagnostic skills in the coroner's office may account for some of this increase, it does not (in the opinion of the University of Southern California student task force report) account for it all. A Harvard student task force used several techniques to estimate the size of the heroin-user population in Boston, and concluded that there was a tenfold increase in the decade of the 1960s. Why that increase occurred and continued into the 1970s is a matter about which one can only speculate. The USC group estimated that there were at least fifty thousand addicts in Los Angeles; the Harvard group estimated that there were six thousand in Boston; various sources conventionally refer (with what accuracy we do not know) to the "hundred thousand" addicts in New York.[1]

No one has proposed a fully satisfactory theory to explain the apparent increase in addiction. There are at least four speculative possibilities, some or all of which may be correct. The rise in real incomes during the prosperity of the 1960s may simply have made possible the purchase of more heroin as it made possible the purchase of more automobiles or color television sets. The cult of personal liberation among the young may have led to greater experimentation with heroin as it led to greater freedom in dress and manners and the development of a rock music culture. The war in Vietnam may have both loosened social constraints and given large numbers of young soldiers easy access to heroin supplies and ample incentive (the boredom, fears, and demoralization caused by the war) to dabble in the drug. Finally, the continued disintegration of the lower-income, especially black, family living in the central city may have heightened the importance of street peer groups to the individual, and thus (in ways to be discussed later in this chapter) placed him in a social environment highly conducive to heroin experimentation. There are, in short, ample reasons to suppose (though few facts to show) that important changes in both the supply of and demand for heroin occurred during the 1960s.

Heavy users of heroin, according to their own testimony, tend to be utterly preoccupied with finding and consuming the drug. Given an unlimited supply (that is, given heroin at zero cost), an addict will "shoot up" three to five times a day. Given the price of heroin on the black market, some addicts may be able to shoot up only once or twice a day. The sensations associated with heroin use by most novice addicts are generally the same: keen anticipation of the fix, the "rush" when the heroin begins to work in the bloodstream, the euphoric "high," the drowsy or "nodding" stage as the "high" wears off, and then the beginnings of the discomfort caused by the absence of heroin. For the veteran addict the "high" may no longer be attainable, except perhaps at the risk of a lethal overdose. For him, the sensations induced by heroin have mainly to do with anesthetizing himself against withdrawal pain—and perhaps against most other feelings as well—together with a ritualistic preoccupation with the needle and the act of injection.

The addict is intensely present-oriented. Though "dabblers" or other episodic users may save heroin for a weekend fix, the addict can rarely save any at all. Some, for example, report that they would like to arise in the morning with enough heroin for a "wake-up" fix, but almost none have the self-control to go to sleep at night leaving unused heroin behind. Others report getting enough heroin to last them for a week, only to shoot it all the first day. How many addicts living this way can manage a reasonably normal family and work life is not known, but clearly many cannot. Some become heroin dealers in order to earn money, but a regular heavy user seldom has the self-control to be successful at this enterprise for long. Addicts turned dealers frequently report a sharp increase in their heroin use as they consume much of their sales inventory.

It is this craving for the drug, and the psychological states induced by its use, that are the chief consequences of addiction; they are also the most important consequences about which one must ultimately have a moral or political view, whatever the secondary effects of addiction produced by current public policy. At the same time, one should not suppose that all of these secondary effects can be eliminated by changes in policy. For example, while there are apparently no specific pathologies (serious illnesses or physiological deterioration) that are known to result from heroin use per se, the addict does run the risk of infections caused by the use of unsterile needles, poisoning as a result of shooting an overdose (or a manageable dose that has been cut with harmful products), and thrombosed veins resulting from repeated injections.[2] Some of these risks could be reduced if heroin were legally available in clinics operated by physicians, but they could not be eliminated unless literally everyone wishing heroin were given it in whatever dosage, short of lethal, he wished. In Great Britain, where pure heroin is legally available at low prices, addicts still have medical problems arising out of their use of the drug—principally unsterile self-injections, involuntary overdoses, and voluntary overdoses (that is, willingly injecting more than they should in hopes of obtaining a new "high"). If, as will be discussed later, heroin were injected under a doctor's supervision (as it is not in England), the risk of sepsis and of overdoses would be sharply reduced, but at the cost of making the public heroin clinic less attractive to addicts who wish to consume not merely a maintenance dose but a euphoria-producing (and therefore risky) one, and to do so in familiar, private settings rather than in forbidding public ones.

Why Heroin?

NO GENERALLY accepted theory supported by well-established facts exists to explain why only some persons become addicts. It is easy to make a list of factors that increase (statistically, at least) the risk of addiction: black males living in low-income neighborhoods, coming from broken or rejecting families, and involved in "street life" have much higher chances of addiction than upper-middle-class whites in stable families and "normal" occupations. But some members of the latter category do become addicted, and many members of the former category do not; why this should be the case, no one is sure. It is easy to argue that heroin use occurs only among people who have serious problems (and thus to argue that the way to end addiction is to solve the underlying problems), but in fact many heavy users seem to have no major problems at all. Isidor Chein and his co-workers in their leading study of addiction in New York found that between one-quarter and one-third of addicts seemed to have no problems for which heroin use was a compensation.[3]

Though we cannot predict with much confidence who will and who will not become an addict, we can explain why heroin is used and how its use spreads. The simple fact is that heroin use is intensely pleasurable, for many people more pleasurable than anything else they might do. Heroin users will have experimented with many other drugs, and when heroin is hard to find they may return to them or to alcohol, but for the vast majority of users heroin remains the drug of choice. The nature of the pleasure will vary from person to person, or, perhaps, the interpretive description of that pleasure will vary, but the desire for it remains the governing passion of the addicts' lives. All of us enjoy pleasure; an addict is a person who has found the supreme pleasure and the means to make that pleasure recur.

This fact helps explain why "curing" addiction is so difficult (virtually impossible for many addicts) and how new addicts are recruited. Addicts sent to state or federal hospitals to be detoxified (that is, to be withdrawn from heroin use) almost invariably return to such use after their release, simply because using it is so much more pleasurable than not using it, regardless of cost. Many addicts, probably a majority, resist and resent oral methadone maintenance because methadone, though it can prevent withdrawal pains, does not, when taken orally, supply them with the euphoric "high" they associate with heroin. (Intravenous use of methadone will produce a "high" comparable to that of heroin. The oral use of methadone is seen by addicts as a way to avoid the pain of heroin withdrawal but not as an alternative source of a "high.") Persons willingly on methadone tend to be older addicts who are "burned out," physically and mentally run down by the burdens of maintaining a heroin habit. A younger addict still enjoying his "run" (which may last five or ten years) will be less inclined to shift to methadone.

The "Contagion" Model

WHEN ASKED how they got started on heroin, addicts almost universally give the same answer: they were offered some by a friend. They tried it, often in a group setting, and they liked it. Although not every person who tries it will like it, and not every person who likes it will become addicted to it, a substantial fraction (perhaps a quarter) of first users become regular and heavy users. Heroin use spreads through peer-group contacts, and those peer groups most vulnerable to experimenting with it are those that include a person who himself has recently tried it and whose enthusiasm for it is contagious. In fact, so common is this process that many observers use the word "contagious" or "contagion" deliberately—the spread of heroin use is in the nature of an epidemic in which a "carrier" (a recent and enthusiastic convert to heroin) "infects" a population with whom he is in close contact.

A study in Chicago revealed in some detail how this process of infection occurs. Patrick H. Hughes and Gail A. Crawford found that a major heroin "epidemic" occurred in Chicago after World War II, reached a peak in 1949, was followed by a decline in the number of new cases of addiction during the 1950s, with signs of a new epidemic appearing in the early 1960s.[4] They studied closely eleven neighborhood-sized epidemics that they were able to identify in the late 1960s, each producing fifty or more new addicts. In the great majority of cases, not only was the new user turned on by a friend, but the friend was himself a novice user still exhilarated by the thrill of a "high." Both recruit and initiator tended to be members of a small group that had already experimented heavily with many drugs and with alcohol. These original friendship groups broke up as the heavy users formed new associations in order to maintain their habits. Strikingly, the new user usually does not seek out heroin the first time he uses it, but rather begins to use it almost fortuitously, by the accident of personal contact in a polydrug subculture. A majority of the members of these groups usually try heroin after it is introduced by one of them, though not all of these become addicted.

Such a theory explains the very rapid rates of increase in a city such as Boston. The number of new users will be some exponential function of the number of initial users. Obviously, this geometric growth rate would soon, if not checked by other factors, make addicts of us all. Since we all do not become addicts, other factors must be at work, though their nature is not well understood. They may include "natural immunity" (some of us may find heroin unpleasant), breaks in the chain of contagion (caused by the absence of any personal linkages between peer groups using heroin and peer groups that are not), and the greater difficulty in some communities of finding a supply of heroin. Perhaps most important, the analogy between heroin use and disease is imperfect: we do not choose to contract smallpox from a friend, but we do choose to use heroin offered by a friend.

The Myth of the "Pusher"

IF HEROIN use is something we choose, then the moral and empirical judgments one makes about heroin become important. If a person thinks heroin use wrong, if he believes that heroin use can cause a serious pathology, then, other things being equal, he will be less likely to use it than if he makes the opposite judgments. Chein found that the belief that heroin use was wrong was a major reason given by heroin "dabblers" for not continuing in its use. The extent to which belief in the wrongness of heroin use depends on its being illegal is unknown, but it is interesting to note that many addicts tend to be strongly opposed to legalizing heroin.

The peer-group/contagion model also helps explain why the fastest increase in heroin use has been among young people, with the result that the average age of known addicts has fallen sharply in the last few years. In Boston the Harvard student group found that one-quarter of heroin users seeking help from a public agency were under the age of eighteen, and 80 percent were under twenty-five. A study done at American University found that the average age at which identifiable addicts in Washington, D.C., began using heroin was under nineteen. Though stories of youngsters under fifteen becoming addicts are commonplace, most studies place the beginning of heavy use between the ages of seventeen and nineteen. It is persons in this age group, of course, who are most exposed to the contagion: they are intensely involved in peer groups; many have begun to become part of "street society" because they either dropped out of or graduated from schools; and they are most likely to suffer from boredom and a desire "to prove themselves." It is claimed that many of those who become serious addicts "mature out" of their heroin use sometime in their thirties, in much the same way that many juvenile delinquents spontaneously cease committing criminal acts when they get older. Unfortunately, not much is known about "maturing out," and it is even possible that it is a less common cause of ending heroin use than death or imprisonment.

If this view of the spread of addiction is correct, then it is pointless to explain heroin use as something that "pushers" inflict on unsuspecting youth. The popular conception of a stranger in a dirty trenchcoat hanging around schoolyards and corrupting innocent children is largely myth— indeed, given what we know about addiction, it would almost have to be myth. No dealer in heroin is likely to risk doing business with strangers. The chances of apprehension are too great and the profits from dealing with friends too substantial to make missionary work among unknown "straights" worthwhile. And the novice user is far more likely to take the advice of a friend, or to respond to the blandishments of a peer group, than to take an unfamiliar product from an anonymous pusher.

An important implication of the peer-group/contagion model is that programs designed to treat or control established addicts may have little effect on the mechanism whereby heroin use spreads. Users tend to be "infectious" only early in their heroin careers (later, all their friends are addicts and the life style seems less glamorous), and at this stage they are not likely to volunteer for treatment or to come to the attention of police authorities. In the Chicago study, for example, Hughes and Crawford found that police efforts directed at addiction were intensified only after the peak of the epidemic had passed, and though arrests increased sharply, they were principally of heavily addicted regular users, not infectious users. No matter whether one favors a medical or a law-enforcement approach to heroin, the optimum strategy depends crucially on whether one's objective is to "treat" existing addicts or to prevent the recruitment of new ones.

Crime and Heroin

THE AMOUNT of crime committed by addicts is no doubt large, but exactly how large is a matter of conjecture. And most important, the amount of addict crime undertaken solely to support the habit, and thus the amount by which crime would decrease if the price of heroin fell to zero, is unknown. Estimates of the proportion of all property crime committed by addicts range from 25 to 67 percent. Whatever the true fraction, there is no reason to assume that property crimes would decline by that fraction if heroin became free. Some addicts are criminals before they are addicts and would remain criminals if their addiction, like their air and water, cost them virtually nothing. Furthermore, some addicts who steal to support their habit come to regard crime as more profitable than normal employment. They would probably continue to steal to provide themselves with an income even after they no longer needed to use part of that income to buy heroin.

Just as it is wrong to suppose that an unwitting youth has heroin "pushed" on him, so also is it wrong to suppose that these youth only then turn to crime to support their habit. Various studies of known addicts have shown that between half and three-quarters were known to be delinquent before turning to drugs. In a random sample of adult black males studied in St. Louis (14 percent of whom turned out to have records for using or selling narcotics), 60 percent of those who tried heroin and 73 percent of those who became addicted to it had previously acquired a police record. Put another way, one-quarter of the delinquents, but only 4 percent of the nondelinquents, became heroin addicts.[5]

That addicts are recruited disproportionately from the ranks of those who already have a criminal history may be a relatively recent phenomenon. The history of heroin use in New York City compiled by Edward Preble and John J. Casey, Jr., suggests that in the period before 1951 heroin use grew slowly and often occurred through "snorting" (inhaling the powder) rather than "mainlining" (injecting liquefied heroin into a vein).[6] The heroin used was of high quality and low cost, and its consumption took place in social settings in which many users were not criminals but rather entertainers, musicians, and so on. The heroin epidemic that began around 1951 was caused by the new popularity of the drug among younger people on the streets, especially street gang members looking for a new "high." (Indeed, one theory of the breakup of those gangs romanticized in *West Side Story* is that heroin use became a status symbol, such that the young man "nodding" on the corner or hustling and dealing in dope, rather than the fighter and the leader of gang wars, became the figure to be emulated. A group of heavy addicts, each of whom is preoccupied with his own "high," will soon find collective action—and thus gang life—all but impossible.) Mainlining became commonplace, increased demand led to a rise in price and decline in quality of the available heroin, and the level of heroin-connected crime increased.

Some supportive evidence for the increase in recruitment of addicts from among the ranks of the criminal is found in a study of white male Kentucky addicts done by John A. O'Donnell.[7] He traced the careers of 266 such persons who had been admitted to the U.S. Public Health Service Hospital in Lexington from its opening in 1935. The earlier the year and the younger the age in which the person first became addicted, the more likely he was to have committed criminal acts before addiction. The proportion of addicts with criminal records, and perhaps the rate of increase of those with such records, would probably be greater among a more typical population of addicts, for example, among urban blacks.

Once addicted, however, persons are likely to commit more crimes than they would have had they not become addicted, sometimes astonishingly more. A study of 243 male addicts in Baltimore, randomly selected from a list of all addicts known to the police, revealed that, according to the addicts' own testimony, the frequency with which they committed crimes was six times higher during those periods when they were "on a run" (that is, using heroin regularly) than it was when they were not heavy users. Another study of addicts in the Denver jail found that their self-reported crime rates were five times higher when addicted than before being addicted. In Miami, 239 male addicts admitted to interviewers having committed an average of 337 offenses each per year. Finally, research among addicts in Philadelphia, Phoenix, San Antonio, and Washington, D.C., produced estimates of crime quite similar to those reported above —an average of 312 crimes per year per addict.[8] Though most addict crimes involved the selling of drugs, a large proportion involved burglary and robbery. For example, among the Miami addicts, half admitted to having committed at least one robbery that year and, of those offenders, the average number of robberies was nearly 30 per year.

The amount of property taken by addicts is large, but probably not as large as some of the more popular estimates would have us believe. Max Singer has shown that those who make these estimates (usually running into the billions of dollars per year in New York City alone) fail to reconcile their figures with the total amount of property known or suspected to be stolen. He estimated that no more than $500 million a year is lost to both addicted and nonaddicted burglars, shoplifters, pickpockets, robbers, and assorted thieves in New York. If all of that were taken by addicts (which of course it isn't) and if there were one hundred thousand addicts in the city, then the average addict would be stealing about $5,000 worth of goods a year—not a vast sum. Even the more conservative figure of sixty thousand addicts would raise the maximum average theft loss per addict to only $8,000.[9]

Despite the fact that many addicts were criminals before addiction and would remain criminals even if they ended their addiction, and despite the fact that the theft losses to addicts are considerably exaggerated, there is little doubt that addiction produces a significant increase in criminality of two kinds: stealing from innocent victims and selling heroin illegally to willing consumers. More accurately, the heroin black market provides incentives for at least two kinds of antisocial acts: theft (with its attendant fear) and spreading the use of heroin further.

Heroin and Law Enforcement

CRITICS of the "punitive" mode of attacking heroin distribution argue that law enforcement has not only failed to protect society against these social costs, it has increased those costs by driving up the price of heroin and thus the amount of criminality necessary to support heroin habits. If by this they mean that law enforcement has "failed" because it has not reduced the heroin traffic to zero—and anything short of this will increase the price of heroin—then of course the statement is true. It would be equally true, and equally misleading, to say that most medical approaches have "failed" because the vast majority of persons who undergo voluntary treatment at Lexington or other hospitals return to heroin use when they are released.

Apart from methadone maintenance, which deserves separate discussion, existing therapeutic methods for treating heroin addiction are extremely expensive and have low success rates. Various investigators have found a relapse rate for addicts discharged from hospitals after having undergone treatment ranging between 90 and 95 percent. Over time, a

certain fraction of those treated will begin to become permanently absti-
nent (Dr. George Vaillant estimates it at about 2 percent a year), but most
of those do not do so voluntarily.[10] The Kentucky males studied by
O'Donnell displayed relatively high rates of abstinence after release from
the hospital, but this was due mostly to the fact that heroin itself became
more or less unavailable in Kentucky. The New York addicts studied by
Vaillant who had been released from the same hospital showed much
lower rates of abstinence, in part because heroin was easy to find in New
York; those who did abstain tended to be those placed under some form
of compulsory community supervision, such as intensive parole. And even
these did not become entirely "clean"—typically they found a substitute
for heroin and most often became alcoholics.

The fact that medical approaches do not "cure" addiction, especially
if the addict must volunteer for them, need not trouble the critics of the
law-enforcement approach if they believe that only the tangible social cost
of addiction (crime) and not addiction itself is a problem, or if they
concede that addiction is a problem but think it wrong for addicts to be
compelled to obtain help.

But if law enforcement at present fails to prevent the "external" costs
of addiction, or even increases those costs, this will also remain true under
any likely alternative public policy, unless one is willing to support complete legalization of heroin for all who wish it. Yet no advocate of "decriminalizing" heroin with whom I am familiar supports total legalization.
Most favor some version of the British system, by which heroin is dis-
pensed at low cost in government-controlled clinics to known addicts in
order to maintain them in their habit. Almost no one seems to favor
allowing any drugstore to sell, or any doctor to prescribe, heroin to anybody who wants it.

The reason for this reluctance is rarely made explicit. Presumably it is
either political expediency (designed to make the British system more
palatable to a skeptical American public) or an unspoken moral reserva-
tion about the desirability of heroin use per se, apart from its tangible
social cost. I suspect that the chief reason is the latter: one's moral
sensibilities are indeed shocked by the prospect of young children buying
heroin at the drugstore the same way they now buy candy. And if one finds
that scene wrong or distasteful, then one should also find the prospect of
an adult nonuser having cheap access to heroin wrong or distasteful, unless
one is willing to make a radical (and on medical grounds, hard to defend)
distinction between what is good for a person under the age of (say)
eighteen and what is good for a person over that age.

The total decriminalization of heroin would lead, all evidence suggests,
to a sharp increase in its use. Indeed, precisely because of such an increase,

the British in 1968 abandoned the practice of allowing physicians to prescribe heroin to anyone they wished.

The British System

UNDER post-1968 British policy, the sale of heroin to nonusers or to novice users is illegal. In clinics authorized to prescribe heroin, the doctor must not do so unless he is certain the patient is addicted and truly needs the drug, and he should then prescribe conservatively. The aim is to maintain the patient with enough heroin to be free of withdrawal pains, but not enough so that he will have any surplus to sell or give to others.

The result is that a black market in heroin still exists in Britain. As Griffith Edwards (of the Addiction Research Unit, Institute of Psychiatry, London) has pointed out, the British system "in fact cuts down but in no way eliminates the potential population of black-market customers."[11] That market, the size of which is unknown but in his view is not negligible, is made up of "customers" of the clinic system who want larger doses in order to get a "high," addicts who for various reasons do not wish to register with the government, and would-be novice users who would like to try heroin.

If this is a problem in Britain, which has only two thousand or so addicts, it would be a much greater problem in the United States, where there are several hundred times as many addicts, a large fraction of whom are quite young. Those willing to be maintained on low dosages in a government clinic are probably those who fear withdrawal pains more than they cherish the heroin "high"; in short, they are likely to be addicts who have passed beyond the stage of missionary zeal about an exciting new thrill. They may be similar to those addicts in the United States who volunteer for methadone maintenance. (This is all supposition, for I know of no detailed comparative studies of British and American addicts. I think it a reasonable supposition, however.) It is possible, in short, that the number of addict-zealots in the United States would be large enough to continue the spread of heroin to new users and to maintain an active black market, even if the United States were to adopt some version of the British clinic method.

It is important to bear in mind that the residual black market need not be large in order to supply novice users and thus continue the infection-recruitment process. Even if the vast majority of confirmed addicts registered to receive government heroin (which is unlikely, unless the govern-

ment were willing to supply euphoria-producing rather than simply maintenance doses), the increase in the number of new addicts among susceptible groups could continue to be quite rapid and to be supplied out of a
black market of modest proportions.

Furthermore, there is some reason to believe that British and American
addicts are sufficiently different so that an American clinic system would
not attract as large a proportion of the total addict population as have the
British clinics. A member of the Addiction Research Institute in London
is quoted by Edgar May as observing that the typical British addict is likely
to be a "middle-class drop-out" rather than a lower-class "oblivion-
seeker."[12] The contemporary British addict, in short, may be more similar
to the American addict before 1920 (when the use of opiates was increasing in the middle classes) than to the American addict of today. The
difference, if correct, may have profound consequences for the efficacy of
control techniques. The use of opiates among middle-class Americans
dropped sharply after they were made illegal and law enforcement got
underway, just as the use of heroin by the British has apparently stabilized
since heroin was made illegal except through licensed clinics.

This possibility is worth bearing in mind when we interpret accounts
of the British system. The success of the plan (that is, the apparent
stabilization in the number of addicts and the absence of addict-related
crime) is in part the result of imposing on a middle-class addict population
stricter controls than had once existed—and doing so after the rather easy
availability of heroin had resulted in a *fortyfold increase* in the number
of known addicts during the preceding fifteen years. If the size of the
American addict population grew rapidly when possession of heroin was
already illegal, it is a bit hard to understand what there is in either the
British experience or our own that would lead one to conclude that the
number of addicts here would be stabilized or reduced if heroin were
made easier to get. At best, decriminalization would reduce somewhat the
size of the black market (while simultaneously lowering prices in that
market) and reduce by an unknown but probably significant fraction the
amount of crime committed by those addicts willing to avail themselves
of the maintenance doses to be obtained at government clinics.

The Effectiveness of Law Enforcement

UNDER ANY conceivable American variant of the British system, then,
a law-enforcement strategy would remain an important component of

government policy. Rather than simply rejecting law enforcement as "punitive" (and therefore "medieval," "barbarian," "counterproductive," or whatever), one ought to consider what it might accomplish under various circumstances.

The assumption that law enforcement has no influence on the size of the addict population but does have an effect on the price of heroin (and thus on crime committed to meet that higher price) rests chiefly on the evidence that the majority of known addicts have been arrested at least once; that during his life expectancy, any addict is virtually certain to be arrested; and that, despite this, the addict returns to his habit and to the criminal life needed to sustain it. These facts are essentially correct. The difficulty lies in equating "law enforcement" with "arrest."

Thousands of addicts are arrested every year; a very large proportion are simply returned to the street—by the police, who wish to use them as informants, or by judges who wish to place them on probation or under suspended sentences because they believe (rightly) that a prison term will not cause their cure or rehabilitation. Only a few addicts are singled out for very severe punishment. We do not know for how many addicts arrest is simply a revolving door. In Boston, however, David Wheat did a careful study of the relationship between the level of law enforcement, defined as the "expected costs" of an arrest to the user, and the number of addicts in the city. By "expected costs," Wheat meant the probability of being arrested multiplied by the probability of being sentenced to prison and the length of the average prison sentence. Though his numerical estimates were complex and open to criticism, the general relationship between the number of heroin users and the expected "costs" to the addict of law enforcement was quite striking—the "costs" declined sharply between 1961 and 1970, while the estimated number of addicts in Boston increased about tenfold. Furthermore, the largest increases in the number of addicts tended to follow years in which the certainty and severity of law enforcement were the lowest.[13]

More specifically: (1) from 1961 to 1965, the estimated proportion of users arrested by the police declined (it started to increase again in 1966); (2) the chances that an arrested user would be sentenced to jail declined from better than one in two in 1960 to only one in ten in 1970; and (3) the length of the average sentence imposed fell from about twenty-three months in 1961 to fewer than fifteen months in 1969, though there were some intervening ups and downs. By 1970, the chance of a heroin addict being sent to jail during any given year was rather remote. We do not know whether similar changes occurred in other cities, though given the cause of the changes—the growing (and erroneous) view among legislators and judges that addicts should be referred to psychiatrists for (nonexistent) "help"—we suspect that many cities, influenced by the same sentiments, may have experienced the same changes. In Chicago, for example, Hughes and his colleagues have shown that the number of arrests of addicts, and the average sentence given to those convicted, rose dramatically during or just after the heroin epidemic of 1947–1950, but by 1955 the length of sentence had begun to fall again, and by 1960 it was almost down to the prewar level.[14]

If there is a relationship between law enforcement and heroin use, it may result from one or both of two processes. An increase in legal penalties may deter the novice user from further use, or it may deter the confirmed addict-dealer (or if he is jailed, prevent him entirely) from selling to a potential user. Lessening the "costs" of the penalty may either embolden the novice users and potential users, or improve their access to a supplier, or both.

There is some clinical evidence that both processes are in fact at work. Robert Schasre's study of forty Mexican-American heroin users who had stopped shooting heroin revealed that over half (twenty-two) did so involuntarily after they had lost their source of supply (their dealer had been arrested or had lost his source, or the user himself had moved to another community where he could find no dealer). Of the remaining eighteen who stopped "voluntarily," most did so in response to some social or institutional pressure; in a third of these cases, that pressure was having been arrested or having a friend who was arrested on a narcotics charge.[15]

Indeed, one could as easily make the argument that law enforcement has not even been tried as the argument that it has been tried and failed. Before making it, please be reassured that such an argument does not bespeak an illusion that prison sentences "cure" addiction nor indicate a desire to "wreak vengeance" on the addict. The same argument could be made if one substituted for "sentences to prison," sentences to Synanon, Daytop, methadone maintenance, or expensive psychiatric clinics. The central point is that only a small proportion of heroin addicts will voluntarily seek and remain in any form of treatment, care, or confinement—unless that care involves free dispensation of heroin itself.

One can imagine a variety of law-enforcement strategies that would have a powerful effect on the number of addicts on the street, and thus on the number of street crimes they might commit and other harm they might do to others and themselves. One could arrest every known addict and send him to a "heroin quarantine center" with comfortable accommodations and intensive care programs. Or one could arrest every known addict and send him back onto the street under a "pledge" system requiring him to submit to frequent urine tests which, if omitted or failed, would then lead to confinement in either center or jail.

American society does not do these things for a number of reasons. One is that, despite popular talk, we did not really take the problem that seriously—or at least did not until white middle-class suburbanites began to suffer from a problem only ghetto blacks once endured. Another is that we think that detaining addicts for the mere fact of addiction is violative of their civil rights. (It is an interesting question. We quarantine people with smallpox without thinking that their rights are violated. The similarities as well as the differences are worth some public debate.) Finally, we do not do these things because we labor under the misapprehension that law enforcement should concentrate on the "pushers" and the "big connections" and not on the innocent user.

The last reason may be the weakest of all, even if among tough-sounding politicians it is the most common. In the first place, the "pusher" is largely a myth, or more accurately, he is simply the addict playing one of his roles. And the "big connections" and "top dealers," who indeed exist and who generally are not users, are in many ways the least important part of the heroin market system, because they are the most easily replaced. A new "connection" arises for every one put out of business. The amount of heroin seized by federal agents is only a fraction of what is imported.

This last fact has led many persons in and out of government to speak critically of the government's effort to eliminate the growing of opium poppies in such places as Turkey and Mexico. There is not much doubt that the present American heroin market can be supplied by alternative, and harder to control, poppy fields in Southeast Asia and elsewhere. One study suggests that the entire estimated American consumption of heroin would require fewer than ten square miles of poppy fields. There may be compelling political reasons, however, for pressing the crop eradication program. It is hard to imagine a president launching a serious effort to constrain heroin users or heroin dealers if he were to ignore the foreign manufacture and importation of heroin. Indeed, he would run the risk of being accused not only of ignoring foreign producers, but perhaps even of actively helping them wage what some would no doubt call "chemical warfare" against America's ghetto poor. Furthermore, elimination of overseas poppy crops was in fact associated with a sharp decline in the amount of illicit morphine base moving through the trafficking networks of Europe and Mexico. Intelligence reports from various cities indicated that heroin manufacturers were experiencing great difficulty in acquiring their raw materials.

Closing down the Turkish fields and French laboratories contributed in the early 1970s to a marked shortage of heroin at the retail level on the streets of our large eastern cities. Prices rose and quality decreased sharply.

By 1973, the price of a bag of heroin had doubled over what it was in the late 1960s, and what one could purchase for the new, higher price was often no more than 2 or 3 percent pure—so weak that regular users of it could often be rather easily detoxified.

At the same time, heroin usage was declining. All the measures used to estimate heroin consumption were down or had leveled off: the number of heroin overdose deaths, the percentage of arrested persons in Washington, D.C., found to have heroin traces in their urine, the rate of serum hepatitis, and the number of persons seeking admission to methadone clinics.

This drop in heroin use, which by 1974 was widely reported by a number of independent sources, cannot be ascribed entirely to law-enforcement pressure or to treatment programs. There had been a substantial element of fad and novelty in the heroin experimentation in the 1960s. The havoc wreaked on the lives of young persons was readily seen by the next generation, and many decided that what once was thought fun was in fact a catastrophe. Many militant black leaders began associating drugs with oppression by the white community, thereby providing their followers with ideological as well as personal reasons for staying clean. Many poor and working-class blacks, terrified of the addict, began supporting punitive countermeasures. But law enforcement and the availability of a variety of treatment programs surely played a role in this decline. The former literally priced heroin out of the market for many users, while the latter provided an alternative way of coping with drug dependence. In time, the scarcity of heroin from France and Turkey was partially offset by the increased importation of heroin manufactured in Mexico. Then, a crop eradication program was begun in Mexico, and again supplies fell and prices rose.

To understand why that happened, one must consider the heroin delivery system at the street level and how it reacts to changes in price and demand.

Containing the Contagion

THE NOVICE or would-be heroin user is quite vulnerable to changes, even small ones, in the availability of heroin. For one thing, a person who has not yet become a heavy user will not conduct an intensive search for a supply. Some studies have suggested that a "dabbler" may use heroin if it is immediately available, but will not use it if it requires two, three, or four hours of searching. Extending the search time for novices may discourage or reduce the frequency of their use of heroin. In addition, a dealer is reluctant to sell to persons with whom he is not closely acquainted for fear of detection and apprehension by the police. When police surveillance is intensified, the dealer becomes more cautious about those with whom he does business. A casual user or distant acquaintance represents a threat to the dealer when police activity is high; when such activity is low, the casual or new customer is more attractive. Heroin customers can be thought of as a "queue" with the heaviest users at the head of the line and the casual ones at the end; how far down the queue the dealer will do business depends on the perceived level of risk associated with each additional customer, and that in turn depends on how strongly "the heat is on."

The price of heroin to the user will be affected by law enforcement in different ways, depending on the focus of the pressure. No one has the data with which to construct anything but a highly conjectural model of the heroin market; at the same time, there is little reason for asserting that the only effect of law enforcement on the heroin market is to drive up the price of the product.

Enforcement aimed at the sources of supply may well drive up the price. The price of a "bag" on the street has risen steeply since the early 1950s, and simultaneously the quality of the product has declined (which means that the real price increase is even higher than the nominal one). This was the result of a vast increase in demand (the heroin "epidemic" of the 1950s and 1960s) coupled with the increase in risks associated with dealing in the product. The long-term effect of law-enforcement pressures on large-scale dealers is probably to force up the price of heroin by either increasing the cash price, decreasing the quality of the product, or requiring dealers to discriminate among their customers in order to avoid risky sales. But in the short term, antidealer law enforcement probably affects access (finding a "connection") more than price.

Suppose that law enforcement were directed at the user and the street-level dealer rather than the top supplier. Taking user-dealers off the streets in large numbers would tend to reduce the demand for, and thus the price of, heroin. Furthermore, with many heavy customers gone, some dealers would have to accept the risks of doing business with novice users who, having smaller habits or no real habits at all, would consume fewer bags per capita and pay lower prices. (Law enforcement aimed merely at known and regular users would not result in the apprehension of many novice users, however, and thus would not take off the streets a large fraction of the sources of heroin "infection.") Suppose, finally, that coupled with law enforcement aimed at known user-dealers there was a selective strategy of identifying and restraining the agents of contagion. This was tried in Chicago on an experimental basis by Hughes and Crawford with promising though not conclusive results. On spotting a neighborhood epidemic, they intervened by seeking quickly to identify the friends and fellow users of an addict. They found in this case that one addict led them to fourteen other addicts and, most important, to seven persons experimenting with heroin. The doctors were able to involve eleven of the fourteen addicts and five of the seven experimenters in a treatment program; the remainder of the experimenters apparently discontinued heroin use, perhaps because the social structure in which their drug use took place was disrupted.[16]

There is, of course, an alternative way to get many confirmed addicts out of the heroin black market, and that is to offer them heroin legally at nominal prices. A black market would still exist for novice users, unregistered regular users, and registered regular users who wish to supplement their government-supplied maintenance dose with an additional dose that would produce a "high." Furthermore, this black market would be in many ways more attractive to the euphoria-seeking user because, due to competition from government suppliers, prices in it would be lower than the price in the existing market. Under this system, the government-maintained users would remain on the street and some fraction of them would continue to serve as contagion agents, thus causing the size of the addict population to continue to grow. Whether it would grow as fast as it has in the past, no one can say. There is little evidence of any rapid growth in England, but as pointed out above, this may be due to the fact that British addicts are different from American ones and the illegal supply of heroin is much smaller there than it is here. Indeed, any estimate of the future size of the addict population under any set of legal constraints is almost meaningless. We simply do not know how many persons are susceptible to heroin use if exposed to it nor what fraction of the population that is at risk is now using heroin.

Methadone Maintenance

METHADONE is an addictive synthetic opiate that has become the basis of the single most important heroin treatment program in the United States. Although methadone itself is addictive (after regular use, withdrawal produces pain), it has advantages over heroin: it may be taken orally; it produces no "high" if used orally; in large doses it seems to "block" the euphoric effect of heroin and prevent the craving for heroin; its effects last for about twenty-four hours (as opposed to about six hours for heroin); and it has no significant harmful side effects. If methadone is injected (as is often the case in Britain), it can produce a "high" and a risk of a harmful overdose. And if taken orally in small dosages, methadone will not block the high that results from injecting heroin, though it may continue to suppress the craving for heroin. Because it will produce a "high" when injected, a black market in methadone has developed and deaths from overdosage have been reported.

There are a number of controversies about the proper use of methadone and indeed about the ethics of using it at all. Doctors disagree over whether the addict should get the large "blockage" dose or only the small "anticraving" dose, over whether the methadone patient should be required to accept various ancillary services (for example, psychiatric help, job counseling), and over whether efforts can or should be made to withdraw the patient from methadone. Others argue over the morality of feeding an addiction and, inevitably, running the risk of addicting some persons who were not addicted when they entered the program. For this reason, most methadone clinics screen candidates carefully to insure that only confirmed heroin users are admitted; this means that young persons tend to be excluded.

Evaluations that have been made of methadone so far generally term it a success. By "success" is meant that the patients tend to stay in the program, those who stay in the program tend to become employable, and those who stay in the program do not return to regular use of heroin (though some may experiment with it from time to time). The evidence as to whether persons on methadone abstain from criminality is not as clear. Dr. Frances Gearing of Columbia University, who headed the largest evaluation program, found that the number of arrests and incarcerations of persons who entered a methadone program fell dramatically.[17] A study in the Bedford-Stuyvesant area of Brooklyn, on the other hand, found some evidence that many successful methadone patients remain employed in criminal occupations (for example, shoplifters, prostitutes), not only because that is the only trade they know, but also because, once they are freed of the need for heroin, that trade becomes even more profitable than before.[18]

The central problem with methadone maintenance, however, is beyond dispute. So long as it remains a voluntary program, methadone is only attractive to those addicts who are tired of the life style of the addict, who no longer cherish the heroin "high" to the exclusion of all else, and who are otherwise "burned out." It is for this reason that the average methadone patient is between thirty and thirty-five years of age, while the average heroin addict is much younger. The typical methadone patient has been a heroin addict for ten to fifteen years and now finds methadone a more attractive choice than heroin. This means that the number of addicts who can be helped by a voluntary methadone program may be no more than one-third or one-half of the total addict population. And most important, it means that voluntary methadone maintenance holds little attraction for the kind of addict who is a contagion agent—young, excited by the heroin "high," and eager to convert his "straight" friends to its use.

Other forms of chemical treatment have been developed for heroin addiction. "Antagonists" that prevent subsequently injected opiates from having any effect and that produce painful withdrawal symptoms in persons who have previously injected heroin exist and are being improved. But since they do not produce a "high," and in addition do not reduce the craving for heroin, relatively few addicts are likely to volunteer for their use.

Possible Policy Directions

IF NOTHING else, this discussion of the complexities of heroin use, marketing, and control should suggest the futility of arguments between the so-called "punitive" and "medical" approaches to addiction, the simplistic nature of unqualified recommendations that we adopt the "British system," and the imprecision of angry disputes between those who wish to "get tough" on "pushers" and those who wish to "decriminalize" heroin.

Beyond that, thinking about heroin requires one first of all to decide how one will handle the underlying philosophical issue; namely, whether the state is ever justified in protecting people from themselves, or whether it can only intervene to protect an innocent party from the actions of someone else. Put another way, the question is whether the state has any responsibility for the quality of human life in those cases where that quality (or lack of it) appears to be the result of freely exercised choice with no external effects on other parties. It is my view that the state does have such responsibilities, though its powers in this regard must be carefully exercised toward only the most important and reasonable goals. Even John Stuart Mill, whose defense of personal liberty was virtually absolute, argued against allowing a man to sell himself into slavery, "for by selling himself as a slave, he abdicates his liberty; he foregoes any future use of it beyond that simple act."

The next question is whether heroin addiction is such a form of "slavery" or is otherwise a state of being which should not be left to free choice. This is a more difficult question to answer in general terms, for somewhat surprisingly, we know rather little about what proportion of all heroin users are seriously incapacitated (or "captured") by it. Obviously, a large number are; but some might remain heavy users and yet hold jobs, lead responsible family lives, and retain other attributes of their humanity. Nobody knows what fraction are in this category, though we do know that the advocates of decriminalization tend to give (with little or no evidence) very generous estimates of it, while proponents of "stamping out" heroin give very small ones. In Great Britain, one study estimated that about 20 percent of the addicts interviewed were "junkies"—that is, unemployed persons who are heavily involved in crime, use heroin regularly, and buy it on the black market (despite its availability from clinics!)—and perhaps another quarter or so were "loners" who use heroin regularly but manage to avoid the underworld.[19] Furthermore, the mortality rate of British addicts, even without the need to steal to support a habit, is twenty-eight times as large as the death rate for the equivalent age group in the British population and twice that of American heroin addicts.[20]

I think it clear that for a sufficiently large number of persons, heroin is so destructive of the human personality that it should not be made generally available. (Defending that view in the context of the current debate is not essential, however, because not even the most zealous advocate of decriminalization supports complete legalization.) I believe this to be the case, though I recognize the rejoinders that can be made. Alcohol, some will say, has consequences for many individuals and for society at least as destructive as those of heroin, yet no one would propose returning to a system of prohibition. Alcohol and heroin are different problems, however, both medically and legally. A far smaller proportion of alcohol users than of heroin users become addicted in any meaningful sense of that term; the risks to the average individual of experimentation are accordingly far less in the former than in the latter case. And of those "addicted" to alcohol, there have been a larger proportion of "cures," although perhaps not as many as one would wish. Finally, alcohol use is so widespread as to be nearly universal, while heroin use remains an exotic habit of relatively few, and thus presents easier problems of control. Perhaps because of this, while no advanced society has been able to eliminate alcohol use, most societies have been able to eliminate, or keep to trifling proportions, heroin use.

If one accepts the view that it is desirable and possible, not only to provide better treatment for present addicts, but to reduce the rate of growth of the addict population, then one must also accept the need for some measure of compulsion; nothing is clearer than the fact that most young addicts enjoying their "run" will not voluntarily choose a life without heroin in preference to a life with it. Such compulsion will be necessary whatever disposition is made of the constrained addict—whether he be put on probation or sent to prison, to a quarantine center, to a methadone program, or to a heroin maintenance program. The compulsion will be necessary to achieve two objectives: to insure that he remains in the appropriate treatment without "cheating" (that is, simply using the treatment center as a cheap source of drugs to be sold on the street), and to insure that while treated he does not proselytize among nonaddicts and spread the contagion. Furthermore, there is some evidence (inconclusive, to be sure) that the possibility of arrest followed by some penalty deters at least some potential users and makes access to heroin more difficult for others.

Finally, to the extent that people voluntarily elect not to use heroin, the fact of its illegality may contribute to the belief that such use is "wrong," and therefore enhance the probability that a nonuser will remain a nonuser. Or put another way, it is difficult to see how society can assert that heroin use is a grave evil if it also must admit that its use is perfectly legal.

A detailed consideration of the legal policies which might most effectively deal with the heroin problem is beyond the scope of this chapter. In general, there are two alternatives—"outpatient" programs (in which the addict is left in the community but under a legally enforced requirement to report periodically for tests and for chemical or other forms of treatment) and "inpatient" programs (in which the addict is separated from the community in detoxification, methadone, or other programs). Each kind of program must deal with both regular addicts and infectious, novice addicts. The legal, medical, and organizational issues involved in these alternatives are complex. The important thing, however, is to consider them seriously—which means in turn to stop thinking of "legal" and "medical" approaches as mutually exclusive or separately viable.

Perhaps the most difficult of these issues is to decide what role heroin maintenance itself can play in an overall addict control program. It seems likely that offering low-cost, high-quality heroin is the one positive inducement that will prove attractive to most young addicts still enjoying their "run." Under the British system, the addict who obtains heroin from clinics is under no other obligations; no doctor or government official has the power to compel (and some doctors do not even have the desire to ask) the addict to accept, as a condition of heroin maintenance, any form of therapy, including the gradual substitution of oral methadone for heroin. In the British context, with a tiny addict population composed of persons apparently quite different from the typical American addict, that policy may work well enough, though experience with it is still too short to permit one to be confident of its value.

But whatever the fate of the British experiment, it seems probable that any larger program will involve real risks of sustaining the habits of contagion agents likely to recruit new addicts, and of supplying, through illegal diversions, the existing black market in drugs. With the best will in the world, it is probably impossible to devise a government program run by ordinary mortals that can provide heroin to several hundred thousand addicts on an outpatient basis in a way that will avoid subsidizing the growth of the addict pool and supplying debilitating (as opposed to mere maintenance) doses.

Ideally, as my colleague Mark Moore has pointed out, we would like to have two heroin markets, each rigidly separated from the other. In the first, designed to reduce the human suffering and criminal activities of confirmed addicts, heroin would be readily available at a very low price. In the other, designed to prevent the creation of new addicts, heroin would be scarce and have a very high price. In the real world, however, it would be impossible to keep separate two such markets—inevitably, supplies from the low-price one would inundate the high-price one. We have chosen to have a single, high-price market. We have done so because we are more interested in preventing the recruitment of new addicts than in improving the lives of confirmed ones. It is a difficult choice, but I think the right one.

PART
IV

CRIME AND THE
AMERICAN REGIME

Chapter 12

Crime and
American Culture

WE OFTEN GET better answers by asking better questions. In no area of inquiry are we in need of better answers than in the effort to explain the relationship between crime and the conditions of American life. For decades we have argued about whether crime rates have gone up because of economic deprivation, family disintegration, population changes, or judicial leniency. Those who claim that deprivation causes crime can point to the fact that street crime is more common in poor than in privileged neighborhoods, but they have difficulty explaining why, in the nation as a whole, crime rates seemed to have been stable or declining during the Great Depression and to have risen sharply during the prosperity of the 1960s. Those who argue that family disintegration leads to crime may take comfort from evidence adduced by some scholars, such as the late Sheldon and Eleanor Glueck, that broken homes are more likely to produce delinquent boys, but they can take scant comfort from the work of other scholars, such as Lee Robins, that finds no relationship between single-parent families and crime.[1] Though it seems clear that a rising proportion of young males in the population, such as resulted from the baby boom of the 1950s, will lead to an increase in crime, it is not at all clear why the age-specific crime rate (that is, the number of crimes committed by young males of a given age) has also increased—so much so that, according to Marvin Wolfgang, a delinquent boy born in Philadelphia in 1958 was five times more likely to commit a robbery than one born in that city in 1945.[2] It is quite possible that changes in the certainty, celerity, or severity of punishment affect the crime rate, but there are some formidable methodological obstacles lying in wait for anyone seeking to prove this.

Instead of trying to explain why crime rates go up, and especially why they go up during a relatively short period of time, let us ask why they go down and remain down for a relatively long period of time. The latter is, in one sense, the more natural question, for unless one believes in the inherent innocence of human nature, what one must explain is how people ever manage to form societies that are not shot through with criminality. The difficulty with asking that question is that we have not had very good crime statistics until the last few decades, and during most of this time crime has been going up, not down. If we are to search for periods in our history when crime was stable or declining, we must rely on inaccurate, fragmentary, often inconsistent data. Until recently, even that was unavailable, but now, thanks to the work of historians such as Ted Robert Gurr, Roger Lane, Eric Monkkonen, and others, we can draw on quite a large number of studies of crime rates during the nineteenth and early twentieth centuries, and these can be supplemented by studies in other nations that have kept better records. No single study alone would be decisive, but what is impressive about the findings we now have is that different scholars, using different methods and investigating different cities and states, have come to conclusions that are, with only a few exceptions, quite consistent.

Crime in the New Nation

ON THE EVE of the Revolutionary War, many colonists (and not only Tories) feared that if rebellion came, "the bands of society would be dissolved, the harmony of the world confounded, and the order of nature subverted."[3] Crime and disorder would surely accompany any challenge to authority, especially one involving a resort to arms.

It did not happen, not, at least during or just after the war. William E. Nelson, analyzing the records of seven populous Massachusetts counties, found an average of twenty-three prosecutions for theft each year before 1776 and twenty-four a year in the five years after 1776—hardly indicative of any crime wave.[4] When the framers of the Constitution gathered in Philadelphia in 1787, crime was not an important issue. The small towns and villages of which the infant republic was composed seemed quite able, by using public opinion to enforce a communal consensus, to maintain an orderly society save for the disruptions occasioned by political protest, such as Shays's Rebellion.

The vision of a tranquil community life on which the new constitutional order could depend was soon destroyed by a sharp rise in crime and disorder in American cities. Though the statistics are inadequate, it seems clear from the best historical inquiries that about the time Andrew Jackson was assuming the presidency, crime rates went up and stayed up through the 1830s and 1840s. Roger Lane has provided evidence of this growth in riotous and criminal behavior in Boston[5] and Philadelphia,[6] and James F. Richardson has told a similar story for New York City.[7] Even in such small and relatively isolated cities as Rochester, New York, there was a marked increase in disorder and crime, as Paul E. Johnson has shown.[8] Ted Robert Gurr has assembled a number of studies that indicate that this crime wave—like later ones, even down to the present—was not a peculiarly American phenomenon, as similar increases occurred at about the same time in London and Stockholm.[9]

All this was what Jeffersonian critics of urbanization had feared. The small communities of pre-Revolutionary America that had controlled behavior by a combination of moral tutelage, reciprocal obligations, and public humiliations were giving way to the individualistic and libertine life styles of the big cities. By 1830, New York City had a quarter of a million inhabitants, and its city fathers were beginning to worry about crime and violence.

But then a striking thing happened, something totally at odds with conventional theories that urbanization or urban problems automatically produce crime. The facts are hard to reconstruct from the available data, but so far as we can tell, the level of crime and public disorder in America began to decrease (or at least to level off) beginning about the middle of the nineteenth century and continuing, with some minor ups and downs, into the twentieth century.[10] The great waves of foreign immigration, the onset of rapid industrialization, the emergence of an urban working class—all the features of postbellum America that one supposes would have contributed to rising crime rates did not, in most of the cities that have been studied, have the predicted effect. Lane noted that late-nineteenth century Boston was a less violent and disorderly place than the Boston of 1840 and that homicide rates in Philadelphia declined throughout much of the late nineteenth century.[11] Monkkonen surveyed all the American studies of crime in the nineteenth century and found that, with perhaps two exceptions, each study discovered a pattern of falling or stable crime rates in industrializing America.[12] Gurr found the same decline occurring generally.[13] Michael B. Katz and his colleagues concluded from a detailed study of Hamilton,

Ontario (Canada), that crimes did not increase to any significant degree in that city between 1850 and 1873 despite rapid industrialization.[14] Nor is the decline (or leveling off) in offense rates confined to serious crimes. Monkkonen presented some evidence that drunkenness and disorderly conduct may also have declined in American cities during the second half of the nineteenth century, and Katz and his colleagues seem to have discovered much the same thing in Hamilton.[15]

How can we explain developments that seem to contradict the predictions of Thomas Jefferson and, even more, of common sense? One possibility is that there were created, during the latter part of the century, urban police forces to replace the older system of volunteer night watchmen. But these fledgling departments would have to have been astonishingly, and implausibly, effective to have stopped the antebellum crime wave dead in its tracks. There is no evidence they were so effective. And the resurgence of crime in the twentieth century, especially in the 1960s, occurred not only after the police had been institutionalized but after they had gone through, in the mid-twentieth century, a determined effort to "professionalize" and upgrade them. No one can explain how a rudimentary police system could have been so powerful and a modernized one so impotent.

A second possibility, suggested by Gurr and others, was the changing age structure of the population. From 1800 to 1900 there was a sharp and more or less continuous drop in the birth rate that led to a slow but steady increase in the average age of the population. In Rochester in 1830, three-fourths of the population of the city was under the age of thirty, and the majority of these were males who had left the farms in search of work and freedom in the rapidly growing cities.[16] Over one quarter of the residents of those cities with populations of one hundred thousand or more in 1840 were in the crime-prone age group of twenty-five to twenty-nine.[17] As the birth rate fell, the proportion of young persons in the cities fell, and this may have helped curb the rise in crime.

But the decline in the birth rate was not the only force at work; counteracting it to some degree was the rapid influx of new immigrants, many of them young men. And though the median age of the population almost doubled between 1800 and 1950,[18] the lessened youthfulness of the population was not enough to explain, by itself, the decline in the crime rates. The crime most carefully studied during the nineteenth century was murder. Theodore Ferdinand estimated that the murder rate (measured as arrests per hundred thousand persons) in Boston dropped from 4.7 around the middle of the century to 2.1 by the end of the century.[19] Lane found a comparable decline in Philadelphia using a somewhat different measure. There were at mid-century about 3.3 murder indictments per hundred thousand persons in that city; by the end of the century, the rate had dropped to 2.1.[20] The estimated murder rate fell by 55 percent in Boston and by 36 percent in Philadelphia, but during this same period the proportion of persons aged twenty to twenty-nine living in large cities such as these fell by only 15 percent.[21] Lane concluded that the changing age structure of the population could not have explained the decline in the rates of violent death in Philadelphia.[22] Scholars trying to understand contemporary crime increases tend to agree that age changes alone cannot account for more than a small fraction of the increase.[23]

A third possibility, suggested by Roger Lane, is that industrialization, far from loosening social ties, actually strengthened them by replacing the lost discipline of the small community with the new discipline of the factory and the public school.[24] Work became regular and not, as in the earlier agricultural and handicraft society, episodic. Economic efficiency required punctuality, industriousness, and habits of cooperative effort; failure to abide by this new regimen condemned the urban worker to destitution or to an inhospitable almshouse. The public school helped inculcate those values, and, in combination with the factory, restored a degree of order that families, churches, and neighborhoods could no longer sustain. The Jacksonian cities of the 1830s and 1840s had been riotous not simply because they brought young men together in large concentrations, but because they brought them together with nothing to do (except to join in the rowdy highjinks of the volunteer fire companies). This explanation may have some merit, but it does not explain the mechanism by which the value of order was instilled (after all, there was plenty of opportunity for brawling and thievery after the factories closed and on Sundays), and it leaves us wondering why the discipline of the factory and the school should have been so effective in the 1870s and 1880s and so ineffective in the 1960s and 1970s.

The second half of the nineteenth century was by no means a tranquil period. There were riots, though these were now more likely to have economic or industrial rather than ethnic origins. Crime would go up and down from year to year. There were small crime waves in many of the newer, frontier towns, and vigilante committees would spring up to deal with them. But despite industrialization, despite the widening of class differences, despite immigration, despite the growth of a propertyless urban proletariat, despite the rising congestion of the inner city, we find nothing to resemble the exceptionally high and sustained levels of crime characteristic either of the emerging cities of the 1830s and 1840s or of the mature and declining cities of the 1960s and 1970s.

Gurr, following the lead of the German sociologist Norbert Elias, has suggested that more important than the modest decline in the proportion of young persons in the population was the growth of the "civilizing process"—that is, of the extent to which people turned away from violence and internalized or displaced aggressive impulses.[25] The process began with the upper classes and was given institutional expression in the drive to eliminate corporal and capital punishment, the abolition of slavery, the elaboration in international law of rules for the conduct of warfare, the rise of the women's movement, the spread of the public school, the growing influence of temperance, and the development of urban police forces whose function, as Lane has noted, was as much to enforce morality (especially laws against drinking) as it was to apprehend criminals.[26]

Monkkonen has advanced a parallel argument. From about 1840 into the early decades of the twentieth century, there took hold a set of essentially Victorian values simultaneously with the advent of industrialization.[27] Bourgeois (that is, middle-class) ideology acquired a remarkable degree of hegemony in England and America.[28] Though much of it can be criticized as hypocritical, especially those parts that pretended at familial virtue and individual improvement while tolerating a libertine subculture and a growing class cleavage, we must remember, as La Rochefoucauld said, that hypocrisy is the homage that vice pays to virtue. Popular literature emphasized the value of thrift, order, industriousness, sobriety, the mastery of passions, and a deep regard for the future. Conduct often departed from these standards, but there was general agreement that such conduct was a departure to be deplored and, if possible, corrected.

The Investment in Impulse Control

PERSONS inclined to think of history as the product of economic forces, military battles, or political choices may balk at accepting such vague notions as "the civilizing process" or the "rise of Victorian morality" as having much explanatory value. I confess that substantiating the existence, to say nothing of the causal power, of such ideas is difficult. Given the present state of historical scholarship, the evidence for the effect of the new moral code is largely circumstantial. But it is not trivial.

In the early decades of the nineteenth century, middle-class Americans were appalled at the disorder and dissolution of their cities. There arose in response to this concern a varied but widespread effort at social reform.

Though its various manifestations had different particular goals, these had at least one thing in common: a desire to alter and strengthen human character. For centuries, young men had been leaving the farms in order to find new opportunities in the villages and towns, but the migration of the 1820s and 1830s had a new and more threatening dimension. Families with many children had often expected, even required, that several of their boys and girls would go to work for the others. In the past this had been accomplished by assigning (or even renting) children out to work and live with another family, perhaps a large landholder but just as often a village artisan or tradesman. Childhood was very short—far shorter than it is today, when we like to think of the family as "weakened" or "nuclear" —and there was no such thing as adolescence, a period of storm and stress experienced by teenage boys and girls living at home and discovering themselves. Those who lived at home, worked; those who did not live at home, lived at somebody else's home and worked there. The growth of the cities in early nineteenth-century America was so rapid, however, and the nature of the productive processes was changing so rapidly, that the young men (and later, the young women) who now left home to go to the city no longer lived in the home of the craftsman or manufacturer for whom they worked, but lived instead in boarding houses, with other young men.[29] Adult supervision of young men was weakened, not, as Joseph Kett and Paul E. Johnson have shown, because the family was weakened, but because the necessary alternative to the family was no longer under adult control.[30]

Young male workers in the cities suddenly acquired an autonomous social life. Americans had always drunk intoxicating beverages in prodigious amounts, but in the past it had been done by young men in the homes of their parents or their masters. Now it was done in the company of other young men, in boarding houses and saloons. If order was to be restored to the cities, some way would have to be found, other than the family, to instill "character."

Different people meant different things by "character." For some, it meant a religious life; for others, merely moderation in drink and circumspection in sex; for still others, orderly habits and a suitable occupation diligently pursued. Joseph F. Kett, in his masterful study of the rise of the concept of adolescence in America, found that all the various uplift and reform movements had in common was a desire to instill "decision of character," by which was meant a "strenuous will" aimed at "inner control" and "self-restraint." The ills that middle-class adults saw all about them arose from a lack of a "self-activating, self-regulating, all-purpose inner control."[31] If young men no longer lived and worked under direct and round-the-clock adult supervision, there was no hope of external control regulating behavior, and though urban police forces were being invented at about this time, few persons had much hope that the police could do more than control the riots and cart away the drunks, and many persons remained fearful of giving even these powers to uniformed officers of the state.

There were many routes to self-control, such as religious revivals, temperance pledges, Sunday school classes, and living with foster families. Americans tried them all, with a vengeance. Paul Boyer has surveyed many of these efforts occurring between 1820 and 1920; though it would be foolish to attempt to supply a summary figure in dollars spent and manhours worked, his account and that of others leaves little doubt that nineteenth-century Americans made an enormous investment in controlling the impulses of the young.[32]

The first few decades of the nineteenth century witnessed a series of religious revivals that have become known as the Second Great Awakening. Most of the converts in this period were young people, in their teens or early twenties, and many revival preachers aimed especially at this group, particularly in the cities.[33] When Charles G. Finney came to Rochester in 1830, his initial appeal was to the proprietors and artisans —in short, to the middle class—but soon he organized, with the aid of the middle-class churches, missions aimed at the workers. He encountered a great deal of success, which arose, according to Paul Johnson, out of a combination of voluntary conversion and social compulsion. Many employers began to insist on membership in a church as a prerequisite for employment and advancement.[34]

One can easily exaggerate the extent to which the Awakening chiefly aimed at, or had the effect of, social control. It was, after all, a religious movement centering around intense debates about God and the Bible. In general, religious conservatives sought to bring man into a right relationship with God, while liberals urged the need to bring man into a right relationship with his fellow man. For the latter, religious conviction had important implications for slavery (revival leaders were also abolitionists). But both sides agreed on the need to find principles of proper conduct that could not be inferred merely from individual wants or rational self-interest. The turmoil of the times gave a sense of urgency to the mission, which had at its heart, as Perry Miller was later to phrase it, "anxiety over the future."[35]

The reach of the religious movements was impressive, especially as they brought people into voluntary associations. In 1820, fewer than 5 percent of the adult males in New York City were on the lay boards of the various Protestant organizations located there; by 1860, that fraction had increased to about 20 percent. In the latter year, something approaching half of all adult Protestant males of the city were members of at least one church-related voluntary association.[36]

It was not originally part of every revival movement to set contemporary human affairs aright or to stimulate the formation of reform associations. But as William G. McLoughlin observed, converts who had "got right with God" felt an almost uncontrollable urge to help others get right with Him.[37] One of the ways in which this might be accomplished was through the Sunday school movement. Though Sunday school often began under denominational control and with religious objectives, it soon took on a life of its own and acquired secular objectives as well. Sunday school in these days was not merely a brief lesson from the Bible, but a day-long exercise in "decorum and restraint" that emphasized, through the minute application of rules and procedures, the duties and obligations of its young members.[38] The enrollment in this effort, both here and in England, was very large. In 1825, the American Sunday School Union claimed to enroll one-third of all the children in Philadelphia between the ages of six and fifteen, while in 1829 in New York City, over 40 percent of the children ages four to fourteen were said to attend Sunday schools.[39] In England, Sunday school enrollment tripled between 1821 and 1851 and accounted for over half of all the children between the ages of five and fifteen and three-fourths of the working-class children of those ages.[40]

Sunday schools were not a device by which the middle class imposed its views on a rebellious working class. As Thomas W. Laqueur has shown for England (and as was apparently true for the United States as well), the Sunday school movement was staffed and financed by working-class persons who sought to inculcate not only literacy but the values of respectable working-class society. Whatever economic cleavages divided society, the great social cleavage was not one that separated occupations but one that separated the "rough and the respectable." What was being inculcated in these schools were as much personal habits as religious or moral values: every detail of the regimen assigned the highest importance to order, punctuality, drill, and regulation. By this means, Laqueur writes, "the bourgeois world view triumphed in the nineteenth century largely through consent, not through force." The middle class established a "moral hegemony."[41]

But Sunday schools did not reach the young men of the factories and shops nor did they reach the children abandoned or neglected by their parents. For the former, the YMCA movement provided one remedy—facilities and courses of instruction in the city intended to serve as a functional alternative to family and village life. Brought to the United States from England in 1851, within a decade there were over two hundred YMCAs with more than twenty-five thousand members.[42] YMCAs, however, tended to offer refuge for those least in need of it, as the young men who joined were already a part of the respectable working class. For the abandoned children, Charles Loring Brace in 1853 started the Children's Aid Society, which stood in opposition to orphanages and asylums, and sought instead to relocate street urchins to farm homes in the West. Unfortunately, rural family life was more attractive to the leaders of the Society than to the children it sought to help, and it eventually proved impossible to relocate a significant number of homeless young people.

Revivals, Sunday schools, moral uplift, YMCAs, and sheltering homeless children represented an enormous investment of social capital, but the order-maintenance value of that investment is impossible to measure and in some instances was directed at persons who were not the immediate cause of crime and disorder. The temperance movement, on the other hand, was directed precisely at behavior that many persons believed, rightly or wrongly, was the cause of the urban distemper, and the effect of that movement can be estimated by noting changes in the alcohol consumption of the nation.

Today, we often think of "temperance" as an effort by Puritanical farm women to obtain passage of the "disastrous" Eighteenth Amendment and the subsequent Volstead Act. In fact, it was much more than this—a century-long, broadly based social movement that may have been the single most effective effort in American history to change human behavior by plan.

In the decades leading up to the tumultuous 1830s, the consumption of alcoholic beverages was rising sharply. Colonial Americans had always drunk a lot for a variety of reasons, such as the shortage of potable water, the unavailability of coffee and the expense of tea, and the belief that alcoholic beverages were good for you. Moreover, the supply of alcohol had been going up and its price had been going down as the perfection of new distillation methods and the abundant grain harvests of western Pennsylvania and elsewhere made it both easy and profitable to produce distilled spirits. Not only easy, but in many cases necessary: the poor quality and high cost of overland transportation often made it unprofitable to move grain to markets in any form other than alcohol. Norman H. Clark estimates that the annual per capita consumption of alcohol in the United States rose from about 2.5 gallons in 1790 to 7 gallons in 1810 and to 10 gallons in 1829.[43] Respectable Americans thought the effect of this increase could be seen in the rowdy, brawling conditions of city streets, the spread of saloons (Paul E. Johnson calculates that there was one establishment selling liquor for every twenty-eight adult males in Rochester, New York, in 1829), and the collapse of familial virtues.[44]

"Temperance" meant different things to different people. To Thomas

Jefferson, it meant drinking beer and wine rather than distilled spirits. To others it meant closing down saloons but allowing home consumption of gin, rum, and whiskey to continue. To still others, it meant total abstinence. Some temperance advocates relied on moral suasion, others embraced legal compulsion. But taking all its forms together, the temperance movement was extraordinarily broad, combining revival preachers and educated philosophers, urban as well as rural leaders, the intelligentsia as well as the common folk. By the thousands, men were induced to sign various temperance pledges. Special programs, such as the Cold Water Army and the Cadets of Temperance, were aimed at youth, and they grew rapidly.[45] In 1851, Maine became the first state to prohibit the manufacture and sale of intoxicating beverages; within four years, thirteen states had such laws, including New York, Massachusetts, and Connecticut. In some places the ban was state-wide, in others it involved local option. It was the effort to enforce these laws that gave rise to intense struggles over the control and enlargement of municipal police departments and that led, in the case of Massachusetts, to the creation of the first state police.[46]

The effect of all this activity was dramatic. William J. Rorabaugh estimates that, beginning around 1830, alcohol consumption began to decline, steeply—between 1830 and 1850, per capita consumption (for persons aged fifteen years and over) fell from 7.1 gallons per year to 1.8 gallons per year.[47] Clark concurs, calculating (using a somewhat different base) that per capita consumption fell from 10 gallons per year in 1829 to 2.1 gallons in 1850.[48] The Civil War caused a setback in the temperance movement, and the growth of beer consumption (owing much to European immigration, the perfection of large-scale production methods, and improved railroad transportation) created further difficulties. But despite all this, the per capita consumption of alcohol never again reached the levels attained in 1830.[49]

We cannot be certain that reduced alcohol consumption contributed to the reduction in crime, but most people at the time believed it did. Were we to have the facts, we would probably learn that lessened drunkenness reduced some crimes and not others and may have had its greatest effect, not by directly reducing crime (it is far from clear that people commit serious crimes because they are drunk), but by restoring a degree of order to urban neighborhoods that permitted the normal and informal processes of social control to manage behavior and thereby to inhibit the criminogenic tendencies of disreputable street life. Even these results were unevenly distributed, with some neighborhoods helped and others, particularly in the teeming Tenderloin districts of the cities, left largely unaffected.[50]

The temperance movement was the most dramatic example of the effort of nineteenth-century Americans to invest in the control of self-indulgent impulses. But it was only a part, as we have seen, of a much wider array of efforts to protect the character-building role of families or to supply substitutes for familial influences at a time of growing personal liberty and rapid social change. These efforts were aimed, as Clark has phrased it, at producing in Americans a "bourgeois interior," whatever their economic exterior.[51] That inner life was organized around the need for self-control, the delay of personal gratification, and the management of social relations on the basis of mutual restraint.

The Triumph of Self-Expression

PAUL BOYER dates the century in which Americans invested so heavily in creating and sustaining a moral order as running from about 1820 to 1920. I agree. The effort, of course, did not end in 1920, nor has it ended today; "uplift" organizations and movements continue all about us. But beginning in the 1920s, or at least becoming visible then, we see the repudiation by the educated classes of moral uplift as it had been practiced for the preceding century.

Religious revivals, once led by liberal college students such as Theodore Weld, were now scorned by college-educated persons as being the province of narrow-minded opportunists such as the real Billy Sunday and the fictional Elmer Gantry. Revivalism became synonymous with fundamentalist Protestantism, and that was discredited, in intellectual minds, by the defense of the doctrine of creationism by William Jennings Bryan at the Scopes trial. Secular public schools had now made unnecessary, or so it was thought, day-long Sunday schools associated with churches. The YMCA movement continued to grow, but now largely because it offered gymnasiums and low-cost rooms rather than because it supplied spiritual and moral uplift.[52]

And temperance had been destroyed by Prohibition. Though national prohibition was not a peculiarly American movement (national laws restricting the use of alcohol were passed at about the same time in Finland, Norway, and Sweden) and temperance had never been simply a rural effort, prohibition came to be seen by intellectuals as an expression of the narrow-mindedness of American farmers and villagers. Though there is not much evidence that crime (except for a few well-publicized gangland killings) went up during Prohibition, many people came to believe that Prohibition had caused a crime wave.[53] Though Prohibition succeeded in reducing alcohol consumption in the United States by between a third and a half, in the eyes of its critics it was a failure.[54] Though the era of "Flaming Youth" and looser moral standards occurred at the same time in European nations that did not have Prohibition, Prohibition was blamed for having created a youth problem in this country (somewhat hypocritically, since the critics of Prohibition were also among those most inclined to celebrate the youth movement).

Where a century or even a half century earlier, intellectuals and urban reformers denounced the saloon, their heirs in the 1920s and 1930s glamorized the "cocktail lounge" and took drinking in public places to be a mark of sophistication. Where a century earlier, intellectuals feared the city as a threat to traditional values, now some were beginning to praise it as the indispensable arena of personal liberty.[55] Whereas in the nineteenth century parents worried when young persons went off to live in boarding houses made up entirely of other young people, by the twentieth century the residential college was regarded as the most desirable place to which young persons could aspire. From 1790 to 1840, children became adults as soon as they began to work, and that happened at a very early age; by the period 1890 to 1920, "adolescence" had been discovered, a period of stress and opportunity that required prolonged education and special nurture.[56] Whereas in the nineteenth century scarcely anyone dissented from the view that the object of character formation was to restrain self-indulgent impulses, by the 1920s popular versions of the psychological theories of Sigmund Freud were widely circulated and generally interpreted as meaning that repressing one's instincts was bad, not good. The children's stories of the first half of the nineteenth century portrayed a world in which there was no conflict between moral correctness and wordly success; a "Christian citizen" would prosper in this world as in the next.[57] In the second half of the nineteenth century such literature had become less moralistic, but still likely to emphasize success. By the 1920s, it had begun to emphasize happiness apart from success.

The almost unbounded self-confidence with which nineteenth-century Americans viewed the value of their culture and its central precepts was replaced, beginning in the 1920s, with the view that this culture was wrong, or at the very least, no better than several competing cultural forms. Franz Boas and his students at Columbia University interpreted their anthropological studies in ways that were critical of middle-class Western civilization. Margaret Mead became a best-selling anthropologist by claiming that the greater happiness of Samoans arose from their being granted greater sexual freedom and from being raised in more nurturant, less repressive families.[58]

One might expect that all these changes in elite views would have an effect on techniques of childrearing and that these in turn would alter youthful behavior in the direction of making it more daring and more impatient of restraints. Unfortunately, it is quite difficult to say much about the changes that occurred in how children were raised and it is almost impossible to say anything about how these changes might have affected youthful behavior. But we can say something about how elites advised mothers to rear their children, and, since this advice was typically distributed through national magazines that competed for the woman's market, presumably it was designed with an eye to what would prove popular. In the mid-nineteenth century, childrearing advice emphasized the supreme importance of inculcating moral and religious principles on the assumption that the child would soon be free of direct adult supervision. Though this moral training was no longer as rigorously Calvinist as it once had been and though corporal punishment was increasingly subject to criticism, the object of childrearing was unchanged—to make the child "at an early age a self-maintaining moral being" so as to guard him from "evil within and without."[59]

This view persisted into the early part of the twentieth century, but by the 1920s it was beginning to be replaced by a different view. The child was once thought to be endowed by nature with dangerous impulses that must be curbed, but now he was seen as equipped with harmless instincts that ought to be developed. Previously it was thought to be a mistake to play with the child too much; now play was beginning to be urged upon mothers. Where once the stress had been on moral development and the decisive importance of the mother's character, now the literature was more likely to emphasize the enjoyable aspects of childrearing in which fun and play were important.[60] In 1890, 1900, and 1910, one-third of the childrearing topics discussed in a sample of articles from the *Ladies Home Journal*, *Woman's Home Companion*, and *Good Housekeeping* were about character development; in 1920, only 3 percent were. By 1930 articles on moral character by and large had been replaced with ones on "personality development." And where the magazines in 1890 had said that the best means to proper character development lay in providing a good home influence, by 1920 the route to acquiring a well-adjusted personality was thought to involve proper feeding.[61]

Except for the well-documented exuberance of the 1920s, it is not clear that this shift in the dominant ethos of the social and intellectual elites had immediate and important practical consequences, perhaps because it still represented a shift only in elite rather than mass attitudes. Perhaps also it was because the shift away from impulse control to self-expression was cut short by the grim realities of the Great Depression.

Though in the early 1930s we still had no national crime statistics and not much in the way of national opinion surveys, the evidence we do have from studies in particular communities suggests that the severe economic dislocations of the Great Depression produced no significant increase in crime and may, in fact, have been associated with a decrease in some forms of law-breaking. Ruth Cavan and Katherine H. Ranck studied one hundred Chicago families in 1934–1935, selected from among those who had been referred to a juvenile agency during the late 1920s because they had difficult or delinquent children. Though this was a group already at risk, Cavan and Ranck found no evidence of any increase in crime among these young people.[62] An inspection of police and court records in Massachusetts, Illinois, and Cleveland during the same period also failed to disclose any evidence of a crime wave.[63] Glen H. Elder was later to analyze data gathered from a group of persons born in Oakland, California, in the early 1920s and coming of age during the Great Depression. For this group, family income fell on the average about 40 percent between 1929 and 1933, and as a result children were pushed out at an early age into the labor market in order to help the families survive. But in spite of this, or perhaps because of it, the children displayed little sign of rebellion and deviance. Though boys were liberated to a degree from parental controls, they were placed almost immediately under other forms of adult supervision in the workplace, while still living at home. The result, according to Elder, was to accelerate the movement of these boys into the adult world and into having a sense of adult responsibility. Though their values changed, the change was almost entirely in the direction of more traditional ones.[64]

Accompanying such changes in attitude and behavior as may have been induced by a depression and two world wars was a declining birth rate in the first decades of the twentieth century. The proportion of males in the crime-prone age group of fifteen to nineteen was 10 percent in 1890 but only 7 percent by 1950, a drop of about one-third.[65] However by the 1960s, as everyone knows, the sharply increased birth rates of the 1950s had produced a baby boom that came of age. But as everyone does not know, that age shift toward increased youthfulness could not by itself have produced the crime increases of the 1960s and 1970s (see chapter 1). One additional factor, I suggest, was the continued spread of the ethic of self-expression that had begun in the 1920s but had been temporarily blunted by national crises and that for a time lacked a large youth market to which it could appeal.

What is distinctive about the contemporary period, in my view, is the collapse of the Victorian popular culture and of the moral legitimacy of the institutions embodying it. The psychology of radical individualism and the philosophy of individual rights has triumphed. I will not try to characterize in detail the contemporary ethos; that has been done by many others and could as well be done by the reader of this chapter. I think its dominant element is individual self-expression and, closely linked with that, immediate gratification. Such an ethos need not lead to selfish behavior (the so-called "Me Generation"), for self-expression can lead to creativity and innovation that entail substantial personal sacrifice, as well as to greed and callousness. But whether self-regarding or other-regarding, contemporary behavior recognizes no limits (at least for most of us) save that it "hurt no one else." This is especially true of the intelligentsia; it is less true of ordinary folk. But if my general argument is correct, it is precisely what the intelligentsia, the upper-middle class, the educated persons, the literati think that provides the central cues for popular culture, especially now that such persons are so large a proportion of the total population.

The contemporary public philosophy emphasizes rights, not duties. A commitment to rights implies a preference for spontaneity over loyalty, conscience over honor, tolerance over conformity, self-expression over self-restraint. Where nineteenth-century elites sought to extend the range of criminal sanctions over behavior (notably with respect to drink and sex), twentieth-century elites seek to decriminalize such behavior. Whereas the nineteenth-century police were expected (and were in large measure created) to enforce public order, the twentieth-century police are expected to arrest criminals. As I have argued in chapter 5, the criminal law has acquired in practice if not in theory an individualist focus—the law defines *my* rights, punishes *his* behavior, and is applied by *that* officer because of *this* harm.[66] This fits well with our philosophical inclinations and makes easier the task of detecting violations of our rights, but it obscures somewhat the earlier view that the criminal law was designed in part to shape conduct and sustain communities.

Obviously, the communal element of our public philosophy has not disappeared; a concern for character, propriety, and duty persists among a majority of the citizenry, and accordingly they lead lives not radically different in substance (though often quite different in style) from what they might have led a century ago. The Protestant ethic, if that is what you wish to call it, is alive and well, though not in public view. Among elites, however, the interest in a communal as opposed to an individualistic public philosophy is now regarded as characteristic of something called the counterculture, not of the culture itself, and is often based on a desire, not to perfect character by moral development, but to repudiate the "philistine" features of the ordinary culture with its commonplace concerns for conventional morality and personal propriety.

The ethos of self-expression and personal liberty has largely been developed and given its persuasive power by young persons. Whether there was ever in the nineteenth century such a thing as a "youth culture," I do not know, but I doubt it. The abnormally large proportion of young persons in the population during the 1840s certainly contributed to public disorder, but I am aware of no evidence that any important institutions deferred to youthful preferences or that older persons sought to ape them. As Albert Parry has shown, "Bohemianism" and a "Bohemian," or artist's, quarter have been a feature of our larger cities since at least 1850, but only in the last few decades have such areas been populated by liberated young people rather than by exotic adults.[67]

The first stirrings of a youth culture occurred in the 1920s when, as Paula Fass observed, "modern youth" was created by the disjuncture between the familial world and the social world and the acceptance, at least among the upper-middle class, of control over the social world being exercised by adolescent peer groups. Parents no doubt worried about the amount of smoking, drinking, and "petting" among their offspring, but they did not challenge the fundamental shift—that from courtship to dating as the appropriate way to organize contact between young men and young women. Courtship had been a stylized system, under close adult control, for finding marriage partners; dating, by contrast, was a method for having fun as well as finding partners, and it was carried out under peer-group control. As with most changes in values, the first tremors had only limited effects. A psychiatrist such as Karl De Schweinitz could proclaim, to applause, that the goal of family life was now "the liberation of the human spirit," but in practice the new forms of self-expression, though marking a profound shift in cultural values, were still placed in service of traditional goals: careers, prosperity, and family formation. As Fass remarked, the college students of the 1920s (the first large youth-culture market) were "optimistic about business and naughty about sex," practicing self-expression less for its own sake than as a means to popularity and success.[68]

Since the 1960s, an increase in the proportion of young persons in the population has been met by the celebration in the marketplace, the churches, and adult life styles of the youth culture. (One measure of the change: a century, or even a half century ago, young boys sought, as soon as they were able, to dress like grown men; today, grown men try to dress like young boys.) This institutionalization in all parts of society of the natural desire of youth for greater freedom may well have given legitimacy to all forms of self-expression, including, alas, those forms that involve crime and violence, and thus helped magnify and sustain what would have been a crime increase in any event.

This transformation of values is not the whole story. A full account of

the current crime wave would have to consider the changes in the allocation of living space, and especially the abandonment of the inner city by
the middle class and thus the removal from those places of the persons
most likely to sustain a social infrastructure—churches, neighborhood
groups, social networks, and small businesses—with a stake in impulse
control. Moreover, the rise in the ethic of self-expression has occurred at
a time when employment opportunities have moved out of the cities faster
than have city people, diminishing opportunities for the young persons
left behind. Racial antagonisms have left their mark on whites and blacks
alike. Though most violent and much property crime is intraracial, the
corrosive effects of racism, real and imagined, undoubtedly play a part in
weakening a sense of obligation to the social order. The increased availability of handguns and the sharpening of consumer instincts by the mass
media contribute to at least the pattern and perhaps the level of criminality.

I give only subordinate attention to these factors for two reasons. First,
many of them are unique to the United States, or nearly so, especially the
pattern of urban out-migration, the availability of handguns, and the
existence of racial cleavages. Nevertheless, the pattern of increase in crime
during the last two or three decades, coming after a half century of decline
in crime, is not a peculiarly American phenomenon, but a feature of
virtually every industrialized society. (Japan is a notable exception, but
Japan is one of the few industrial nations that has managed to retain a
traditional and communal ethos, though that may be changing.[69]) A true
understanding of crime requires us to know what these nations have in
common, not what differentiates them. Second, most of the factors
related to crime that are common to all nations—the consumer society,
the advent of television—are not factors operating independently of the
ethos of self-expression, but are reflections and instrumentalities of it.

Crime, Politics, and Policy

THE GREAT IRONY is that the ethos of individual self-expression not
only helps explain the contemporary rise in crime, it also governs our
policies toward crime. When crime and disorder first became a problem
in the new republic, the solution embraced by almost all persons, including the most progressive minds, was to search for ways to reduce misconduct by reasserting, or finding substitutes for, the constraints of family and
village. Though more attention was paid to our rudimentary police and

to the emergent penal system, the great social investment was in devices (religious revivals, moral uplift, temperance movements, advice to mothers) designed to shape character and induce self-control. And even the penitentiary system was initially conceived in the spirit of communal reform as a mechanism for reeducating the offender by exposing him to solitary reflection and spiritual guidance.

Our policy toward crime then, as now, was shaped in large measure by our understanding of human nature. At least two theories were in competition. One, the individualistic, found its clearest expression in the writings of Thomas Hobbes; the other, the communal, had an older provenance but was given its most forceful modern expression by Jean Jacques Rousseau. Each is best known for his political philosophy, but each based that philosophy on a theory of human nature.

Hobbes gives us a picture of man as a creature of his senses, responding to stimuli in his environment. Man does not respond randomly, however, for there are active forces in him by which he evaluates these stimuli.[70] These forces are human passions, three of which are of special importance: a desire for wealth, a desire for glory, and a fear of violent death. Because of these passions, men in the state of nature are in conflict with one another, the appetite for gain leading to theft, that for glory leading to exercising power, and that for safety leading to violence. Unchecked, these passions will bring about a perpetual war of all against all in which the life of man will be "solitary, poor, nasty, brutish, and short." To avoid a violent death, men will combine to create a superior force, a Leviathan, that will protect each man from the other. With his safety guaranteed by government, man will be able to use his calculating nature to his advantage, and thereby help bring into being an orderly commercial society.

To Rousseau, man is not naturally an amoral calculator, but naturally good (or at worst "pre-moral").[71] He is not driven by any fixed passions; though he loves himself, it is not a selfish love. Man does not naturally fear death, nor love glory, nor seek wealth; all these things he is taught by society. Alongside a reasonable and moderate self-love, man is moved by the sentiment of pity and thus finds friendship rewarding and human compassion natural. The bourgeois and commercial society that Hobbes anticipates, Rousseau loathes, for it corrupts the soul. To create men who are not corrupted and societies that are not corrupting requires great exertions. One such exertion is to acquire a proper education, that, as Rousseau describes it in *Emile,* emphasizes self-discovery and the cultivation of a decent self-love and sentiments of pity. Correspondingly, there is a proper organization of society, a matter on which Rousseau was not entirely clear but that seemed to involve a rough equality of wealth, a rigorous rule of law, and the inculcation of a sense of community that would shape and sustain human character.

I ask the indulgence of serious philosophers for my simplistic rendering of complex distinctions and subtle arguments. But even simply stated, it is apparent what kind of psychology underlies the moral and political elements of an individualistic and a communal view of man. The consequences of supposing that man is either a rational calculator or a creature of sentiments, that human nature is either fixed or pliable, are both great and obvious. We can trace from Hobbes (or in less stark form, from John Locke) a theory of government that begins with a compact among rationally self-interested persons worried about their lives and property but determined to use the state simply as a mechanism (either all-powerful in the case of Hobbes, or tempered by restraints in the case of Locke) to make possible life, liberty, and the possession of property. The government, in short, will facilitate the pursuit of the private ends of individuals. When those individuals break the law, they cause practical difficulties for others by lessening their security and upsetting their calculations. But since criminal citizens are fundamentally no different than law-abiding ones, save, perhaps, in their willingness to run risks or the impatience with which they pursue practical advantages, they can be dealt with by procedures not fundamentally different from the arrangements that animate and justify the regime.

Thus, beginning with Hobbes, we find a utilitarian criminology first elaborated by Jeremy Bentham and Cesare Beccaria (now called, for unimportant reasons, "classical" criminology), a criminology based on adjusting the costs and benefits of alternative courses of action so as to maximize the probability that the law-abiding, and not the law-violating, course will be followed. The Benthamite calculus, marvelously elaborated, has been refined by the tools of modern mathematics into the calculus of deterrence, whereby we estimate the amount of crime that can be prevented by increasing the swiftness, the certainty, or the severity of the penalties for crime, or by increasing the availability and value of alternatives to crime (such as jobs or leisure), or by doing both. An especially skilled practitioner of this line of analysis once calculated that for every murderer executed, eight murders are prevented.[72]

We can trace from Rousseau (and, of course, from even earlier writers) a theory that government is not a device to facilitate the pursuit by individuals of their private ends, but a device to shape those ends and the character of the individuals seeking them. A good society is one that forms in its citizens a good character. This, obviously, is an ancient notion of government, and it need not be done by the rather odd mechanism of the "general will" or in the self-governing commune proposed by Rousseau;

I take him as my example because he was among the first to give to the character-forming view of government a modern tone—that is, one that tries to link character formation with egalitarianism and democracy.

From Rousseau and his argument that modern society tends to corrupt naturally good men comes the view that crime is not the result of choice and calculation, but rather the consequence of some defect in social arrangements. Crime is, in short, "caused," in ways over which the individual has little control. Modern criminologists refer to this as the "positivist" tradition. It can be found, implicitly or explicitly, in the writings of proponents of various structural, cultural, or psychological strategies for preventing crime and rehabilitating criminals. The precise shape of the strategy varies: early proponents of curing the causes of crime stressed religious and moral instruction; contemporary criminologists are now an almost entirely secular profession and so the emphasis has shifted to such institutions as schools, halfway houses, or neighborhoods. And do not think that positivists are always tender minded: one of the first monuments to the rehabilitative urge was the American penitentiary.

The two opposing theories of human nature that underly American attitudes toward crime also underly our political arrangements. Our national constitution was written with an eye to the view of man found in Locke and Hobbes. We are all familiar with those phrases of Publius (chiefly, of James Madison) found in the *Federalist* that explained how our political arrangements were intended to use the calculating and self-seeking nature of man to protect liberty. "Ambition must be made to counteract ambition," Madison wrote, because men are not angels.[73] Factions are inevitable, because the "latent causes of faction are . . . sown in the nature of man."[74] To control the effects of faction and of human ambition, the Founders not only separated the powers of government but gave "to those who administer each department the necessary constitutional means and personal motives to resist encroachments of the others."[75] It was, Madison said, a "policy of supplying, by opposite and rival interests, the defect [that is, the lack] of better motives."[76] Madison's view of human nature was not wholly Hobbesian; it was, as the late Martin Diamond put it, not a pessimistic view so much as a sober one. "As there is a certain degree of depravity in mankind which requires a certain degree of circumspection and distrust," Madison wrote, "so there are other qualities in human nature which justify a certain portion of esteem and confidence."[77] But—and this is the crucial point—it was not to be the business of the federal government to create or sustain these "other qualities"; rather, the new government "presupposes the existence" of them.[78]

George Will, in his recent Godkin Lectures at Harvard, has argued that, from a conservative point of view, this presupposition that man is good enough to make free government work is an error. The government, in his phrase, is "ill-founded." No free government can exist unless it exercises some responsibility for the cultivation of virtue among its citizens. If it merely presupposes the existence of these virtues and confines itself to managing arrangements designed to harness self-interest to serve public purposes, it will in time discover that the government and the society are no longer capable of serving anything but self-interest. Will's view was anticipated by critics of Madison at the time.

The Antifederalists, as we know, chiefly opposed the new Constitution because it claimed to do what they believed was impossible—reconcile the national government of a large republic with the protection of liberty. It was in the small community that men could truly be free. The late Herbert Storing summarized the Antifederalist commitment to the small republic as involving three arguments: only a small republic could enjoy voluntary obedience to the laws, secure the genuine accountability of the government to the people, and "form the kind of citizens who will maintain republican government."[79] He does not go so far as Gordon Wood to argue that the Antifederalists were inheritors of the old Puritan tradition that required the sacrifice of individual interest to the common good.[80] The critics of the new Constitution were not in any obvious sense the descendants of either Jonathan Edwards or Rousseau: like the authors of the Constitution, they chiefly valued liberty. The central difference between the two groups appears to have been a dispute over the means to achieve this goal. The Antifederalists believed that liberty would only be secure if society deliberately promoted civic virtue and the subordination of individual interests to the commonwealth, and this promotion could only occur, safely, in small republics.[81]

A small republic—or a small community—could only promote civic virtue if its population was relatively homogenous, culturally, ethnically, and economically. The Swiss cantons were an oft-cited model. The new national government, with its capital city, its standing army, its openness to intercourse with foreign nations and foreign habits, its inclination to aristocratic manners and European luxury, would be the antithesis of civic virtue. In particular, the Antifederalists noted the nonreligious, perhaps even antireligious, character of the new Constitution. They were quite aware that many of the emerging national leaders (Madison, Jefferson, Franklin) were children of the Enlightenment who believed, at best, in a vague deism that looked for guidance to the orderly patterns of nature rather than to the strict commands of God. Madison and Jefferson went much further than almost any other national figures in attempting to separate church and state. In the former's *Memorial and Remon-*

strance and the latter's *Notes on the State of Virginia,* they argued not only against coercion of religious beliefs, but against any state support of churches—against, that is, making religion an "engine of Civil policy." Though the Supreme Court has largely adopted the Madisonian view of church-state relations, that is probably not what most persons at the time believed (and certainly not what the authors of the First Amendment thought they were enacting).[82] The Antifederalists, to be sure, favored freedom of conscience, but expected that government would foster religion, support it, and make passing a religious test a qualification for office. Religion ought to be an "engine of Civil policy," though it could only be so, in a nation as diverse as America, at the local level.

My argument thus far, stripped of important qualifications, is that we grafted a Lockean (and in part, Hobbesian) national government onto a communal life that was explained and defended in the language of Rousseau, and we did so over the objections of many persons who thought the engrafted national limb would destroy the sturdy communal trunk. The graft was successful in large measure because the defenders of small communal republics could think of no practical alternative, given the need for national defense and orderly commerce, and because the defenders of the national constitution assumed that the center of our collective lives would remain at the community level wherein would be nurtured that civic virtue on which the national order to some degree depended.

The assumption was not an unreasonable one. The national government, after all, had limited powers and modest responsibilities; the governance of the nation would remain chiefly the duty of towns, cities, and states. If governance required the formation of character by education, religion, or the force of communal opinion, then all this would be done, to the extent it could be done at all, by the many small republics of which the new nation would be composed.

The events of the Jacksonian era were to reveal the error of that assumption. The small republics were becoming teeming cities in which young men freed of adult supervision by either father or master were becoming rowdy libertines. Andrew Jackson himself was worried about the moral health of the nation over which he was elected to preside; as Marvin Meyers has argued, Jackson's appeal to "the people" was not merely an appeal against the "money power" of the banks and corporations, it was more profoundly an appeal for the restoration of civic virtue that he thought was exemplified in the industrious and economical lives of planters, farmers, mechanics, and laborers. That virtue consisted of self-reliance and simplicity. The country, he felt, was in a moral crisis.[83]

The response to that crisis, as we have seen, was also cast in moral and communal terms. If the cities and the factories were a new challenge, redoubled efforts would be made to meet that challenge. For the better part of a century, the struggle was waged. It had its ups and downs; wars and panics interrupted and even, for a while, reversed it, and it was aided to a degree by a slow rise in the average age of the population. But not until this century was the effort formally abandoned.

Today, and for the last few decades, enlightened people scoff at moral uplift, reject temperance as an effort of bluenoses, and are skeptical (with good reason) about the prospects of using prisons (or much of anything else) for rehabilitating offenders. Having replaced the Victorian commitment to controlling impulses with the modern commitment to individual choice, liberal and conservative students of crime alike have turned their attention to finding better ways of manipulating the incentives facing individuals who might choose crime. The chief difference of opinion among these thinkers is whether it is better to manipulate the costs of crime (by stressing the deterrent or incapacitative effects of criminal sanctions) or the benefits of noncrime (by stressing the need for better employment and income-maintenance opportunities).

Advocates of manipulating costs are usually regarded as tough minded while advocates of manipulating benefits are often thought to be tender minded; in fact, there is no important philosophical difference between them (though they imagine there is). Both assume that the would-be offender is reasonably rational and generally self-interested, and that he chooses between crime and noncrime on the basis of the opportunities each offers to satisfy his needs. Indeed, if the model of human nature each school embraces is correct, then it follows that a sound public policy would try to alter both costs and benefits. Of course, the tough minded may believe that it is the attractiveness of crime that leads people to prefer it even to available jobs, whereas the tender minded may think that it is the unavailability of jobs that "forces" people into crime regardless of its costs. These differences have important political implications but only modest scientific or philosophical ones. The tough minded stress getting tough and the tender minded stress doing good, but scientifically all they are arguing about is the relative efficiency of sanctions and their alternatives (which is only a matter of more or less); philosophically, they embrace the same theory of human nature.

The older debate about crime involved very different assumptions about human nature. Both liberals and conservatives (those terms, of course, were not in use at the time) agreed that crime was the result of failure in the moral development of men, in particular the failure of some men to learn how to control their impulses. In the nineteenth century, "conservatives" thought that human nature was fundamentally evil and that the family and church must work hard to overcome, by rigorous discipline, these base impulses; "liberals" thought human nature was at worst neutral and perhaps good and the task of the family and church was to guide those benign impulses into a "Christian character."

The current ascendancy of the rational choice view of human nature —the view first sketched by Hobbes and then elaborated by Bentham— is in part the result of the disappointment experienced by so many persons who have sought in vain for dependable evidence that criminals could be rehabilitated by plan, in large numbers, and at reasonable cost. But science alone rarely shapes our conceptions of human psychology; there were cultural and political reasons as well for the declining acceptability of the communal approach to crime. That view seemed, to many of its adherents, to require an intrusion into personal lives that was quite out of keeping with the rising commitment to the ideology of personal liberation and radical individualism.

The ending of Victorian morality and the inability of the state, except at great and unacceptable cost, to recreate that morality, combined with the growth in personal freedom and social prosperity, have produced an individualistic ethos that both encourages crime and shapes the kind of policies we are prepared to use to combat it. A liberal, commercial society committed to personal self-expression thus discovers that it must rely more, not less, on the criminal justice system and on efforts to manage the labor market. Since 1960, we have invested heavily in trying to improve the criminal justice system and to solve the problem of young adult unemployment. Partisans of one strategy or another argue, with more heat than light, about which tactic has received or should receive the greater emphasis, but in the long view this is little more than a quibble.

The factors that most directly influence crime—family structure, moral development, the level of personal freedom—are the very things that we cannot easily change or for persuasive reasons do not wish to change. The factors that we can change (though perhaps not as much as we wish) are the factors that have only a marginal influence on crime—laws, police and prosecutorial strategies, and government-created job programs. It is possible that very large changes in these formal institutions would make a larger difference, but we are reluctant to risk having a more oppressive police or a more meddlesome state. Besides, we are constrained by a sense of justice: when many are unemployed, it seems unfair to give criminals or would-be criminals priority access to jobs.

Societies that are not free need not rely as much as we on the police apparatus to control crime for, if they manage their "unfreedom" skill-fully, they can use schools, neighborhoods, communes, political parties, and mutual spying to control behavior. Societies that are free need to rely more heavily on the police apparatus and economic management because they have foresworn the use of other methods. Law becomes more important as informal social control becomes less important.

The people are impatient with so bleak a choice and have, by their actions, indicated their continuing attachment to a more communal form of crime control. Hundreds, probably thousands, of neighborhood organizations and civic enterprises have arisen spontaneously out of a desire to reduce crime, or at least to mitigate its effects, by direct popular action. It is a measure of our times that these efforts are often resisted by the police as an intrusion into their official domain and criticized by the intelligentsia as giving expression to the vigilante spirit. In truth, this recourse to informal, communal action is nothing more than a reaffirmed allegiance to a communal theory of social control and a repetition of a manner of exercising that control noted by Tocqueville when he visited this country (at a time when crime was beginning to become a problem). He wrote:

> In America the means that the authorities have at their disposal for the discovery of crimes and the arrest of criminals are few. A state police does not exist, and passports are unknown. The criminal police of the United States cannot be compared with that of France; the magistrates and public agents are not numerous; they do not always initiate the measures for arresting the guilty; and the examinations of prisoners are rapid and oral. Yet I believe that in no country does crime more rarely elude punishment. The reason is that everyone conceives himself to be interested in furnishing evidence of the crime and in seizing the delinquent. During my stay in the United States I witnessed the spontaneous formation of committees in a county for the pursuit and prosecution of a man who had committed a great crime. In Europe a criminal is an unhappy man who is struggling for his life against the agents of power, while the people are merely a spectator of the conflict; in America he is looked upon as an enemy of the human race, and the whole of mankind is against him.[84]

Today, the dominant ethos does not easily support such methods or such views. We have become a nation that takes democracy to mean maximum self-expression, though it never meant that originally, and to be suspicious of anything that looks like an effort to state or enforce a common morality. Democracy has become an end, though it originally was embraced as a means to other ends—a way (to quote the Constitution) of forming a more perfect union, establishing justice, insuring domestic tranquillity, providing for the common defense, promoting the general welfare, and securing the blessings of liberty. In the hands of reasonable, decent people, a devotion to self-actualization is at best artistic or inspiring and at worst banal or trivial. In the hands of persons of weak character, with a taste for risk and an impatience for gratification, that ethos is a license to steal and mug.

We have made our society and we must live with it. If the philosophy of Hobbes and Bentham governs our explanations of history and our definitions of policy, so be it; no one, least of all fundamentalist ministers, is going to change that. And so we must labor as patiently as we can to make a liberal society work and to make the best and sanest use of our laws to control behavior without feeling embarrassed that by invoking "The Law," we are denying our liberal creed. Far from it; we are reaffirming it.

Chapter 13

Crime and
Public Policy

IF we are to make the best and sanest use of our laws and liberties, we must first adopt a sober view of man and his institutions that would permit reasonable things to be accomplished, foolish things abandoned, and utopian things forgotten. A sober view of man requires a modest definition of progress. A 20 percent reduction in the number of robberies would still leave us with the highest robbery rate of almost any Western nation but would prevent over one hundred thousand robberies. A small gain for society, a large one for the would-be victims. But even this gain is unlikely if we do not think clearly about crime and public policy.

The quest for the causes of crime is an intellectually stimulating, though, thus far, rather confusing, endeavor. To the extent we have learned anything at all, we have learned that the factors in our lives and history that most powerfully influence the crime rate—our commitment to liberty, our general prosperity, our childrearing methods, our popular values—are precisely the factors that are hardest or riskiest to change. Those things that can more easily and safely be changed—the behavior of the police, the organization of neighborhoods, the management of the criminal justice system, the sentences imposed by courts—are the things that have only limited influence on the crime rate.

If the things we can measure and manipulate had a large effect on the crime rate, then those effects would by now be evident in our statistical studies and police experiments. If crime were easily deterred by changes in the certainty or severity of sanctions, then our equations would probably have detected such effects in ways that overcome the criticisms now made of such studies. If giving jobs to ex-offenders and school dropouts readily prevented crime, the results of the Manpower Demonstration Research Corporation experiments would not have been so disappointing. If new police patrol techniques made a large and demonstrable difference, those techniques would have been identified.

In a sense, the radical critics of American society are correct: if you wish to make a big difference in crime, you must make fundamental changes in society. But they are right only in that sense, for what they propose to put in place of existing institutions, to the extent they propose anything at all except angry rhetoric, would probably make us yearn for the good old days when our crime rate was higher but our freedoms were intact. Indeed, some versions of the radical doctrine would leave us yearning for the good old days when not only were our freedoms intact, but our crime rate was lower.

I realize that some people, not at all radical, find it difficult to accept the notion that if we are to think seriously about crime, we ought to think about crime and not about poverty, unemployment, or racism. Such persons should bear two things in mind. The first is that there is no contradiction between taking crime seriously and taking poverty (or other social disadvantages) seriously. There is no need to choose. Quite the contrary; to the extent our efforts to measure the relationships among crime, wealth, and sanctions can be said to teach any lessons at all, it is that raising the costs of crime while leaving the benefits of noncrime untouched may be as shortsighted as raising the benefits of noncrime while leaving the costs of crime unchanged. Anticrime policies are less likely to succeed if there are no reasonable alternatives to crime; by the same token, employment programs may be less likely to succeed if there are attractive criminal alternatives to working. If legitimate opportunities for work are unavailable, some people may turn to crime, but if criminal opportunities are profitable, some persons will not take the legitimate jobs that exist.

Some persons may believe that if legitimate jobs are made absolutely more attractive than stealing, stealing will decline even without any increase in penalties for it. That may be true provided there is no practical limit on the amount that can be paid in wages. Since the average "take" from a burglary or mugging is quite small, it would seem easy to make the income from a job exceed the income from crime. But this neglects the advantages of a criminal income: one works at crime at one's convenience, enjoys the esteem of colleagues who think a "straight" job is stupid and skill at stealing is commendable, looks forward to the occasional "big score" that may make further work unnecessary for weeks, and relishes the risk and adventure associated with theft. The money value of all these benefits (that is, what one who is not shocked by crime would want in cash to forego crime) is hard to estimate but is almost certainly far larger than either public or private employers could offer to unskilled or semiskilled young workers. The only alternative for society is to so increase the risks of theft that its value is depreciated below what society can afford to pay in legal wages, and then take whatever steps are necessary to insure that those legal wages are available.

The desire to reduce crime is the worst possible reason for reducing poverty. Most poor persons are not criminals; many either are retired or have regular jobs and lead conventional family lives. The elderly, the working poor, and the willing-to-work poor could benefit greatly from economic conditions and government programs that enhance their incomes without there being the slightest reduction in crime (indeed, if the experience of the 1960s is any guide, there might well be, through no fault of most beneficiaries, an increase in crime). Reducing poverty and breaking up the ghettoes are desirable policies in their own right, whatever their effects on crime. It is the duty of government to devise other measures to cope with crime, not only to permit antipoverty programs to succeed without unfair competition from criminal opportunities, but also to insure that such programs do not inadvertently shift the costs of progress, in terms of higher crime rates, onto innocent parties, not the least of whom are the poor themselves.

One cannot press this economic reasoning too far. Some persons will commit crimes whatever the risks; indeed, for some, the greater the risk the greater the thrill, while others (the alcoholic wife beater, for example) are only dimly aware that there are any risks. But more important than the insensitivity of certain criminals to changes in risks and benefits is the impropriety of casting the crime problem wholly in terms of a utilitarian calculus. The most serious offenses are crimes not simply because society finds them inconvenient, but because it regards them with moral horror. To steal, to rape, to rob, to assault—these acts are destructive of the very possibility of society and affronts to the humanity of their victims. Parents do not instruct their children to be law abiding merely by pointing to the risks of being caught, but by explaining that these acts are wrong whether or not one is caught. I conjecture that those parents who simply warn their offspring about the risks of crime produce a disproportionate number of young persons willing to take those risks.

Even the deterrent capacity of the criminal justice system depends in no small part on its ability to evoke sentiments of shame in the accused. If all it evoked were a sense of being unlucky, crime rates would be even higher. James Fitzjames Stephens makes the point by analogy. To what extent, he asks, would a man be deterred from theft by the knowledge that by committing it he was exposing himself to one chance in fifty of catching a serious but not fatal illness—say, a bad fever? Rather little, we would imagine—indeed, all of us regularly take risks as great or greater than that: when we drive after drinking, when we smoke cigarettes, when we go hunting in the woods. The criminal sanction, Stephens concludes, "operates not only on the fears of criminals. [A] great part of the general detestation of crime . . . arises from the fact that the commission of offenses is associated . . . with the solemn and deliberate infliction of punishment wherever crime is proved."[1]

Much is made today of the fact that the criminal justice system "stigmatizes" those caught up in it, and thus unfairly marks such persons and perhaps even furthers their criminal careers by "labeling" them as criminals. Whether the labeling process operates in this way is as yet unproved, but it would indeed be unfortunate if society treated a convicted offender in such a way that he had no reasonable alternative but to make crime a career. To prevent this, society should insure that one can "pay one's debt" without suffering permanent loss of civil rights, the continuing and pointless indignity of parole supervision, and the frustration of being unable to find a job. But doing these things is very different from eliminating the "stigma" from crime. To destigmatize crime would be to lift from it the weight of moral judgment and to make crime simply a particular occupation or avocation which society has chosen to reward less (or perhaps more!) than other pursuits. If there is no stigma attached to an activity, then society has no business making it a crime. Indeed, before the invention of the prison in the late eighteenth and early nineteenth centuries, the stigma attached to criminals was the major deterrent to and principal form of protection from criminal activity. The purpose of the criminal justice system is not to expose would-be criminals to a lottery in which they either win or lose, but to expose them in addition and more importantly to the solemn condemnation of the community should they yield to temptation.

If we grant that it is proper to try to improve the criminal justice system without apologizing for the fact that those efforts do not attack the "root causes" of crime, the next thing to remember is that we are seeking, at best, marginal improvements that can only be discovered through patient trial-and-error accompanied by hardheaded and objective evaluations.

There are, we now know, certain things we can change in accordance with our intentions, and certain ones we cannot. We cannot alter the number of juveniles who first experiment with minor crimes. We apparently cannot lower the overall recidivism rate, though within reason we should keep trying. We are not yet certain whether we can increase significantly the police apprehension rate. We may be able to change the teenage unemployment rate, though we have learned by painful trial-and-error that doing this is much more difficult than once supposed. We can probably reduce the time it takes to bring an arrested person to trial, even though we have as yet made few serious efforts to do so. We can certainly reduce any arbitrary exercise of prosecutorial discretion over whom to charge and whom to release, and we can most definitely stop pretending that judges know, any better than the rest of us, how to provide "individualized justice." We can confine a larger proportion of the serious and repeat offenders and fewer of the common drunks and truant children. We know that confining criminals prevents them from harming society, and we have grounds for suspecting that some would-be criminals can be deterred by the confinement of others.

Above all, we can try to learn more about what works and, in the process, abandon our ideological preconceptions about what ought to work. This is advice, not simply or even primarily to government—for governments are run by men and women who are under irresistible pressures to pretend they know more than they do—but to my colleagues: academics, theoreticians, writers, advisers. We may feel ourselves under pressure to pretend we know things, but we are also under a positive obligation to admit what we do not know and to avoid cant and sloganizing.

In the last decade or so, we have learned a great deal, perhaps more than we sometimes admit. But we have learned very little to a moral certainty. Any effort to reduce crime is an effort to alter human behavior at moments when it is least well observed and by methods (deterrence, incapacitation, rehabilitation) whose effect is delayed and uncertain. Under these circumstances, we may never know "what works" to a moral certainty. Why, then, gamble on what we (or at least I) think we know? I offer Pascal's wager. If altering the rewards and penalties of crime affects the rate of crime, and I act on that belief, I reduce crime. If such strategies do not work, and I act on the false belief that they do, I have merely made swifter, more certain, or more severe the penalties that befall a person guilty in any event and to that extent have served justice, though not utility. But if I do not believe in them, and they do in fact work, then I have condemned innocent persons to suffer needlessly and have served neither justice nor utility.

But what, precisely, ought we to do if we act on the belief that we know, though with some uncertainty, how to reduce crime marginally? The purpose of this book is not to offer a detailed set of anticrime policies, it is only to teach people how to think about crime (and especially how to think about the kind of research that is done about crime control). But it would be unfair to the reader to leave him or her to guess what the author believes ought to be done after learning to think this way.

The policy implications of what I have learned are in many ways so obvious that many readers will wonder why it is necessary to struggle through all these facts, regression equations, and experiments to accept them. There are many reasons why it is necessary to find evidence for the obvious, not the least of which is that many people still do not find them obvious, or even reasonable. If you doubt this, attend a city council meeting on the police budget, a legislative debate on the criminal laws, a convention of judges discussing sentencing, or a conference of criminologists.

A reasonable set of policies would, to me, include the following. Neighborhoods threatened with crime or disorder would be encouraged to create self-help organizations of citizens who, working in collaboration with the police, patrol their own communities to detect, though not to apprehend, suspicious persons. Densely settled neighborhoods would make extensive use of foot patrol officers and would hire off-duty police and, perhaps, private security guards to help maintain order and to prevent disreputable behavior in public places from frightening decent persons off the sidewalks or from encouraging predatory offenders to use the anarchy and anonymity of the streets as an opportunity for serious crime. Drug dealers would be driven off the streets.

The police would organize their patrol units to help maintain order and to identify and, where possible, arrest high-rate offenders. Detectives and patrol officers would make thorough, on-the-spot investigations of recent, serious offenses. As much information as possible would be gathered about the records and habits of high-rate offenders and officers would be given strong incentives to find and arrest them. Even when they are caught committing a relatively minor crime, these career criminals would be the object of intensive follow-up investigations so as to make the strongest possible case against them.

All persons arrested for a serious offense and all high-rate offenders arrested for any offense would be screened by prosecutors who would have immediately accessible the juvenile and adult criminal records of such persons so that a complete picture of their criminal history could be readily assessed. Those who commit very serious offenses and high-rate offenders who have committed any offense would be given priority treatment in terms of prompt follow-up investigations, immediate arraignment, bail recommendations to insure appearance at trial, and an early trial date so that those who cannot post bail will have their cases disposed of swiftly. One prosecutor would handle each priority case from intake to final disposition. Victims and witnesses would be given special assistance, including counseling on procedures, money aid (where appropriate) to compensate them for their time away from work, and the early return of any stolen property that has been recovered.

Well-staffed prosecutorial and public defender's offices would be prepared for an early trial (or plea-bargain) in these priority cases; judges would be loath to grant continuances for convenience of counsel. Sentencing would be shaped, though not rigidly determined, by sentencing guidelines that take into account not only the gravity of the offense and the prior conviction record of the accused, but also the full criminal history, including the juvenile record and the involvement, if any, of the accused with drug abuse. The outer bounds of judicial discretion would be shaped by society's judgment as to what constitutes a just and fair penalty for a given offense; within those bounds, sentencing would be designed to reduce crime by giving longer sentences to high-rate offenders (even when convicted of a less serious offense) and shorter sentences to low-rate offenders (even if the offense in question is somewhat more serious).

Persons convicted of committing minor offenses who have little or no prior record would be dealt with by community-based corrections: in particular, by supervised community service and victim restitution. Probation officers would insure that these obligations are in fact met; individuals failing to meet them would promptly be given short jail sentences.

Offenders sentenced to some period of incarceration would be carefully screened so that young and old, violent and nonviolent, neurotic and psychotic offenders would be assigned to separate facilities and, within those facilities, to educational and treatment programs appropriate to their personalities and needs. Progress in such programs would have nothing to do, however, with the date on which the offenders are released. Time served would be set by the judge, perhaps with stated discounts for good behavior; rehabilitation, to the extent that it occurs at all, would be a benefit of the programs but not a circumstance determining the length of the sentence. Parole boards might make recommendations to the sentencing judge or to the governor about sentences that ought to be commuted or shortened in the manifest interests of justice, but they would not determine release dates. Parole officers would continue to assist ex-offenders in returning to the community, especially with jobs and limited financial assistance, but there would be no assumption that these services would reduce the recidivism rate or that the parole officer would oversee the behavior of the offender in the community.

Prisons would be of small to moderate size and in no facility housing violent or high-rate offenders would double-bunking occur. Contraband flowing into or out of the prisons would be strictly controlled. The first objective of the guards would be to protect society by maintaining secure custody; their second (and perhaps equally important) objective would be to protect the inmates from one another. Guards would be sufficiently numerous so that they were not forced to choose between controlling the prison by terror or abdicating control of it to organized groups of inmates.

People will disagree with one or more elements of this sketchy set of proposals; I myself may change my mind about the details as I learn more about what works and think harder about what justice requires. But in broad outline, it strikes me neither as an unreasonable set of ideas nor one likely to be rejected by most citizens. There is no idea on this list that is not now being implemented in at least one jurisdiction, and large numbers of these ideas are being practiced in a few jurisdictions. But in general, and in most places, this package of ideas is resisted in practice just as it may be applauded in theory. The blunt fact is that the criminal justice system in this country does not, for the most part, operate as I have suggested.

Neighborhood and citizen patrols are often resisted by the police who fear a loss of their monopoly of power, by individual officers who fear a loss of their jobs, and by citizens who are quickly bored with volunteer work. Community-involved foot patrol is resisted by many police supervisors who fear loss of control of the beat officers. Assigning officers to neighborhoods on the basis of levels of public disorder and concentrating police investigations on high-rate offenders are resisted by citizens who judge the police entirely on the basis of how swiftly they dispatch a patrol car in response to a telephone call reporting a burglary that might have occurred many hours or even many days earlier.

Supporters of the family court system resist making juvenile criminal records routinely available in adult courts and many prosecutors who, in fact, could obtain such records often do not because of the expense and bother. Prosecutors have come to embrace the idea of "career criminal" programs, but most of these are limited to adult offenders and even to those adult offenders who have committed very serious crimes, regardless of whether they are in fact high-rate offenders. The offices of prosecutors and public defenders are often so thinly staffed that asking for court continuances is absolutely essential. And even where it is not essential, it is usually convenient. Postponing cases is for prosecutors a way of evening out the workload and for defenders a way of making the evidence turn cold and the witnesses lose interest.

Many probation departments have created victim restitution and community service programs, but they often discover that persons ordered to participate in them ignore the order with impunity, because judges are not inclined (or are too busy) to enforce the order with appropriate sanctions. If a large fraction of all fines levied by judges are not paid in full, is it any wonder that community-based corrections so often result in offenders walking away from them?

Judges are by and large opposed to any substantial restriction on their right to sentence as they see fit, whatever the cost in crime control or fairness. They favor "guidelines," but only those they themselves have developed and that they are free to ignore. Some thoughtful legislators support more restrictive guidelines, but these are often based merely on the gravity of the instant offense and take little account of the crime-control possibilities of selectively incapacitating high-rate offenders. And less thoughtful legislators find it much more appealing to call for massively severe sentences without regard to whether they will ever be imposed.

Taxpayers overwhelmingly want the system to crack down on serious and repeat offenders, but they regularly vote down bond issues designed to build the necessary additional prisons and they oppose having new facilities located in their neighborhoods. These taxpayer revolts are aided and abetted by pressure groups that are hostile to incarceration, retaining in the face of all evidence to the contrary a faith in rehabilitation and reserving their feelings of vengeance for "white-collar" criminals (especially those who might have served in conservative administrations).

In short, the entire criminal justice system, from citizen to judge, is governed by perverse incentives. Though many of its members agree on what they wish to achieve, the incentives faced by each member acting individually directs him or her to act in ways inconsistent with what is implied by that agreement.

In evidence of this, consider the following. Police officers want to arrest serious offenders—they are "good collars"—but making such arrests in ways that lead to conviction is difficult. Those convictions that are obtained are usually the result of the efforts of a small minority of all officers. Arrests that stand up in court tend to involve stranger-to-stranger crimes, to occur soon after the crime, and to be accompanied by physical evidence or eyewitness testimony. The officers who look hard for the perpetrators of stranger-to-stranger crimes, who gather physical evidence, and who carefully interview victims and potential witnesses are a small minority of all officers. Recall the account in chapter 6 of the study by Brian Forst. He found, in six police jurisdictions, that about one-half of all convictions resulted from arrests made by only one-eighth of all officers. Indeed, one-quarter of the officers who made arrests produced zero convictions. Though these differences were in part the result of differences in duty assignments, they persisted after controlling for assignments.[2] For many officers, it is much easier to take reports of crimes, mediate disputes, and turn big cases over to detectives who often take up the trail when it is cold. Despite these differences in behavior, Forst found that the most productive officers tend to get about the same number of commendations and awards as the least productive ones.

Prosecutors also behave in many cases in ways inconsistent with a crime-control objective. In the 1960s, many of them tooks cases to court more or less in the order in which the arrests had been made. Then they began to assign higher priority to grave offenses. While an improvement, this still resulted in resources being concentrated on persons who had committed serious offenses, rather than on high-rate offenders. As we saw in chapter 8, these are not necessarily the same persons. By the late 1970s, many career criminal programs had become quite sophisticated: they gave highest priority to grave offenses and to offenders with long or serious records. But even now, many jurisdictions limit the selection of cases to persons with serious adult records, ignoring the high predictive value of the juvenile record and the drug-abuse history. Some prosecutors will concentrate their follow-up investigations on persons who have committed serious crimes and neglect the crime-control value of investigating suspected high-rate offenders who may have been caught for a nonserious offense.

Judges must manage a crowded docket, dispose of cases quickly, and make decisions under uncertainty. Some are also eager to minimize their chances of being reversed on appeal. These managerial concerns, while quite understandable, often get in the way of trying to use the court hearing as a means of establishing who is and who is not a high-rate offender and of allowing such distinctions, as well as the facts about the gravity of the case, to shape the sentence.

To the extent the incentives operating in the criminal justice system have perverse and largely unintended effects, it is not clear what can be done about it. The "system" is not, as so many have remarked, in fact a system—that is, a set of consciously coordinated activities. And given the importance we properly attach to having an independent judiciary and to guaranteeing, even at some cost in crime control, the rights of accused by means of the adversarial process, there is no way the various institutions can be made into a true system. The improvements that can be made are all at the margin and require patient effort and an attention to detail. Sometimes a modest leap forward is possible, as when prosecutors began using computers to keep track of their cases and to learn about the characteristics of the defendants, or when legislators began experimenting with various kinds of sentencing guidelines. But mostly, progress requires dull, unrewarding work in the trenches. There is no magic bullet.

Throughout all this, our society has been, with but few exceptions, remarkably forebearing. We have preserved and even extended the most comprehensive array of civil liberties found in any nation on earth despite rising crime rates and (in the 1960s) massive civil disorder. Though proposals are now afoot to modify some of these procedural guarantees—especially those having to do with the exclusionary rule, the opportunity for unlimited appeals, and the right to bail—they constitute, at most, rather modest changes. If adopted, they would still leave our criminal justice system with a stronger set of guarantees than one could find in most other nations, including those, such as Great Britain and Canada, that we acknowledge to be bastions of freedom. We have chosen, as I think we should, to have a wide-ranging bill of rights, but we must be willing to pay the price of that choice. That price includes a willingness both to accept a somewhat higher level of crime and disorder than we might otherwise have and to invest a greater amount of resources in those institutions (the police, the prosecutors, the courts, the prisons) needed to cope with those who violate our law while claiming its protections.

For most of us, the criminal justice system is intended for the other fellow, and since the other fellow is thought to be wicked, we can easily justify to ourselves a pinch-penny attitude toward the system. It is, after all, not designed to help us but to hurt him. If it is unpleasant, congested, and cumbersome, it is probably only what those who are caught up in its toils deserve. What we forget is that the more unpleasant the prisons, the less likely judges will be to send people to them; the more congested the prosecutor's office, the less likely that office will be to sort out, carefully, the serious and high-rate offender from the run-of-the-mill and low-rate offender; the more cumbersome the procedures, the less likely we and our neighbors will be to take the trouble of reporting crimes, making statements, and testifying in court.

Wicked people exist. Nothing avails except to set them apart from innocent people. And many people, neither wicked nor innocent, but watchful, dissembling, and calculating of their chances, ponder our reaction to wickedness as a clue to what they might profitably do. Our actions speak louder than our words. When we profess to believe in deterrence and to value justice, but refuse to spend the energy and money required to produce either, we are sending a clear signal that we think that safe streets, unlike all other great public goods, can be had on the cheap. We thereby trifle with the wicked, make sport of the innocent, and encourage the calculators. Justice suffers, and so do we all.

Appendix

A Note on Gun Control

EVERY publicized shooting revives the debate about gun control without bringing the debaters closer together.* The deaths of Dr. Michael Halberstam and John Lennon, and the attempted assassination of President Reagan, like the death of Robert F. Kennedy and the assault on George Wallace, stir emotions but produce no consensus. When people think an issue important but can make no progress toward resolving it, it is probably time to rethink the way in which they define it.

Essentially three views are in contention. One is to do nothing: guns do not kill, people kill. A second is that a handgun exists only to kill and its production and possession should be tightly restricted. A third is that certain kinds of violent encounters are more likely to have lethal consequences if guns happen to be readily available and that society ought to devise ways of reducing that availability among people likely to be involved in those encounters.

The first view is correct but misleading. People pull triggers. And some triggers are pulled by people so determined that the gun is merely a tool. But many crimes are committed by persons without clear or strong intentions—persons who are enraged, drunk, or looking for trouble. In such cases, people let the means at hand determine what kind of force they will employ and against whom. A substantial body of research, such as that by Franklin Zimring, confirms that the availability of a gun influences the

*Original version of this appendix written with Mark H. Moore.

261

outcomes of angry encounters.[1] Fights that occur in settings where guns are present are more likely to be fatal than those that occur where guns are absent.

The second view is wrong, unfeasible and impolitic. There are handguns in at least one-fifth of all American households. The vast majority of these weapons are never used to threaten or injure anyone. Banning the production of new handguns might prevent that stock from increasing. Buying back existing guns might reduce that stock slightly, but it would be enormously expensive and, without production controls, futile. Larger reductions would require confiscation. And even if all these policies were adopted, and even if the reductions in ownership were great (say, by 50 percent), the remaining guns would easily support for a decade current rates of robberies at gunpoint.

But none of these policies is likely to be adopted, and for reasons having nothing to do with the presumed power of the National Rifle Association. The average legislator simply cannot afford to come before his or her constituents with the following proposal: "Your government, having failed to protect you against crime, now proposes to strip from you what you regard as an effective means of self-defense as well as an enjoyable hobby." Never mind whether the belief about self-defense is true; gun ownership, from the First Lady to the average citizen, is testimony to the unshakable power of that belief.

The third view is one that policy-makers ought to take more seriously than they have. We should recognize that people have a right to own guns but do not have the right to use them criminally. Moreover, people who are found in possession of guns while committing a crime or participating in a violent dispute should lose both the gun and their freedom. Finally, the police should be more active in intercepting the traffic in contraband guns and apprehending people carrying unlicensed guns in public places, and judges should deal with those persons more severely.

Federal and state laws now make it unlawful for convicted felons, ex-addicts, and mental defectives to possess a handgun. Moreover, in many states and most big cities, it is illegal to carry a concealed handgun (except for a small number of people with police permits). The laws governing possession might usefully be tightened even further—for example, by denying handguns to people convicted of violent misdemeanors (such as assault) or of chronic public drunkenness. The Attorney General's Task Force on Violent Crime, in its 1981 report, recommended measures that would tighten the controls on gun ownership without denying law-abiding persons the right to purchase and own a handgun. If adopted, those recommendations would require that states provide for a mandatory waiting period to allow for a records check to ascertain whether a prospective handgun purchaser is a convicted offender or an ex-addict and would further require that individuals report to local law enforcement agencies the theft or loss of a handgun.[2] In these and other ways, the casual purchasing of guns by dangerous persons and the difficulty of tracing guns that have been stolen might be reduced. I doubt that such changes would have major effects, but it is hard to see why one should oppose them. After all, we have little difficulty with the idea that the states should be allowed to check the driving records of persons applying for drivers' licenses or that people should be required (for insurance purposes at least) to report the theft of an automobile.

But the real problem is to motivate the criminal justice system to take these or better laws more seriously. To see what this involves, it is first necessary to understand the different situations in which a weapon affects the outcome of a violent encounter. The first involves disputes—family quarrels, barroom fights, street corner brawls among "friends." The traditional police response to such disputes is to pacify the opponents, perhaps separate them for the night, and occasionally make an arrest if the assault seems to be serious, the officer's authority is challenged, or the "victim" clearly intends to press charges. (Who is the "victim" and who the assailant in these disputes is often hard to decide. The victim may simply be the person who lost the fight.)

There is strong evidence that the presence of a gun in these situations raises dramatically the chance of a lethal outcome, and that people who regularly engage in such disputes are much more likely than others of similar incomes and circumstances to be responsible for, or the victim of, a homicide. Yet there is equally strong evidence that communal disputes are not taken seriously by the criminal justice system. Either no arrest is made or the charges are dropped or the sentence is trivial. This is understandable, given the constraints: if only a simple assault (a misdemeanor) has occurred, the police cannot lawfully make an arrest without a signed complaint. And even if a complaint is forthcoming, the victim is likely to change her (sometimes his) mind the next day. Without an arrest, a search for a seizure of weapons is difficult, if not impossible.

I suggest that state law and police practice be amended so as to take violent disputes more seriously. Following the lead of Minnesota and other states, the police should be empowered to make arrests in these cases if they have probable cause to believe an assault has occurred, even if the assault is not felonious. Following the policy of the New York Police Department and the evidence of the Minneapolis spouse-assault experiment described in chapter 7, officers should be encouraged to make arrests both to protect the victim and to deter, if possible, future assaults.[3] And, incident to these arrests, valid searches should be made for guns improperly in the possession of the disputants. Both the assault and the illegal possession of a weapon in these circumstances should be dealt with more sternly than now is the custom with judges who tend not to regard such matters as "real crime." That attitude may encourage a real crime later because a predisposition to violence is unchecked by sanctions. These sanctions may involve jail or they may involve posting peace bonds, intensive probation or the like. The key is a clear penalty and the removal of the gun.

The second situation is the stranger-to-stranger violent crime—muggings and robberies. The guns used by such criminals are often already possessed in violation of the law. For them, the problem is not tightening the laws involving carrying a weapon, but blocking the access these people have to supplies of guns and increasing the risks from carrying weapons. Mark Moore's research indicates that the largest sources of supply of handguns to people who use them for stranger-to-stranger crimes are thefts and the black market.[4] In short, armed robbers usually violate gun laws in two ways: they have stolen their handgun, or bought it from somebody who did, and they are carrying it without a permit.

To reduce the black-market traffic in guns, the police should consider mounting more undercover "buy and bust" operations (much as they now do with respect to heroin and dangerous drugs) in order to make illegal gun dealers wary of dealing with strangers, to raise the price and difficulty of acquiring illegal guns (perhaps beyond the point that opportunistic, teenage robbers will find it worthwhile) and to deter some people from going into the illegal gun business at all.

To inhibit the carrying of handguns, the police should become more aggressive in stopping suspicious people and, where they have reasonable grounds for their suspicions, frisking (that is, patting down) those stopped to obtain guns. Hand-held magnetometers, of the sort used by airport security guards, might make the street frisks easier and less intrusive. All this can probably be done without changing the law.

The success of undercover buys and aggressive patrolling depends partly on the extent to which judges will seriously penalize the unauthorized carrying of concealed weapons. Though judges often give more severe sentences to people who commit a crime *using* a gun, the available data suggest that a person convicted of illegally carrying or possessing a handgun is generally treated leniently. This is a serious mistake: a person in a public place with a gun and without a permit is often a person looking for trouble.

The Bartley-Fox law in Massachusetts requires a mandatory one-year jail sentence for any unlicensed person who carries a firearm. It was opposed by those who said the law would not be enforced and by those who said it would not have the desired effect. As we saw in chapter 7, both criticisms appear to have been wrong—the criminal justice system did not engage in wholesale evasions of the requirements of the law, and the three studies that have been done of its effect all point to some decline in the proportion of the assaults that were committed with firearms. Assaults as a whole increased; firearm assaults decreased. The effect of Bartley-Fox might have been even greater if the police had been more aggressive in enforcing it (or less if it had not been so heavily publicized).

Note what I am suggesting: not "gun control" in any comprehensive sense, but rather increased pressure on the particular circumstances and people whose illegal behavior is most likely to be affected by the availability of a gun. Note also that to do these things requires action chiefly by state and local, not federal, agencies. Bear in mind that motivating police and prosecutors to act in these ways is not easy. And note finally that real progress in reducing gun violence almost certainly requires methods—aggressive patrolling, undercover operations, tougher sentences—that liberals instinctively dislike. I think, however, there is no way around these tough choices, and it is time we face up to them.

Notes

Introduction

1. Harry G. Johnson, "The Alternative Before Us," *Journal of Political Economy* 80 (May–June, 1972): S280–S289.

Chapter 1 Crime Amidst Plenty

1. Crime rates used in this chapter are taken from Donald J. Mulvihill and Melvin M. Tumin, eds., *Crimes of Violence*, vol. 11 of a staff report to the National Commission on the Causes and Prevention of Violence (Washington, D.C.: U.S. Government Printing Office, 1969), p. 54.

2. Data on drug use from *Quantitative Analysis of the Heroin Addiction Problem*, a report to the Office of Science and Technology, Executive Office of the President (Arlington, Va.: Institute for Defense Analyses, 1972).

3. The official title of the "Moynihan Report" was *The Negro Family: The Case for National Action* (Washington, D.C.: Office of Policy Planning and Research, U.S. Department of Labor, March 1965). The more recent AFDC figures are from the National Center for Social Statistics, U.S. Department of Health, Education, and Welfare (private communication).

4. Employment figures are from U.S. Department of Labor, Bureau of Labor Statistics, "Youth Unemployment and the Minimum Wage," Bulletin No. 1657 (Washington, D.C.: U.S. Government Printing Office, 1970), pp. 1–6. The phrase quoted appears on p. 5.

5. The figures and comments from Professor Ryder are taken with his permission from a memorandum prepared by him for the President's Science Advisory Committee.

6. The data on Washington, D.C., were supplied by Dr. Robert L. DuPont, M.D., then head of the Narcotics Treatment Administration of that city.

7. Marvin E. Wolfgang, Robert M. Figlio, and Thorsten Sellin, *Delinquency in a Birth Cohort* (Chicago: University of Chicago Press, 1972).

8. Arnold Barnett, Daniel J. Kleitman, and Richard C. Larson, "On Urban Homicide," working paper WP–04–74 (Operations Research Center, Massachusetts Institute of Technology, March 1974).

9. Theodore Ferdinand, "Reported Index Crime Increases Between 1950 and 1965 Due to Urbanization and Changes in the Age Structure of the Population Alone," app. 3 to *Crimes of Violence*, ed. Mulvihill and Tumin, pp. 145–152. See also Llad Phillips, Harold L. Votey, Jr., and Darold Maxwell, "Crime, Youth, and the Labor Market," *Journal of Political Economy* 80 (May–

June 1972): 491–504, and compare Roland Chilton and Adele Spielberger, "Is Delinquency Increasing? Age Structure and the Crime Rate," *Social Forces* 47 (1971): 487–493.

10. Analyses of the epidemic patterns of heroin addiction include Leon Gibson Hunt, *Heroin Epidemics: A Quantitative Study of Current Empirical Data*, Monograph MS-3 (Washington, D.C.: Drug Abuse Council, 1973); Robert L. DuPont and Mark H. Greene, "The Dynamics of a Heroin Addiction Epidemic," *Science* 181 (August 1973): 716–722; and Robert L. DuPont, "Profile of a Heroin-Addiction Epidemic," *New England Journal of Medicine* 285 (August 1971): 320–324. See also the references for chapter 11.

Chapter 2 Crime and Community

1. Roger Beardwood, "The New Negro Mood," *Fortune* 78 (January 1968): 146–151. For some contradictory findings, see Peter K. Eisinger, "The Urban Crisis as a Failure of Community," *Urban Affairs* 9 (June 1974): 437–461, and my rejoinder on pp. 462–465.

2. Commission on Law Enforcement and the Administration of Justice, *Task Force Report: Assessment of Crime* (Washington, D.C.: U.S. Government Printing Office, 1968), pp. 85–89.

3. I treat here the function of community in regulating public behavior through face-to-face contact, and stress the rational elements of this regulatory process. There are other meanings—and functions—of community. See, for example, Robert Nisbet, *The Quest for Community* (New York: Oxford University Press, 1953).

4. Daniel Elazar, "Are We a Nation of Cities?" in *A Nation of Cities*, ed. Robert A. Goldwin (Chicago: Rand McNally & Co., 1968), pp. 89–97.

5. "Crime in the Nation's Five Largest Cities," an advance report of the Law Enforcement Assistance Administration, U.S. Department of Justice, Washington, D.C. (April 1974).

6. Sar A. Levitan, William Johnston, and Robert Taggart, *Still a Dream: A Study of Black Progress, Problems, and Prospects* (Cambridge: Harvard University Press, 1975), chap. 7.

7. Levitan, *Still a Dream*, chap. 9, and Thomas Sowell, *Black Education: Myths and Tragedies* (New York: David McKay Co., Inc., 1972), p. 119.

8. Orde Coombs, "Three Faces of Harlem," *New York Times Magazine*, November 3, 1974, pp. 32 ff.

Chapter 3 Thinking About Crime

1. President's Commission on Law Enforcement and Administration of Justice, *The Challenge of Crime in a Free Society* (Washington, D.C.: U.S. Government Printing Office, 1967), p. 6.

2. Ramsey Clark, *Crime in America* (New York: Simon and Schuster, 1970), chap. 4.

3. Edwin H. Sutherland and Donald R. Cressey, *Principles of Criminology*, 7th ed. rev. (Philadelphia: J. B. Lippincott Co., 1966); Richard A. Cloward and Lloyd E. Ohlin, *Delinquency and Opportunity* (New York: Free Press, 1960).

4. Private communication from Professor Ohlin.

5. Sutherland and Cressey, *Principles*, p. 59.

6. Ibid., p. 55.

7. Ibid., pp. 95, 241, 265.

8. Ibid., pp. 150–151.

9. Albert K. Cohen, *Delinquent Boys: The Culture of the Gang* (New York: Free Press, 1955), p. 129.

10. Sheldon and Eleanor Glueck, *Unraveling Juvenile Delinquency* (Cambridge: Harvard University Press, 1950), pp. 279–281.

11. Walter B. Miller, "Lower Class Culture as a Generating Milieu of Gang Delinquency," *Journal of Social Issues* 14 (1958): 15–19. Miller, rare among social scientists, has written insightfully about the relationship of science, ideology, and policy with respect to crime. See, for example, his "Ideology and Criminal Justice Policy: Some Current Issues," *Journal of Criminal Law and Criminology* 64 (1973): 141–162.

12. Cohen, *Delinquent Boys*, p. 25.

13. Sutherland and Cressey, *Principles*, p. 684.

14. Ibid., p. 685.

15. Ibid., pp. 692–693. See also William McCord and Joan McCord, *Origins of Crime* (New York: Columbia University Press, 1959), p. vii, and Edwin Powers and Helen L. Witmer, *An Experiment in the Prevention of Delinquency* (New York: Columbia University Press, 1951).

16. McCord and McCord, *Origins of Crime*, p. 179.

17. Ibid., pp. 181–184.

18. Sutherland and Cressey, *Principles*, p. 367.

19. Ibid., p. 369.

20. Ibid., p. 682.

21. See, for example, Leslie T. Wilkins, *Evaluation of Penal Measures* (New York: Random House, 1969), and Robert Martinson, "What Works? Questions and Answers About Prison Reform," *The Public Interest* (Spring 1974): 22–54.

22. Charles R. Tittle and Charles H. Logan, "Sanctions and Deviance: Evidence and Remaining Questions," *Law and Society Review* (Spring 1973): 371–392.

23. Walter C. Reckless, *The Crime Problem*, 4th ed. (New York: Appleton-Century-Crofts, 1967), p. 508.

24. Tittle and Logan, "Sanctions and Deviance," p. 385.

25. Cloward and Ohlin, *Delinquency and Opportunity*, p. 86.

26. Ibid., p. 93.

27. Ibid., p. 211.

28. Ibid., p. 150.

29. Ibid., pp. 152, 154.

30. Lloyd E. Ohlin, "Report on the President's Commission on Law Enforcement and Administration of Justice" (Paper presented to the American Sociological Association, August 1973), p. 26.

31. Ibid., pp. 27–28.

32. Ibid., p. 29.

33. Robert Martinson, "Letter to the Editor," *Commentary* 58 (October 1974): 12.

34. Ohlin, "Report," p. 32.

Chapter 4 The Police and Crime

1. See, for example, Albert J. Reiss, Jr., *The Police and the Public* (New Haven: Yale University Press, 1971), p. 71.

2. The report on Operation 25 is from a brochure published by the New York City Police Department.

3. J. A. Bright, *Beat Patrol Experiment*, Report N. 8/69 of the Police Research and Development Branch, Home Office, London, England (July 1969).

4. S. J. Press, *Some Effects of an Increase in Police Manpower in the 20th Precinct of New York City*, Report No. R–704–NYC (New York: Rand Institute, 1971).

5. Jan M. Chaiken, Michael W. Lawless, and Keith A. Stevenson, *The Impact of Police Activity on Crime: Robberies in the New York City Subway System*, Report No. R–1424–NYC (New York: Rand Institute, 1974).

6. Philip H. Ennis, *Criminal Victimization in the United States: A Report of a National Sur-*

vey, a report to the President's Commission on Law Enforcement and Administration of Justice (Washington, D.C.: U.S. Government Printing Office, 1967).

7. An overview of team policing efforts is Lawrence W. Sherman et al., *Team Policing* (Washington, D.C.: The Police Foundation, 1973).

8. Data supplied by the New York City Police Department.

9. Tony Pate, Robert A. Bowers, and Ron Parks, *Three Approaches to Criminal Apprehension in Kansas City: An Evaluation Report* (Washington, D.C.: The Police Foundation, 1976).

10. John E. Boydstun, *San Diego Field Interrogation: Final Report* (Washington, D.C.: The Police Foundation, 1975).

11. Tony Pate et al., *Police Response Time: Its Determinants and Effects* (Washington, D.C.: The Police Foundation, 1976); William Spelman and Dale K. Brown, *Calling the Police: Citizen Reporting of Serious Crime* (Washington, D.C.: Police Executive Research Forum, 1981); Michael T. Farmer, ed., *Differential Police Response Strategies* (Washington, D.C.: Police Executive Research Forum, 1981).

12. Alfred I. Schwartz et al., *Evaluation of Cincinnati's Community Sector Team Policing Program: A Progress Report After One Year,* Working Paper 3006-18 (Washington, D.C.: The Urban Institute, 1975).

13. Peter B. Bloch and James Bell, *Managing Investigations: The Rochester System* (Washington, D.C.: The Police Foundation, 1976).

Chapter 5 Broken Windows: The Police and Neighborhood Safety

1. Police Foundation, *The Newark Foot Patrol Experiment* (Washington, D.C.: Police Foundation, 1981).

2. Philip G. Zimbardo, "The Human Choice: Individuation, Reason, and Order Versus Deindividuation, Impulse, and Chaos," in *Nebraska Symposium on Motivation,* ed. W. J. Arnold and D. Levine (Lincoln, Nebraska: University of Nebraska Press, 1969), vol. 17, pp. 237–307.

3. Ellen Hochstedler, *Crime Against the Elderly in 26 Cities,* Analytic Report SD–VAD–10 (Washington, D.C.: Department of Justice/Bureau of Justice Statistics, 1981).

4. David Yaden, Susan Folkestad, and Peter Glazer, *The Impact of Crime in Selected Neighborhoods: A Study of Public Attitudes in Four Portland, Oregon, Census Tracts* (Portland, Oregon: Campaign Information Counselors, 1973); Richard Harris, *Fear of Crime* (New York: Praeger, 1969); Fred DuBow, Edward McCabe, and Gail Kaplan, "Reactions to Crime," unpub. ms., Center for Urban Affairs, Northwestern University; Wesley G. Skogan and Michael G. Maxfield, *Coping With Crime* (Beverly Hills, Calif.: Sage Publications, 1981), chap. 7.

5. Robert Wasserman, "Security in Public Housing: A Report for the Boston Housing Authority."

6. Nathan Glazer, "On Subway Graffiti in New York," *The Public Interest* (Winter 1979), p. 4.

7. James Q. Wilson, "What Makes a Better Policeman," *Atlantic* (March 1969), pp. 129–135; Roger Lane, *Policing the City: Boston, 1822–1885* (Cambridge, Mass.: Harvard University Press, 1967).

8. Elinor Ostrom and Gordon P. Whitaker, "Community Control and Governmental Responsiveness: The Case of Police in Black Neighborhoods," in *Improving the Quality of Urban Management,* ed. David Rogers and Willis Hawley, vol. 8 of Urban Affairs Annual Review (Beverly Hills, Calif.: Sage Publications, 1974), pp. 303–334.

9. Richard Maxwell Brown, "The American Vigilante Tradition," in *Violence in America: Historical and Comparative Perspectives,* ed. Hugh Davis Graham and Ted Robert Gurr, a report to the National Commission on the Causes and Prevention of Violence (Washington, D.C.: Government Printing Office, 1969), vol. 1, pp. 121–169.

10. B. Latané and J. M. Darley, *The Unresponsive Bystander: Why Doesn't He Help?* (New York: Appleton-Century-Crofts, 1970).

Notes

Chapter 6 The Police and Community Relations

1. Gary T. Marx, *Protest and Prejudice* (New York: Harper & Row, 1967), p. 36.
2. Philip H. Ennis, *Criminal Victimization in the United States*, a research study submitted to the President's Commission on Law Enforcement and Administration of Justice (Chicago: National Opinion Research Center, 1967), p. 56.
3. President's Commission on Law Enforcement and Administration of Justice, *Task Force Report: The Police* (Washington, D.C.: U.S. Government Printing Office, 1967), p. 146.
4. Albert D. Biderman et al., *Report on a Pilot Study in the District of Columbia on Victimization and Attitudes Toward Law Enforcement*, a research study submitted to the President's Commission on Law Enforcement and Administration of Justice (Washington, D.C.: U.S. Government Printing Office, 1967), p. 145.
5. Albert J. Reiss, Jr., "Public Perceptions and Recollections About Crime, Law Enforcement, and Criminal Justice," in *Studies in Crime and Law Enforcement in Major Metropolitan Areas*, a research study submitted to the President's Commission on Law Enforcement and Administration of Justice (Ann Arbor: University of Michigan Survey Research Center, 1967), vol. 1, sec. 2, p. 55.
6. Angus Campbell and Howard Schuman, "Racial Attitudes in Fifteen American Cities," in *Supplemental Studies for the National Advisory Commission on Civil Disorders* (Washington, D.C.: U.S. Government Printing Office, 1968), pp. 41–45.
7. President's Commission, *Task Force Report: The Police*, p. 147.
8. Campbell and Schuman, "Racial Attitudes," p. 44.
9. Ibid.
10. President's Commission, *Task Force Report: The Police*, p. 148.
11. *Fortune*, January 1968, p. 148.
12. *New York Times*, December 13, 1968.
13. *Detroit News*, February 25, 1969.
14. Ennis, *Criminal Victimization*, pp. 55–56.
15. James Q. Wilson, "Police Morale, Reform, and Citizen Respect: The Chicago Case," in *The Police*, ed. David J. Bordua (New York: John Wiley & Sons, 1967), p. 17. See also Jerome H. Skolnick, *Justice Without Trial* (New York: John Wiley & Sons, 1966), pp. 9–65.
16. Peter H. Rossi et al., "Between White and Black: The Faces of American Institutions in the Ghetto," in *Supplemental Studies*, p. 104.
17. Ibid., p. 106. See also David H. Bayley and Harold Mendelsohn, *Minorities and the Police* (New York: Free Press, 1969), pp. 45–46.
18. Rossi, "Between White and Black," p. 106.
19. Ibid., pp. 109, 111.
20. Donald J. Black and Albert J. Reiss, Jr., "Police Control of Juveniles," *American Sociological Review* 35 (February 1970): 63–77.
21. Frank F. Furstenberg, Jr., and Charles F. Wellford, "Calling the Police: The Evaluation of Police Service," *Law and Society Review* 7 (Spring 1973): 402.
22. Paul E. Smith and Richard O. Hawkins, "Victimization, Types of Citizen-Police Contacts, and Attitudes Toward the Police," *Law and Society Review* 8 (Fall 1973): 140.
23. Ibid., p. 142.
24. Furstenberg and Wellford, "Calling the Police," p. 402.
25. Richard O. Hawkins, "Who Called the Cops?: Decisions to Report Criminal Victimization," *Law and Society Review* 7 (Spring 1973): 441, and Richard L. Block, "Police Action, Support for the Police, and Support for Civil Liberties" (Paper delivered at the annual meeting of the American Sociological Association, September 1970).
26. Reiss, "Police Perceptions," pp. 20, 39, 47, 55, 75.
27. Albert J. Reiss, Jr., *The Police and the Public* (New Haven: Yale University Press, 1971), p. 77.
28. Lawrence W. Sherman and Robert H. Langworthy, "Measuring Homicide by Police Officers," *Journal of Criminal Law and Criminology* 70 (1979): 554, 559.
29. Catherine H. Milton et al., *Police Use of Deadly Force* (Washington, D.C.: The Police Foundation, 1977).
30. James J. Fyfe, "Geographic Correlates of Police Shootings: A Microanalysis," *Journal of Research in Crime and Delinquency* 17 (1980): 101–113; Fyfe, "Officer Race and Police Shooting," paper delivered at the annual meeting of the American Society of Criminology (November 1979).
31. Milton et al., *Police Use of Deadly Force*.

32. James J. Fyfe, "Administrative Interventions on Police Shooting Discretion: An Empirical Analysis," *Journal of Criminal Justice* 7 (1979): 309–323.

33. Arthur Niederhofer, *Behind the Shield* (Garden City, N.Y.: Doubleday & Company, 1967), p. 235.

34. Herbert A. Shepard, "Changing Interpersonal and Intergroup Relations in Organizations," in *Handbook of Organizations,* ed. James G. March (Chicago: Rand McNally & Co., 1965), pp. 1132–1141.

35. Harold J. Leavitt, "Applied Organizational Change in Industry," in March, *Handbook of Organizations,* p. 1167, and Morton A. Lieberman et al., *Encounter Groups: First Facts* (New York: Basic Books, 1973), chap. 16.

36. Charles Sklarsky, "The Police-Community Relations Program" (Senior honor's thesis, Department of Government, Harvard University, March 1968).

37. David Wellman, "Putting on the Poverty Program," Radical Education Project, Ann Arbor, Mich., n.d.

38. Reiss, *The Police and the Public,* pp. 207–212, and James Q. Wilson, *Varieties of Police Behavior* (Cambridge: Harvard University Press, 1968), pp. 288–290.

39. Bernard Cohen and Jan M. Chaiken, *Police Background Characteristics and Performance,* Report No. R-999-DOJ (New York: Rand Institute, 1972). See also Melany E. Baehr et al., *Psychological Assessment of Patrolman Qualifications in Relation to Field Performance,* a report to the Office of Law Enforcement Assistance of the U.S. Department of Justice from the Industrial Relations Center of the University of Chicago, mimeographed, 1968.

40. I have been impressed, for example, with the work of the Applied Psychology Workshop of the Police Academy of the Chicago Police Department, although I am not aware of any systematic evaluation of its effects.

41. Brian Forst et al., *Arrest Convictability as a Measure of Police Performance* (Washington, D.C.: INSLAW, 1981).

42. David J. Bordua and Larry L. Tifft, "Citizen Interviews, Organizational Feedback and Police Community Relations Decisions," *Law and Society Review* 6 (November 1971): esp. 162–168.

43. Donald J. Black and Albert J. Reiss, Jr., "Patterns of Behavior in Police and Citizen Transactions," in *Studies of Crime and Law Enforcement in Major Metropolitan Areas,* a research study submitted to the President's Commission on Law Enforcement and Administration of Justice (Ann Arbor: University of Michigan Survey Research Center, 1967), vol. 2, p. 87.

Chapter 7 Penalties and Opportunities

1. Isaac Ehrlich, "Participation in Illegitimate Activities: A Theoretical and Empirical Investigation," *Journal of Political Economy* 81 (1973): 521–565.

2. Alfred Blumstein, Jacqueline Cohen, and Daniel Nagin, eds., *Deterrence and Incapacitation: Estimating the Effects of Criminal Sanctions on Crime Rates* (Washington, D.C.: National Academy of Sciences, 1978). Isaac Ehrlich responds to this report and its criticisms of his work in Ehrlich and Mark Randall, "Fear of Deterrence," *Journal of Legal Studies* 6 (1977): 293–316.

3. Colin Loftin, "Alternative Estimates of the Impact of Certainty and Severity of Punishment on Levels of Homicide in American States," in *Indicators of Crime and Criminal Justice: Quantitative Studies,* ed. Stephen E. Feinberg and Albert J. Reiss, report number NCJ-62349 of the Bureau of Justice Statistics (Washington, D.C.: U.S. Department of Justice, 1980), pp. 75–81.

4. Stephen S. Brier and Stephen E. Feinberg, "Recent Econometric Modeling of Crime and Punishment: Support for the Deterrence Hypothesis?" in Feinberg and Reiss, *Indicators of Crime and Criminal Justice,* pp. 82–97.

5. Itzhak Goldberg, "A Note on Using Victimization Rates to Test Deterrence," Technical Report CERDCR-5-78, Center for Econometric Studies of the Justice System, Stanford University (December 1978); James Q. Wilson and Barbara Boland, "Crime," in *The Urban Predicament,* ed. William Gorham and Nathan Glazer (Washington, D.C.: Urban Institute, 1976).

6. Blumstein et al., *Deterrence and Incapacitation,* p. 23.

7. Isaac Ehrlich and Mark Randall, "Fear of Deterrence," *Journal of Legal Studies* 6 (1977): 304–307.

8. Alfred Blumstein and Daniel Nagin, "The Deterrent Effect of Legal Sanctions on Draft Evasion," *Stanford Law Review* 28 (1977): 241–275.

9. Kenneth I. Wolpin, "An Economic Analysis of Crime and Punishment in England and Wales, 1894–1967," *Journal of Political Economy* 86 (1978): 815–840.

10. Harvey Brenner, "Estimating the Social Costs of National Economic Policy," vol. 1, paper number 5 of *Achieving the Goals of the Employment Act of 1946,* a study prepared for the Joint Economic Committee, U.S. Congress (94th Cong., 2d Sess.), October 26, 1976.

11. Michael Block and Fred Nold, "A Review of Some of the Results in Estimating the Social Cost of National Economic Policy," unpub. paper, Center for Econometric Studies of the Justice System, Stanford University, 1979.

12. Carl P. Simon and Ann D. Witte, *Beating the System: The Underground Economy* (Boston: Auburn House, 1982).

13. Brenner, "Estimating the Social Costs of National Economic Policy," pp. 70–71, 76–77, 141–146.

14. Robert W. Gillespie, *Economic Factors in Crime and Delinquency* (Washington, D.C.: National Institute of Law Enforcement and Criminal Justice, 1975).

15. Thomas Orsagh and Ann Dryden Witte, "Economic Status and Crime: Implications for Offender Rehabilitation," *Journal of Criminal Law and Criminology* 72 (1981): 1055–1071.

16. Philip J. Cook, "Research in Criminal Deterrence: Laying the Groundwork for the Second Decade," *Crime and Justice*, vol. 2, ed. Norval Morris and Michael Tonry (Chicago: University of Chicago Press, 1980), p. 219.

17. Ann Dryden Witte, "Estimating the Economic Model of Crime with Individual Data," *Quarterly Journal of Economics* 94 (1980): 57–84.

18. Charles A. Murray and Louis A. Cox, Jr., *Beyond Probation: Juvenile Corrections and the Chronic Delinquent* (Beverly Hills, Calif.: Sage Publications, 1979).

19. Matthew Silberman, "Toward a Theory of Criminal Deterrence," *American Sociological Review* 41 (1976): 442–461.

20. Maynard L. Erickson, Jack P. Gibbs, and Gary F. Jensen, "The Deterrence Doctrine and the Perceived Certainty of Legal Punishment," *American Sociological Review* 42 (1977): 305–317. See also Charles R. Tittle, *Sanctions and Social Deviance: The Question of Deterrence* (New York: Praeger, 1980).

21. H. Laurence Ross, "Law, Science, and Accidents: The British Road Safety Act of 1967," *Journal of Legal Studies* 2 (1973): 1–78.

22. H. Laurence Ross, "Deterrence Regained: The Cheshire Constabulary's 'Breathalyzer Blitz,'" *Journal of Legal Studies* 6 (1977): 241–249.

23. Lawrence W. Sherman and Richard A. Berk, "The Specific Deterrent Effects of Arrest for Domestic Assault: Preliminary Findings," unpub. paper, Police Foundation, Washington, D.C., March 28, 1983.

24. Joint Committee on New York Drug Law Evaluation, *The Nation's Toughest Drug Law: Evaluating the New York Experience* (New York: Association of the Bar of the City of New York, 1977), part I, esp. pp. 13–18.

25. James A. Beha II, "And Nobody Can Get You Out: The Impact of a Mandatory Prison Sentence for the Illegal Carrying of a Firearm on the Use of Firearms and the Administration of Criminal Justice in Boston," *Boston University Law Review* 57 (1977): 98–146, 289–333.

26. Glenn I. Pierce and William J. Bowers, "The Bartley-Fox Gun Law's Short-Term Impact on Crime in Boston," *Annals* 455 (1981): 120–137; Stuart Jay Deutsch and Francis B. Alt, "The Effect of Massachusetts' Gun Control Law on Gun-Related Crimes in the City of Boston," *Evaluation Quarterly* 1 (1977): 543–568; Philip J. Cook, "The Role of Firearms in Violent Crime," unpub. paper, Institute of Policy Sciences, Duke University (May 1981); Beha, "And Nobody Can Get You Out."

27. Milton Heumann and Colin Loftin, "Mandatory Sentencing and the Abolition of Plea Bargaining: The Michigan Felony Firearm Statute," *Law and Society Review* 13 (1979): 393–430.

28. Colin Lofton, Milton Heumann, and David McDowall, "Mandatory Sentencing and Firearms Violence: Evaluating an Alternative to Gun Control," *Law and Society Review* 17 (1983): 287–318.

29. Allan F. Williams et al., "The Legal Minimum Drinking Age and Fatal Motor Vehicle Crashes," *Journal of Legal Studies* 4 (1975): 219–239.

30. Allan F. Williams et al., "The Effect of Raising the Legal Minimum Drinking Age on Fatal Crash Involvement," *Journal of Legal Studies,* forthcoming.

31. Alexander C. Wagenaar, "Effects of the Raised Legal Drinking Age on Motor Vehicle Accidents in Michigan," *HSRI Research Review* (January–February, 1981).

32. Terry M. Klein, "The Effect of Raising the Minimum Legal Drinking Age on Traffic Accidents in the State of Maine," National Highway Traffic Safety Administration Technical Report (December, 1981).

33. H. Laurence Ross, *Deterring the Drunk Driver* (Lexington, Mass.: Lexington Books–D.C. Heath, 1982), pp. 102–115. Ross notes that the deterrent effect decays over time unless reinforced by periodic and well-publicized enforcement efforts. He speculates that this decay occurs because the actual risk of apprehension for drunk driving is so slight that deterrence can only work when people form an exaggerated opinion of the risk they face.

34. Franklin E. Zimring, "Of Doctors, Deterrence, and the Dark Figure of Crime: A Note on Abortions in Hawaii," *University of Chicago Law Review* 39 (1972): 699–721.

35. Gerald D. Robin, "Anti-Poverty Programs and Delinquency," *Journal of Criminal Law and Criminology* 60 (1969): 323–331.

36. William E. Wright and Michael C. Dixon, "Community Prevention and Treatment of Juvenile Delinquency," *Journal of Research in Crime and Delinquency* 14 (1977): 35–67.

37. Evaluation of the Job Corps cited in Orsagh and Witte, "Economic Status and Crime," p. 1066 n 71.

38. Philip J. Cook, "The Correctional Carrot: Better Jobs for Parolees," *Policy Analysis* 1 (1975): 11–54.

39. Gordon R. Waldo and Theodore G. Chiricos, "Work Release and Recidivism," *Evaluation Quarterly* 1 (1977): 87–107. An earlier evaluation of a California work-release program found a crime-reduction effect, but it was methodologically inferior to the Waldo-Chiricos evaluation because it did not randomly assign the inmates to experimental and control groups. Robert Jeffrey and Stephen Woolpert, "Work Furlough as an Alternative to Incarceration," *Journal of Criminal Law and Criminology* 65 (1974): 405–415.

40. Ann Witte, *Work Release in North Carolina: An Evaluation of its Post-Release Effects* (Chapel Hill, N.C.: Institute for Research in Social Science, 1975).

41. *Unlocking the Second Gate: The Role of Financial Assistance in Reducing Recidivism Among Ex-Prisoners*, R & D Monograph No. 45 (Washington, D.C.: U.S. Department of Labor, Employment and Training Administration, 1977); Charles D. Mallar and Craig V. D. Thornton, "Transitional Aid for Released Prisoners: Evidence From the LIFE Experiment," *Journal of Human Resources* 13 (1978): 208–236.

42. Richard A. Berk, Kenneth J. Lenihan, and Peter H. Rossi, "Crime and Poverty: Some Experimental Evidence From Ex-Offenders," *American Sociological Review* 45 (1980): 766–786; Peter H. Rossi, Richard A. Berk, and Kenneth J. Lenihan, *Money, Work, and Crime: Experimental Evidence* (New York: Academic Press, 1980). The claim that there was any crime-reduction effect from the financial aid is disputed in Hans Zeisel, "Disagreement Over the Evaluation of a Controlled Experiment," *American Journal of Sociology* 88 (1982): 378–389. There is a rejoinder by Rossi, Berk, and Lenihan in the same journal (pp. 390–393) and a surrejoinder by Zeisel (pp. 394–396). I think Zeisel gets the better of the argument.

43. Peter Kemper et al., *The Supported Work Evaluation: Final Benefit-Cost Analysis*, vol. 5 of the Final Report of the National Supported Work Demonstration (New York: Manpower Demonstration Research Corp., 1981), pp. 69–77.

44. Irving Piliavin and Rosemary Gartner, *The Impact of Supported Work on Ex-Offenders*, vol. 2 of the Final Report of the Supported Work Evaluation (New York: Manpower Demonstration Research Corp., 1981), pp. 88–92.

45. Ibid., pp. 43–52; Rebecca Maynard, *The Impact of Supported Work on Young School Dropouts*, vol. 1 of the Final Report of the Supported Work Evaluation (New York: Manpower Demonstration Research Corp., 1980), pp. 62–66.

46. Marvin Wolfgang, Robert M. Figlio, and Thorsten Sellin, *Delinquency in a Birth Cohort* (Chicago: University of Chicago Press, 1972), pp. 54, 65, 162.

47. Ibid., chap. 6.

48. The concept of a "stake in conformity" is from Jackson Toby, "Social Disorganization and Stake in Conformity," *Journal of Criminal Law and Criminology* 48 (1957): 12–17.

49. Cf. Richard B. Freeman, "Crime and Unemployment," in James Q. Wilson, ed., *Crime and Public Policy* (San Francisco: Institute for Contemporary Studies, 1983), ch. 6.

50. An egregious example of the double standard at work is Charles Silberman, *Criminal Violence, Criminal Justice* (New York: Random House, 1978), wherein the studies on deterrence are closely criticized (pp. 182–195) in a way that leads the author to conclude that "more punishment is not

the answer" (p. 197) but "community development programs" are found (on the basis of virtually no data whatsoever) to lead to "community regeneration" and a virtual absence of criminal violence (pp. 430–466).

Chapter 8 Incapacitation

1. "Prisons and Prisoners," Bureau of Justice Statistics *Bulletin,* January, 1982.
2. Ernest van den Haag, *Punishing Criminals* (New York: Basic Books, 1975), pp. 52–60.
3. Mark A. Peterson and Harriet B. Braiker, *Doing Crime: A Survey of California Prison Inmates* (Santa Monica, Calif.: Rand, 1980), pp. x, 50.
4. James Q. Wilson, *Thinking About Crime* (New York: Basic Books, 1975), p. 201; Shlomo and Reuel Shinnar, "The Effects of the Criminal Justice System on the Control of Crime: A Quantitative Approach," *Law and Society Review* 9 (1975): 581–611; Benjamin Avi-Itzhak and Reuel Shinnar, "Quantitative Models in Crime Control," *Journal of Criminal Justice* 1 (1973): 196–197.
5. David F. Greenberg, "The Incapacitative Effect of Imprisonment: Some Estimates," *Law and Society Review* 9 (1975): 566, 570.
6. Ibid., p. 572.
7. Stevens Clarke, "Getting 'Em Out of Circulation: Does Incarceration of Juvenile Offenders Reduce Crime?" *Journal of Criminal Law and Criminology* 67 (1974): 528–535.
8. Stephan Van Dine et al., "The Incapacitation of the Dangerous Offender: A Statistical Experiment," *Journal of Research in Crime and Delinquency* 14 (1977): 22–34.
9. Jacqueline Cohen, "The Incapacitative Effect of Imprisonment: A Critical Review of the Literature," in *Deterrence and Incapacitation: Estimating the Effects of Criminal Sanctions on Crime Rates,* ed. Alfred Blumstein et al. (Washington, D.C.: National Academy of Sciences, 1978), p. 201.
10. Ibid., p. 203.
11. Ibid., p. 206.
12. Barbara Boland, "Incapacitation of the Dangerous Offender: The Arithmetic is Not So Simple," *Journal of Research in Crime and Delinquency* 15 (1978): 126–129; Jan Palmer and John Salimbene, "The Incapacitation of the Dangerous Offender: A Second Look," *Journal of Research in Crime and Delinquency* 15 (1978): 130–134; P.M. Johnson, "The Role of Penal Quarantine in Reducing Violent Crime," *Crime and Delinquency* 24 (1978): 465–485.
13. S. Van Dine et al., "Response to Our Critics," *Journal of Research in Crime and Delinquency* 15 (1978): 135–139; Stephan Van Dine et al., *Restraining the Wicked: The Dangerous Offender Project* (Lexington, Mass.: Lexington/D.C. Heath, 1979).
14. Cohen, "The Incapacitative Effect of Imprisonment," p. 206.
15. Alfred Blumstein and Jacqueline Cohen, "Estimation of Individual Crime Rates From Arrest Records," *Journal of Criminal Law and Criminology* 70 (1979): 585.
16. Peterson and Braiker, *Doing Crime*, pp. vii, 32.
17. Ibid., p. 35.
18. Peter W. Greenwood, *Selective Incapacitation* (Santa Monica, Calif.: Rand, 1982), pp. 43–44.
19. Ibid., p. 46.
20. Brian Forst et al., "Targeting Federal Resources on Recidivists," Final Report of the Federal Career Criminal Research Project (Washington, D.C.: INSLAW, 1982), pp. 18–19.
21. Shinnar and Shinnar, "The Effects of the Criminal Justice System," pp. 605–606.
22. Cohen, "The Incapacitative Effect of Imprisonment," p. 218.
23. Joan Petersilia and Peter W. Greenwood, "Mandatory Prison Sentences: Their Projected Effects on Crime and Prison Populations," *Journal of Criminal Law and Criminology* 69 (1978): 604–615.
24. Ibid., p. 615.
25. For a survey of such findings, see *Research on Sentencing: The Search for Reform,* a report of the Panel on Sentencing Research of the National Research Council (Washington, D.C.: National Academy Press, 1983), chap. 2.
26. Greenwood, *Selective Incapacitation*, pp. 52–53.
27. Ibid., p. 99.

28. Forst et al., "Targeting Federal Resources."

29. Blumstein and Cohen, "Estimation of Individual Crime Rates," p. 581; Peterson and Braiker, *Doing Crime*, p. 40; Marvin Wolfgang et al., *Delinquency in a Birth Cohort* (Chicago: University of Chicago Press, 1972), p. 206.

30. Forst, "Targeting Federal Resources."

31. Greenwood, *Selective Incapacitation*, Figure 5–2.

32. Jan M. Chaiken and Marcia R. Chaiken, *Varieties of Criminal Behavior* (Santa Monica, Calif.: Rand, 1982).

33. Andrew von Hirsch, *Doing Justice: The Choice of Punishments*, a report of the Committee for the Study of Incarceration (New York: Hill and Wang, 1976).

34. James Q. Wilson, "Who Is in Prison?" *Commentary* (November, 1976), p. 57.

35. Alfred Blumstein, Jacqueline Cohen, and Harold D. Miller, "Demographically Disaggregated Projections of Prison Populations," *Journal of Criminal Justice* 8 (1980): 22.

36. Bureau of Justice Statistics, "Prisons and Prisoners," in *Bulletin*.

37. Ibid.

38. Kenneth I. Wolpin, "An Economic Analysis of Crime and Punishment in England and Wales, 1894–1967," *Journal of Political Economy* 86 (1978): 819–820. See also James Q. Wilson, "Crime and Punishment in England," *The Public Interest* (Spring 1976): 18–19.

39. This argument, along with other, equally dubious ones, was put forward in William G. Nagel, *The New Red Barn: A Critical Look at the Modern Prison* (New York: Walker and Co., 1973).

40. Kenneth Carlson, *Population Trends and Projections*, vol. 2 of *American Prisons and Jails* (Washington, D.C.: National Institute of Justice, 1980), pp. 53–56, 173–186.

41. National Research Council, *Research on Sentencing: The Search for Reform*, chap. 5.

42. Alfred Blumstein, Jacqueline Cohen, and W. Gooding, "The Influence of Capacity on Prison Population: A Critical Review of Some Recent Evidence," *Crime and Delinquency*, forthcoming.

Chapter 9 Rehabilitation

1. Robert Martinson, "What Works?—Questions and Answers About Prison Reform," *The Public Interest* (Spring 1974): 22–54.

2. Douglas Lipton, Robert Martinson, and Judith Wilks, *The Effectiveness of Correctional Treatment: A Survey of Treatment Evaluation Studies* (New York: Praeger, 1975).

3. Martinson, "What Works," p. 25.

4. R. G. Hood, "Research on the Effectiveness of Punishments and Treatments," in *Crime and Justice*, vol. 3, ed. Leon Radzinowicz and Marvin E. Wolfgang (New York: Basic Books, 1971), pp. 159–182.

5. Walter C. Bailey, "Correctional Outcome: An Evaluation of 100 Reports," in Radzinowicz and Wolfgang, *Crime and Justice*, p. 190.

6. Leslie T. Wilkins, *Evaluation of Penal Measures* (New York: Random House, 1969), p. 78.

7. Citizens' Inquiry on Parole and Criminal Justice, *Report on New York Parole* (March 1974). See also Robert W. Kastenmeier and Howard C. Eglit, "Parole Release Decision-Making," *American University Law Review* 22 (Spring 1973): 477–525.

8. *The Challenge of Crime in a Free Society*, A Report by the President's Commission on Law Enforcement and Administration of Justice (Washington, D.C.: U.S. Government Printing Office, 1967), p. 170.

9. Ted Palmer, "Martinson Revisited," *Journal of Research in Crime and Delinquency* 12 (July 1975): 133–152.

10. Robert Martinson, "California Research at the Crossroads," *Journal of Research in Crime and Delinquency* 13 (April 1976): 180–191.

11. Paul Lerman, *Community Treatment and Social Control* (Chicago: University of Chicago Press, 1975), p. 67.

12. Ted Palmer, *Correctional Intervention and Research* (Lexington, Mass.: Lexington Books/D.C. Heath, 1978). Some hesitant support for Palmer's position is provided in a review of the Lerman book by Eugene Bardach in *Policy Analysis* 3 (1977): 129–136.

Notes

13. Lee Sechrest et al., eds., *The Rehabilitation of Criminal Offenders* (Washington, D.C.: National Academy of Sciences, 1979); Lee Sechrest et al., *New Directions in the Rehabilitation of Criminal Offenders* (Washington, D.C.: National Academy of Sciences, 1981).

14. Sechrest, *The Rehabilitation of Criminal Offenders*, p. 5.

15. David F. Greenberg, "The Correctional Effects of Corrections: A Survey of Evaluations," in *Corrections and Punishment,* ed. David F. Greenberg (Beverly Hills, Calif.: Sage Publications, 1977), pp. 111–148.

16. S. R. Brody, *The Effectiveness of Sentencing—A Review of the Literature,* Home Office Research Report No. 35 (London: HMSO, 1976).

17. Sechrest et al., *The Rehabilitation of Criminal Offenders,* p. 31.

18. Daniel Glaser, "Remedies for the Key Deficiency in Criminal Justice Evaluation Research," *Journal of Research in Crime and Delinquency* 11 (July 1974): 144–153.

19. Stuart Adams, "The PICO Project," in *The Sociology of Punishment and Correction,* ed. Norman Johnston, Leonard Savitz, and Marvin E. Wolfgang (New York: John Wiley & Sons, 1962), pp. 213–224.

20. H. J. Eysenck, "The Effects of Psychotherapy: An Evaluation," *Journal of Consulting Psychology* 16 (1952): 319–324; Eysenck, "The Effects of Psychotherapy," *International Journal of Psychiatry* 1 (1965): 99–144.

21. Mary Lee Smith and Gene V. Glass, "Meta-Analysis of Psycho-Therapy Outcome Studies," *American Psychologist* 32 (September 1977): 752–760.

22. Charles A. Murray and Louis A. Cox, Jr., *Beyond Probation* (Beverly Hills, Calif.: Sage Publications, 1979).

23. Michael D. Maltz, Andrew C. Gordon, David McDowall, and Richard McCleary, "An Artifact in Pretest-Posttest Designs: How It Can Mistakenly Make Delinquency Programs Look Effective," *Evaluation Review* 4 (1980): 225–240.

24. LaMar T. Empey and Maynard L. Erickson, *The Provo Experiment* (Lexington, Mass.: Lexington Books/D.C. Heath, 1972).

Chapter 10 The Death Penalty

1. Ernest van den Haag, *Punishing Criminals* (New York: Basic Books, 1975), chaps. 13, 14; Walter Berns, *For Capital Punishment* (New York: Basic Books, 1979); Richard O. Lempert, "Desert and Deterrence: An Assessment of the Moral Bases of the Case for Capital Punishment," *Michigan Law Review* 79 (May 1981): 1177–1231; Charles L. Black, Jr., *Capital Punishment* (New York: Norton, 1974).

2. Thorsten Sellin, *Capital Punishment* (New York: Harper & Row, 1967), esp. pp. 135–160.

3. Robert H. Dann, "The Deterrent Effect of Capital Punishment," Bulletin 29, Friends Social Service Series (Philadelphia, 1935); Leonard D. Savitz, "A Study in Capital Punishment," *Journal of Criminal Law, Criminology, and Police Science* 49 (1959): 338–341; William E. Graves, "A Doctor Looks at Capital Punishment" in *The Death Penalty in America,* ed. Hugo Adam Bedau (Chicago: Aldine, 1964), pp. 322–332. See also David F. Phillips, "New Evidence on an Old Controversy," *American Journal of Sociology* 86 (1980): 139–147.

4. Donald R. Campion, "Does the Death Penalty Protect State Police?" in Bedau, *The Death Penalty,* pp. 301–315.

5. Hans Zeisel, "The Deterrent Effect of Capital Punishment: Facts vs. Faith," *Supreme Court Review* (1976): 317–343.

6. Arnold Barnett, "Crime and Capital Punishment: Some Recent Studies," *Journal of Criminal Justice* 6 (1978): 299–300.

7. Isaac Ehrlich, "Capital Punishment and Deterrence: Some Further Thoughts and Additional Evidence," *Journal of Political Economy* 85 (1977): 741–788; Dale O. Cloninger, "Deterrence and the Death Penalty: A Cross-Sectional Analysis," *Journal of Behavioral Economics* 6 (Summer/Winter 1977): 87–106.

8. Peter Passell, "The Deterrent Effect of the Death Penalty: A Statistical Test," *Stanford Law*

Review 61 (1975): 61–80; Brian E. Forst, "The Deterrent Effect of Capital Punishment: A Cross-State Analysis of the 1960s," *Minnesota Law Review* 61 (1977): 743–767.

9. Richard M. McGahey, "Dr. Ehrlich's Magic Bullet: Economic Theory, Econometrics, and the Death Penalty," *Crime and Delinquency* 26 (1980): 485–502; William J. Boyes and Lee R. McPheters, "Capital Punishment as a Deterrent to Violent Crime: Cross-Sectional Evidence," *Journal of Behavioral Economics* 6 (Summer/Winter 1977): 67–86; Arnold Barnett, "The Deterrent Effect of Capital Punishment: A Test of Some Recent Studies," *Operations Research* 29 (1981): 346–370.

10. Isaac Ehrlich, "The Deterrent Effect of Capital Punishment: A Question of Life and Death," *American Economic Review* 65 (1975): 397–417.

11. Kenneth I. Wolpin, "Capital Punishment and Homicide: The English Experience," unpub. paper, Yale University Department of Economics, November 1978. A much-condensed version of this paper appeared in the *American Economic Review: Papers and Proceedings*, May 1978. The unpublished manuscript should be consulted for Wolpin's full analysis.

12. Lempert, "Desert and Deterrence," p. 1210.

13. Peter Passel and John B. Taylor, "The Deterrent Effect of Capital Punishment: Another View," *American Economic Review* 67 (1977): 445–451; Lawrence R. Klein, Brian Forst, and Victor W. Filatov, "The Deterrent Effect of Capital Punishment: An Assessment of the Estimates," in *Deterrence and Incapacitation*, ed. Alfred Blumstein et al. (Washington, D.C.: National Academy of Sciences, 1978), pp. 353–355.

14. Klein et. al., "The Deterrent Effect of Capital Punishment," p. 346.

15. Wolpin, "Capital Punishment and Homicide."

16. Kenneth L. Avio, "Capital Punishment in Canada," *Canadian Journal of Economics* 12 (1979): 647–676.

17. Wolpin, "Capital Punishment and Homicide."

18. Barnett, "The Deterrent Effect of Capital Punishment," pp. 354–355.

19. *Furman v. Georgia*, 408 U.S. 238 (1972).

20. Marvin E. Wolfgang and Marc Reidel, "Race, Judicial Discretion, and the Death Penalty," *Annals* 407 (1973): 119–133.

21. Marvin E. Wolfgang, Arlene Kelly, and Hans C. Nolde, "Comparison of the Executed and Commuted Among Admissions to Death Row," *Journal of Criminal Law, Criminology, and Police Science* 53 (1962): 301–311.

22. *Gregg v. Georgia*, 428 U.S. 153 (1976).

23. Gary Kleck, "Racial Discrimination in Criminal Sentencing," *American Sociological Review* 46 (1981): 783–805.

24. Charles L. Judson et al., "A Study of the Penalty Jury in First Degree Murder Cases," *Stanford Law Review* 21 (1969): 1297–1431.

25. Steven D. Arkin, "Discrimination and Arbitrariness in Capital Punishment," *Stanford Law Review* 33 (1980): 75–101.

26. Franklin E. Zimring, Joel Eigen, and Sheila O'Malley, "Punishing Homicide in Philadelphia: Perspectives on the Death Penalty," *University of Chicago Law Review* 43 (1976): 227–252.

27. William J. Bowers and Glenn L. Pierce, "Arbitrariness and Discrimination under Post-*Furman* Capital Statutes," *Crime and Delinquency* 26 (1980): 563–635.

28. *Coker v. Georgia*, 433 U.S. 584 (1977).

29. Kleck, "Racial Discrimination in Criminal Sentencing."

30. Panel on Sentencing Research, National Research Council, *Research on Sentencing: The Search for Reform* (Washington, D.C.: National Academy Press, 1983) vol. 1, p. 13.

31. *The Penalty of Death*, Final Report of the Annual Chief Justice Earl Warren Conference on Advocacy in the United States (Washington, D.C.: Roscoe Pound-American Trial Lawyers Foundation, 1980).

Chapter 11 Heroin

1. Student task force reports prepared at Harvard University, American University, the University of Southern California, the University of Pennsylvania, Southern Methodist University, Washington

University, and the University of California at Berkeley are on file at the Sloan Foundation, New York City.

2. Thomas H. Bewley et al., "Mortality and Morbidity from Heroin Dependence," *British Medical Journal* 1 (March 23, 1968): 725–732.

3. Isador Chein et al., *The Road to H.* (New York: Basic Books, 1964).

4. Patrick H. Hughes and Gail A. Crawford, "A Contagious Disease Model for Researching and Intervening in Heroin Epidemics," *Archives of General Psychiatry* 27 (August 1972): 149–155, and Patrick Hughes et al., "The Natural History of a Heroin Epidemic," *American Journal of Public Health* 62 (July 1972): 995–1001. See also Leon Gibson Hunt, *Recent Spread of Heroin Use in the United States*, Monograph MS-10 (Washington, D.C.: Drug Abuse Council, 1974).

5. Lee Robins and G. Murphy, "Drug Use in a Normal Population of Young Negro Men," *American Journal of Public Health* 57 (September 1967): 1580–1596.

6. E. Preble and J. Casey, "Taking Care of Business—The Heroin User's Life on the Street," *International Journal of the Addictions* 4 (March 1969): 1–24.

7. John A. O'Donnell, "Narcotic Addiction and Crime," *Social Problems* 13 (Spring 1966): 374–385.

8. J. C. Ball et al., "The Criminality of Heroin Addicts," in *The Drugs-Crime Connection*, ed. J. A. Inciardi (Beverly Hills, Calif.: Sage Publications, 1981), pp. 39–65; J. A. Inciardi, "Heroin Use and Street Crime," *Crime and Delinquency* 25 (1979): 335–348; J. C. Wesimann et al., "Addiction and Criminal Behavior," *Journal of Drug Issues* 6 (1976): 153–165; C. D. Chambers et al., "Criminal Involvements of Minority Group Addicts," in *The Drugs-Crime Connection*, pp. 125–154.

9. Max Singer, "The Vitality of Mythical Numbers," *The Public Interest* (Spring 1971): 3–9.

10. George Vaillant, "A Twelve Year Follow-Up of New York Narcotic Addicts: I. The Relation of Treatment to Outcome," *American Journal of Psychiatry* 122 (1966): 727–737.

11. Griffith Edwards, "The British Approach to the Treatment of Heroin Addiction," *Lancet* 1 (1969): 768–772.

12. Edgar May, "Drugs Without Crime," *Harpers* (July 1971): 60–65.

13. I. David Wheat, Jr., "Heroin Abuse in Boston," in *Heroin Abuse in Boston*, a report of a Harvard University task force (Public Policy Program, Kennedy School of Government, Harvard, 1972).

14. Hughes and Crawford, "A Contagious Disease Model"; Hughes et al., "The Natural History."

15. Robert Schasre, "Cessation Patterns Among Neophyte Heroin Users," *International Journal of the Addictions* 1 (1966): 23–33.

16. Hughes, "A Contagious Disease Model." See also Patrick H. Hughes et al., "The Medical Management of a Heroin Epidemic," *Archives of General Psychiatry* 27 (November 1972): 585–591.

17. Frances R. Gearing, "Successes and Failures in Methadone Maintenance Treatment of Heroin Addiction in New York City," *Proceedings*, Third National Conference on Methadone Treatment (NIMH), Public Health Service Publication No. 2172 (1970).

18. James Vorenberg and Irving F. Lukoff, "Addiction, Crime, and the Criminal Justice System," *Federal Probation* 37 (December 1973): 3–7. See also Gila J. Hayim, Irving Lukoff, and Debra Quatrone, *Heroin Use and Crime in a Methadone Maintenance Program* (Washington, D.C.: U.S. Department of Justice, Law Enforcement Assistance Administration, February 1973).

19. G. V. Stimson, *Heroin and Behaviour* (New York: John Wiley & Sons, 1973).

20. Bewley, "Mortality and Morbidity," and Stimson, *Heroin and Behaviour*.

Chapter 12 Crime and American Culture

1. Sheldon Glueck and Eleanor T. Glueck, *Unraveling Juvenile Delinquency* (Cambridge: Harvard University Press, 1950), pp. 89–91; Lee N. Robins, *Deviant Children Grown Up* (Baltimore: William and Wilkins Co., 1966), pp. 79, 111, 172.

2. Marvin E. Wolfgang and Paul E. Tracy, "The 1945 and 1958 Birth Cohorts: A Comparison of the Prevalence, Incidence, and Severity of Delinquent Behavior," unpub. paper delivered at the Conference on Public Danger, Dangerous Offenders, and the Criminal Justice System, Harvard University, 1982.

3. Quoted in Gordon S. Wood, *The Creation of the American Republic* (Chapel Hill, N.C.: University of North Carolina Press, 1976), p. 66.

4. William E. Nelson, *Americanization of the Common Law* (Cambridge: Harvard University Press, 1975), p. 117.

5. Roger Lane, "Urban Police and Crime in Nineteenth-Century America," in *Crime and Justice: An Annual Review of Research*, vol. 2, ed. Norval Morris and Michael Tonry (Chicago: University of Chicago Press, 1980), p. 27.

6. Roger Lane, *Violent Death in the City: Suicide, Accident, and Murder in Nineteenth-Century Philadelphia* (Cambridge: Harvard University Press, 1979), p. 71.

7. James F. Richardson, *The New York Police, Colonial Times to 1901* (New York: Oxford University Press, 1970), chap. 2.

8. Paul E. Johnson, *A Shopkeeper's Millennium: Society and Revivals in Rochester, New York, 1815–1837* (New York: Hill and Wang, 1978), pp. 55–60.

9. Ted Robert Gurr, "Contemporary Crime in Historical Perspective: A Comparative Study of London, Stockholm, and Sydney," *Annals* 434 (November 1977): 114–136.

10. Lane, "Urban Police and Crime," pp. 23–39.

11. Lane, "Urban Police and Crime," p. 27; Lane, *Violent Death in the City*, p. 71.

12. Eric H. Monkkonen, quoted in Lane, "Urban Police and Crime," p. 35.

13. Ted Robert Gurr, "Historical Trends in Violent Crime: A Critical Review of the Evidence," in *Crime and Justice: An Annual Review of Research*, vol. 3, ed. Michael Tonry and Norval Morris (Chicago: University of Chicago Press, 1981), pp. 295–353.

14. Michael B. Katz et al., *The Social Organization of Early Industrial Capitalism* (Cambridge: Harvard University Press, 1982), p. 206.

15. Eric H. Monkkonen, "A Disorderly People? Urban Order in the Nineteenth and Twentieth Centuries," *Journal of American History* 68 (December 1981): 536–559; Katz et al., *The Social Organization*, pp. 208–209.

16. Johnson, *A Shopkeeper's Millennium*, p. 37.

17. Warren S. Thompson and P. K. Whelpton, *Population Trends in the United States* (New York: McGraw-Hill Book Co., 1933), p. 362.

18. Joseph F. Kett, *Rites of Passage: Adolescence in America, 1790 to the Present* (New York: Basic Books, 1977), p. 38.

19. Theodore N. Ferdinand, "The Criminal Patterns of Boston Since 1846," *American Journal of Sociology* 73 (July 1967): 84–99.

20. Lane, *Violent Death in the City*, p. 71.

21. Calculated from data in Thompson and Whelton, *Population Trends*, p. 362.

22. Lane, *Violent Death in the City*, pp. 152–153.

23. *Crimes of Violence*, a staff report to the National Commission on the Causes and Prevention of Violence (Washington, D.C.: U.S. Government Printing Office, 1969), vol. 11, p. 61. This finding has been criticized in Alfred Blumstein and Daniel S. Nagin, "Analysis of Arrest Rates for Trends in Criminality," *Socio-Economic Planning Sciences* 9 (1975): 221–227. However, a comparison of the rate and seriousness of criminality among two cohorts of Philadelphia boys, the first born in 1945, the second in 1958, who have been studied by Marvin Wolfgang, suggests that though the boys in the later cohort are no more likely to commit a crime than those in the earlier one, those who do commit crimes in the later group do so at a much higher rate, and commit more serious crimes, than was true of the offending boys in the earlier group (Wolfgang and Tracy, "The 1945 and 1958 Birth Cohorts").

24. Lane, *Violent Death in the City*, chap. 6.

25. Gurr, "Historical Trends in Violent Crime"; Norbert Elias, *The Civilizing Process: The History of Manners* (New York: Urizen, 1978 [originally published in 1939]).

26. Lane, *Policing the City*.

27. Monkkonen, "A Disorderly People?"

28. Daniel Walker Howe, ed., *Victorian America* (Philadelphia: University of Pennsylvania Press, 1976), p. 6.

29. Johnson, *A Shopkeeper's Millennium*, chap. 2.

30. Kett, *Rites of Passage*, pp. 29, 60; Johnson, *A Shopkeeper's Millennium*, pp. 38, 55–60.

31. Kett, *Rites of Passage*, p. 107.

32. Paul Boyer, *Urban Masses and Moral Order in America, 1820–1920* (Cambridge: Harvard University Press, 1978).

33. Kett, *Rites of Passage*, p. 64.

34. Johnson, *A Shopkeeper's Millennium*, pp. 121–128.

35. Perry Miller quoted in William G. McLoughlin, *Revivals, Awakenings, and Reform* (Chicago: University of Chicago Press, 1978), p. 104.

36. Gregory H. Singleton, "Protestant Voluntary Organizations and the Shaping of Victorian America," in Howe, *Victorian America*, pp. 49–50.

37. McLoughlin, *Revivals*, p. 128.

38. Boyer, *Urban Masses*, pp. 43–49.

39. Ibid., p. 41.

40. Thomas W. Laqueur, *Religion and Respectability: Sunday Schools and Working Class Culture, 1780–1850* (New Haven: Yale University Press, 1976), p. 44.

41. Ibid., pp. 219–227, 239, 241.

42. Boyer, *Urban Masses*, p. 113.

43. Norman H. Clark, *Deliver Us From Evil: An Interpretation of American Prohibition* (New York: Norton, 1976), p. 20.

44. Ibid., p. 40; Johnson, *A Shopkeeper's Millennium*, p. 82.

45. Joseph F. Kett, "Adolescence and Youth in Nineteenth-Century America," in *The Family in History: Interdisciplinary Essays*, ed. Theodore K. Rabb and Robert I. Rotberg (New York: Harper Torchbooks, 1973), p. 104.

46. Roger Lane, *Policing the City: Boston, 1822–1885* (Cambridge: Harvard University Press, 1967), p. 137.

47. William J. Rorabaugh, *The Alcoholic Republic* (New York: Oxford University Press, 1979), p. 233.

48. Clark, *Deliver Us From Evil*, p. 20.

49. Rorabaugh, *The Alcoholic Republic*, pp. 7–9.

50. Brian Harrison argues that in England the temperance movement, apart from the effects of the business cycle, did not reduce the consumption of alcohol. Harrison, *Drink and the Victorians: The Temperance Question in England, 1815–1872* (Pittsburgh: University of Pittsburgh Press, 1971), pp. 311–316.

51. Clark, *Deliver Us From Evil*, p. 13.

52. Mayer N. Zald, *Organizational Change: The Political Economy of the YMCA* (Chicago: University of Chicago Press, 1970), pp. 44–45.

53. Clark, *Deliver Us From Evil*, pp. 148–149; John Burnham, "New Perspectives on the Prohibition 'Experiment' of the 1920s," *Journal of Social History* 2 (1968): 51–68.

54. Clark, *Deliver Us From Evil*, pp. 146–148; Irving Fisher, *The Noble Experiment* (New York: Alcohol Information Committee, 1930); Joseph R. Gusfield, "Prohibition: The Impact of Political Utopianism," in *Change and Continuity in Twentieth Century America: The 1920's*, ed. John Braeman et al. (Columbus, Ohio: Ohio State University Press, 1968), pp. 257–308.

55. Boyer, *Urban Masses*, chap. 20.

56. Kett, *Rites of Passage*, pp. 5–6, 232–258.

57. Bernard Wishy, *The Child and the Republic: The Dawn of Modern American Child Nurture* (Philadelphia: University of Pennsylvania Press, 1968), pp. 58ff.

58. Stanley Coben, "The Assault on Victorianism in the Twentieth Century," in Howe, *Victorian America*, pp. 161–163.

59. Robert Sunley, "Early Nineteenth-Century American Literature on Child Rearing," in *Childhood in Contemporary Cultures*, ed. Margaret Mead and Martha Wolfenstein (Chicago: University of Chicago Press, 1955), pp. 162–163.

60. Martha Wolfenstein, "Fun Morality: An Analysis of Recent American Child-training Literature," in Mead and Wolfenstein, *Childhood*, pp. 168–178.

61. Celia B. Stendler, "Sixty Years of Child Training Practices," *Journal of Pediatrics* 36 (1950): 122–134.

62. Ruth S. Cavan and Katherine H. Ranck, *The Family and the Depression* (Freeport, N.Y.: Books for Libraries Press, 1969), pp. 178, 198 (first published in 1938).

63. V. Jones, "Relation of Economic Depression to Delinquency, Crime, and Drunkenness in Massachusetts," *Journal of Social Psychology* 3 (1932): 259–282; M. E. Kirkpatrick, "Delinquency in Cleveland and Cuyahoga County During the Depression Period," *American Journal of Orthopsychiatry* 4 (1934): 383–386; Roy M. Simpson, "The Employment Index, Arrests, Court Actions, and Commitments in Illinois," *Journal of Criminal Law and Criminology* 24 (1934): 914–922.

64. Glen H. Elder, *Children of the Great Depression* (Chicago: University of Chicago Press, 1974), pp. 275, 279, 287.

65. *Historical Statistics of the United States: Colonial Times to 1970* (Washington, D.C.: Bureau of the Census, 1975), Part I, p. 16.

66. See also James Q. Wilson and George L. Kelling, "Broken Windows: The Police and Neighborhood Safety," *Atlantic* (March 1982), p. 36.

67. Albert Parry, *Garretts and Pretenders* (New York: Covici-Friede, 1933).

68. Paula S. Fass, *The Damned and the Beautiful: American Youth in the 1920s* (New York: Oxford University Press, 1977), pp. 56, 115, 262–270, 368–375.

69. David H. Bayley, "Learning About Crime: The Japanese Experience," *Public Interest,* no. 44 (Summer 1976), pp. 55–68. But compare recent accounts of rising juvenile crime in Japan in the *Times* (of London), February 3, 1982, p. 7.

70. Thomas Hobbes, *Leviathan,* chaps. 13, 14, 15.

71. Jean-Jacques Rousseau, *Emile.* I draw also on the interpretative essay by Allan Bloom, "The Education of Democratic Man: *Emile,"* *Daedalus* 107 (Summer 1978): 135–153.

72. The literature is summarized and criticized in Alfred Blumstein, Jacqueline Cohen, and Daniel Nagin, eds., *Deterrence and Incapacitation: Estimating the Effects of Criminal Sanctions on Crime Rates* (Washington, D.C.: National Academy of Sciences, 1978). The estimate of murders averted is Isaac Ehrlich, "The Deterrent Effect of Capital Punishment: A Question of Life and Death," *American Economic Review* 65 (1975): 397–417.

73. *Federalist,* no. 51.

74. *Federalist,* no. 10.

75. *Federalist,* no. 51.

76. Ibid.

77. *Federalist,* no. 55.

78. Ibid.

79. Herbert J. Storing, *What the Anti-Federalists Were For* (Chicago: University of Chicago Press, 1981), chap. 3.

80. Wood, *Creation of the American Republic,* chap. 2.

81. Storing, *What the Anti-Federalists Were For.*

82. Walter Berns, *The First Amendment and the Future of American Democracy* (New York: Basic Books, 1976).

83. Marvin Meyers, *The Jacksonian Persuasion: Politics and Belief* (Stanford, Calif.: Stanford University Press, 1957), chap. 2.

84. Alexis de Tocqueville, *Democracy in America,* ed. Phillips Bradley (New York: Alfred Knopf, 1944), vol. 1, p. 95.

Chapter 13 Crime and Public Policy

1. James Fitzjames Stephens, *A History of the Criminal Law of England* (New York: Burt Franklin, 1973), vol. 2, pp. 80–81 (first published in 1883).

2. Brian Forst et al., *Arrest Convictability as a Measure of Police Performance* (Washington, D.C.: INSLAW, 1981).

Appendix   A Note on Gun Control

1. Franklin E. Zimring, "The Medium is the Message: Firearm Caliber as a Determinant of Death From Assault," *Journal of Legal Studies* 1 (1972): 97–123; and Zimring, "Is Gun Control Likely to Reduce Violent Killings?" *University of Chicago Law Review* 35 (1967): 721–737.

2. Attorney General's Task Force on Violent Crime, *Final Report* (Washington, D.C.: Department of Justice, 1981), pp. 29–33.

Notes

3. James Q. Wilson, "What Can the Police Do About Violence?" *Annals of the American Academy* 452 (1980): 13–21.

4. Mark H. Moore, "Keeping Handguns From Criminal Offenders," *Annals of the American Academy* 455 (1981): 92–109.; and Moore, "The Bird in Hand: A Feasible Strategy for Gun Control," *Journal of Policy Analysis and Management* 2 (1983): 185–195.

INDEX

with unemployment, 125; cross-sectional analysis of, 184, 187; deterrent effect of prison on, 122–23; historical, 226–27
Murray, Charles A., 130–31, 142, 171–72, 173–74, 175–77

Nagin, Daniel, 123
National Academy of Sciences, 121, 166, 193
National Association for the Advancement of Colored People (NAACP), 93–95
National Center for Health Statistics, 101
National Opinion Research Center, 66, 95
National Research Council, 120–21, 122; Panel on Research on Deterrent and Incapacitative Effects, 120–21, 122, 124, 132*n*, 148–49; Panel on Research on Rehabilitation Techniques, 166–67, 170, 173; Panel on Sentencing Research, 161
National Rifle Association, 262
Negro Family, The (Moynihan), 17–18
neighborhood(s), 29–30, 32–33, 34, 39–40, 88; at city government and, 37–38; and police-community organization, 107–9; safety of, 10, 75–89; self-help organizations in, 250, 255, 257; *see also* community
neighborhood police team, 68
Neighborhood Youth Corps, 138
Nelson, William E., 224
New Jersey, 179*n*; "Safe and Clean Neighborhoods Program," 75
New York City, 16, 39, 80, 91, 93–95, 106, 111, 231; crime rates, 225; heroin users, 198, 200, 204–5, 207; police strategies, 68, 69; police use of deadly force, 102–3, 104; subway crime, 65–66, 73–74, 87, 131, 132; tests of increased police manpower, 62–66, 73–74
New York City Police Department, 62–63, 69–70, 104, 127, 263
New York State: board of parole, 164; drug laws, 133–35, 137; individual offense rate, 148; prison population, 151–52; prohibition of alcohol, 233
New York State Governor's Committee on Criminal Offenders, 162
Newark, N.J., 76–78, 86, 88–89
Nold, Fred, 125
North Carolina, 139

Oakland, Calif., 103–4, 237
O'Donnell, John A., 205, 207
offenders: amenable to rehabilitation, 167–70; high-rate, 151–53, 154–56, 255, 256, 257, 258, 259, 260; juvenile, 148 (*see also* delinquency, delinquents); low-rate, 153, 155, 156; new, 146; repeat, 146, 152–53 (*see also* recidivism); surveillance of known, 74; would-be, 9, 118–19; youthful, 140–42, 148; *see also* individual offense rate; persons at risk of committing crime; prior record

offense, seriousness of, 193; and death penalty, 190–91
Ohio, 148, 149, 182, 191
Ohlin, Lloyd, 42–43, 53, 54, 56; and Cloward, Richard A., *Delinquency and Opportunity*, 42, 52
"Operation Identification," 69
"Operation 25," 62–63, 73–74
order maintenance function of police, 37, 61–62, 74, 76–78, 81–85, 86, 87–88, 89, 90, 111–12, 230, 255; and attitude toward police, 99; shift from, to arresting criminals, 238; *see also* social order
Orsagh, Thomas, 126
Ostrom, Elinor, 86

Packer, Herbert, 196
Palmer, Ted, 165, 166, 168, 170
Palo Alto, Calif., 78
parents, 7, 44, 48
parole, 207; boards, 164, 256; officers, 256
Parry, Albert, 239
Passell, Peter, 184, 186, 187, 188
Pate, Tony, 70
peer groups, 46, 52, 239; and spread of heroin addiction, 201–4
penalties, 6–7, 25, 137, 242, 256; certainty and severity of, 8, 50, 117, 142, 144; delayed, uncertain, 118, 119, 121–22, 123, 186; nonprison, 159; and opportunities, 10, 117–44; *see also* costs of crime vs. benefits of noncrime; punishment
penitentiary, 243
Peoria, Ill., 71
perpetrator-oriented patrol (POP), 70
personal liberation, cult of, 24, 198
personal liberty, 217–18, 235, 238–39, 250; and crime control, 247, 251; protection of, 244
persons at risk of committing crime, 9, 24, 127–31, 142, 154–55
Petersilia, Joan, 152
Philadelphia, Pa., 148, 205, 225, 231; death penalty, 189, 191; murder rate, 225, 226–27
Phoenix, Ill., 86, 205
Pierce, Glenn L., 191
Pilot Intensive Counseling Organizations (PICO), 169, 170
plea bargaining, 133, 134, 135, 157, 256
police, 3, 10, 25, 57, 61, 71, 109, 156, 195, 250; adequacy of protection by, 7, 26–27, 93–95, 97, 98, 109; arrests by, 258–59 (*see also* arrests); black, 96–97, 102–3, 105; change in role of, 81, 83–84, 88–89, 109–10, 111–12, 238; citizen views of, 91–95; college-educated, 105–6; and communal action, 248; community service function of, 47–48, 61–62, 68–69, 71–74, 89, 95, 111–12; constraints on effectiveness of, 83, 90; and crime, 61–74; crime prevention function of, 61–62, 73–74, 97–98; criminal information strategy, 69, 70; effec-

About the Author

JAMES Q. WILSON is Henry Lee Shattuck Professor of Government at Harvard University. He has served on various presidential task forces and national advisory commissions on crime, law enforcement, and drug abuse prevention and is the author of, among other works, *Political Organizations* (1973), *The Investigators: Managing the FBI and Narcotics Agents* (1978), and *The Politics of Regulation* (1980), an edited volume.